Pages from a Worker's Life

William Z. Foster

International Publishers, New York

COPYRIGHT, 1939, BY

INTERNATIONAL PUBLISHERS CO., INC.

DESIGNED BY ROBERT JOSEPHY

PRINTED IN THE U.S.A.
This Printing, 1970

Library of Congress Catalog Card Number: 72-130864

TO ESTHER

CONTENTS

BOOKS AND PAMPHLETS by William Z. Foster

FOREWORD

My earlier book, *From Bryan to Stalin*, although it dealt in a general way with my experiences in the class struggle, was only partly autobiographical. The main purpose of that book was to serve as a contribution to the history of left-wing trade unionism in the United States during the past forty years. It also offered an outline of the development of the Communist Party.

The present book is a sequel to *From Bryan to Stalin*. It contains personal material which did not fit into the scheme of the preceding volume, but which throws light on the forces that made me arrive at my present political opinions. The subject matter is entirely true, taken from my own actual experience and presented without exaggeration or elaboration. In the numerous sketches, recollections and snapshots that comprise this book I have tried to picture, as I lived through them, the hopes and illusions, the comedy and tragedy, the exploitation and struggles of an American worker's life.

PAGES FROM A WORKER'S LIFE

CHAPTER I . . . . WORK

I began work at the age of seven, selling newspapers—the old Philadelphia Evening Star, News, Item and Call, all four of which have long since expired. At nine I applied for a job at Wanamaker's store, but the man told me to grow up first. At ten I finally managed to "go to work." This was the beginning of twenty-six years (from 1891 to 1917) in lumber, agriculture, building, chemical, metal, mining, transport, etc.—during which time I rambled all over the country. The following are true pictures from this industrial experience.

THE BULLDOGS

A few months before the famous blizzard of '88 our family moved from Taunton, Mass., where I was born, to Philadelphia. I was about six years old. Philadelphia was then a city of gas and kerosene street lights, horse and cable cars and cobble-paved streets. There were no skyscrapers, no trolley cars, no street electric lights; telephones were downtown curiosities, the railroads were in the link-and-pin stage, and automobiles, moving pictures and, of course, the radio and airplane, were not yet dreamed of.

A poor worker's family, from 1890 to 1900 we lived at 17th and Kater Streets, a typical slum area of the old "West End" of Philadelphia. Kater Street (called "Skittereen" by us) between 16th and 17th was a noisome, narrow side street, made up of several stables, a woodyard, a carpet cleaning works, a few whore-houses and many ramshackle dwellings. There were also two horrible blind slum alleys made up of ancient and decrepit shacks, without gas, running water or bathrooms, with outside privies, and inhabited by poverty-stricken people—half-starved, diseased, hopeless—who lived by casual labor, begging, petty thieving and what not. Even an insane woman and two idiots lived there.

In those days the tradition of the Civil War was still vividly alive, many war veterans being only in their forties, and their G. A. R. organization was everywhere. The old unpaid fire companies, with lurid records of gang feuds, thieving, arson and corrupt politics, still functioned as political-social clubs. Every neighborhood had its gang, and the poorer the locality the stronger and more vicious the gang. The gangs were named after animals, rivers, streets, districts, parks, etc., as for example: "Lions," "Park Sparrows," "Reedies," "Schuylkill Rangers."

Our gang was the "Bulldogs." Old-timers said it was in full operation long before the Civil War. Its boundaries extended from 16th to 17th Streets, and from South Street to Fitzwater. The families of the neighborhood were large, six to eight children being not unusual, and when the gang was mobilized it counted some five hundred members, a formidable force.

Between the many Philadelphia gangs a constant state of warfare existed. Any boy away from his "corners" could expect to "shell out," that is, to be robbed of his skates, cap, swimming tights, pocket-knife or whatever else he had of value. Often rival gangs fought pitched battles with fists, sticks, stones and knives, but guns were seldom or never used.

Ours was an especially tough neighborhood and the Bulldogs boasted that no gang had ever licked them. Almost all were Irish, a minority of whom were Protestants. Between these Orangemen and the Catholics bad blood existed, and one March 17th and July 12th this broke out into open fights. Kater Street had such a bad reputation that police seldom ventured there, except in groups of two or three.

The Bulldogs "ran" in three age groups. First there were the young boys, then the youths and finally the grown men up to about forty. These sub-gangs operated as separate units unless there was a general mobilization on Election night, Halloween, New Year's Eve, to fight some other gang, or for some other deviltry. Leadership was established simply on the basis of who was the best scrapper.

The parents of the gang members were mostly immigrant workers and all very poor—teamsters, longshoremen, building laborers. Many of the gang members, like myself, were also workers. But there were many who, declassed by hard social conditions, never worked, and lived by their wits.

The Bulldogs carried on many activities. We younger boys organized sports and games on the streets. We had a social club, a good ball team and a fife and drum band, said to be the best boys' band in the United States. The older gang members had a strong baseball nine, a big social-political club and a "New Year's Shooters" association (mummers) known as "The Bright Star" and one of the toughest outfits in the whole city.

In the poverty-bred slum atmosphere of Kater Street, indolence, ignorance, thuggery, crime, disease, drunkenness and general social degeneration flourished. The younger boys drank, smoked, shot craps, indulged in petty thievery and also considerable sex perversion. They broke street gas lamps, pilfered hucksters' trucks and stoned the "horseless carriages" that ventured into our lawless neighborhood. Many refused to attend school and grew up to manhood unable to read or write. The middle gang of youths had more developed forms of vice. They filled the pool halls, patronized the whore-houses as pimps or customers, and carried on law-breaking upon a more ambitious scale. The older Bulldogs were the ripe fruit of the slums. Sometimes they would do a day's work, but they were always ready to "roll" a drunk or commit a burglary or stickup. They were real toughs, barroom fighters, and a few were second-rate "pugs." On election day they sold their votes as a matter of course, became repeaters and helped the Republican bosses mobilize the slum vote. Their social club was a gambling layout and a Sunday "speakeasy," a hang-out for bums, crooks, pimps, gamblers, racetrack touts, political henchmen and idle workers. The Bulldogs were an efficient school for crime, and a steady stream of them went into the reform schools and penitentiaries. They were a typical foundation of the corrupt Republican Party in Philadelphia.

Some of the grown-up gangsters, though still relatively young in years, were made so degenerate by their rotten environment that they could no longer work, fight, steal or even beg. They were broken physically and morally. Their winters they spent in the County poorhouse and their summers in the Kater Street stables—lousy, ragged and half-starved. "Rum-dumbs," we called these unfortunates. Dopetaking had not yet developed in the slums, but these men were hopeless slaves to whiskey, which they begged for or cleaned spittoons to get. What little they ate they usually scoured from neighborhood swill buckets. From time to time, in the Kater Street stable haylofts, we would find one of these miserable "rum-dumbs," frozen to death in the winter months, or dead of tuberculosis or delirium tremens.

The Bulldogs were animated by religious, national and race prejudices. They hated the Jews. Strong parties of gang members would go tearing along South Street, upsetting and stealing displayed goods, breaking shop windows and punching the heads of little Jewish business men. These raids were pogroms in miniature. With the Negroes it was still worse. They were deadlined at Lombard Street, one square north, and at Broad Street, two squares east, and strictly forbidden to cross over into white, Bulldog territory. The Negro man or boy who ventured across these rigid deadlines was unmercifully slugged.

Yet there was much real proletarian spirit in our gang. As far as I ever heard, scabs were never recruited in our neighborhood. Indeed, during the fierce street-car strike of the middle 'nineties the Bulldogs mobilized in full force and wrecked every car that came through our territory, although each one was manned by several armed policemen.

In 1900 we moved away from this neighborhood, fine flower of capitalist civilization that it was. I did not visit it again for thirty years. At that time I found the old Bulldogs had been wiped out, but the slums were more horrible even than before. The deadlined Negroes had broken through the barriers and flooded the once so jealously defended district. After years of bitter struggle the whites had fled before the invading Negroes. The only former Bulldog whom I could locate was now a ward leader for the corrupt Vare political machine. The notorious Bulldogs had vanished and even their tradition was unknown to the new crop of poverty-stricken slum dwellers along "Skittereen."

AN APPRENTICESHIP TO ART

Old Kretchman was a German sculptor and an artist of many crafts. His studio was at Franklin and Noble Streets in Philadelphia. I went to work for him in 1891 at the age of ten. It was my first real job.

Kretchman modeled in clay and wax, carved wood and cut stone. He had created many Civil War monuments for Gettysburg and other battlefields. He had also helped Calder build the gigantic statue of William Penn atop the Philadelphia City Hall. When I worked with him most of his sculpture consisted in making bronze busts of the Philadelphia aristocracy, and he also painted their portraits.

Kretchman was getting old, and the most important art piece he did while I was with him was a bas-relief panel of President Lincoln and his Cabinet. It measured about eight feet by ten, and the highest point stood out only five-eighths of an inch above the flat. The panel was eventually rolled in plate glass by a Pittsburgh company and exhibited at the Chicago World's Fair.

The old artist was also an outstanding steel die-sinker. In his craft he acknowledged only one superior, a man who worked in the Federal Mint. Kretchman was sometimes approached by counterfeiters with propositions that he cut steel dies to make false coins, but without avail. Nevertheless, the government kept a sort of friendly check-up on his activities. He employed his die-sinking ability chiefly to produce memorial medals, for sale at various conventions and celebrations. He took me with him to such gatherings in New York, Boston, Washington and other cities to sell souvenir medals on the street, an occupation that filled me with loathing. I liked these trips around the country very much, but the idea of selling anything went a hundred per cent against my grain, as it has done throughout my life.

Another of Kretchman's many specialties was electro-plating. This craft was then in its infancy, and Kretchman was one of the cleverest in the country at it. He plated gold, silver, copper and nickel. Once he made a big stir locally by copper-plating a glass wine set, metal plating on glass being at that time practically unknown. Tragically enough for me, I accidentally broke one of the precious glasses, which were six weeks in plating and made to order for a rich Philadelphia family. With characteristic versatility, Kretchman often beautifully engraved his finely plated pieces, engraving being one of his many accomplishments.

Towards the end of my time with him, this clever artist practically gave up his many crafts. He was a bad business man and could not turn his great abilities into dollars and cents. He was finally forced to earn his living by modeling huge teeth, a foot high, for the Pennsylvania College of Dental Surgery, to serve as study models for the dental students.

Taking a strong liking to me, Kretchman gave me lessons in all the arts of which he was a master: clay modeling, plaster of paris work, wood carving, stone cutting, drawing and painting, electro-plating, die-sinking, engraving, etc. But I felt no call to a life of art. I wanted to become an industrial worker and was drawn as by a magnet to the shops. So, after three years of it, I left my art job and went to work in a Philadelphia type foundry. When I quit Kretchman I dropped my artistic training as one would discard an unfitting garment. Nor did I afterward ever feel the slightest remorse. I made no mistake in becoming an industrial worker.

FERTILIZER

Nearly every industry festers with occupational diseases, and these reap a harvest of suffering and death among the workers. I have seen much of workers being ruthlessly ruined in health for the sake of employers' profits. After quitting Kretchman, I worked three years for the American Type Founders Company, where I got myself saturated with lead. Next I got work as a fireman at the Harrison White Lead works in Philadelphia. One department in this plant, where they mixed pulverized lead, was so destructive to health that the workers called it the "death house." The most dangerous work was done by green immigrants, unaware of the menace to their lives.

The other workers used to say that if a man working in the "death house" saved his money diligently he could buy himself a coffin by the time the lead poisoning finished him.

But the most unhealthy conditions I ever experienced were in fertilizer. I worked in this industry during the years 1898-1900, in various plants and localities, as laborer, steam-fitter, fireman, engineer and skilled fertilizer mixer.

One of the most noisome and unhealthy phases of the fertilizer industry was the disposal of city garbage. The plant of the American Reduction Company at West Reading, Pa., was a typical example. In this place some of the garbage was burned in furnaces and the rest was boiled in huge kettles, then dried, mixed and sold for fertilizer.

The plant was indescribably filthy, a menace to the health of its workers and the whole community. Within the place garbage was indiscriminately littered about and allowed to decompose, and I often saw whole sections of the dumping floor a living, creeping carpet of maggots. In summer, when garbage collections were heaviest, the plant was swamped, and hundreds of tons of rotting swill, besprinkled with decaying cats, dogs, etc., was left to fester outside in the blazing sun. With the stench, flies and maggots it was a sickening mess. The plant stank to the high heavens for a mile in all directions, and it sent forth millions of filthy, disease-laden flies to endanger the population round about.

Another sweet flower of the fertilizer industry was the disposal of dead animals. I also worked at this, in Wyomissing, Pa. The plant was owned by a veterinary. This doctor got paid for treating sick horses, cows and pigs, collected fees for removing them when they were dead and, finally, made fat profits in selling their remains to farmers as fertilizer. The workers believed that the old doctor, in tending sick animals, carefully developed his other activities as a remover of dead animals and fertilizer manufacturer. The fertilizer was a glaring fake. It was composed of at least fifty per cent yellow clay, and the half dozen brands, differing only in their fancy names, coloring and prices, all came out of the same bin.

In this plant horses and other dead animals were skinned, hacked to pieces, boiled down into tankage, their bones ground, and the whole business mixed with guano, kainit, potash, sheep manure, phosphate rock, lime, clay (especially clay) and other chemicals that go to make up fertilizer. The dead animals in summer were usually in a high stage of "ripeness" when they reached the factory. This plant, with its own special unspeakable smells and unaccountable myriads of flies, outdid in noisomeness, if possible, the West Reading beauty rose garbage plant.

The dead animals were prepared for the boiling tanks by men working in a room filled with stifling steam and crawling with maggots. The horrible odor of the cooking, putrefying flesh would gag a skunk. The men ran grave danger of contracting diseases of which the animals had died. Shortly before my time, one man died from glanders caught from an infected horse. The butcher, although young, was a weazened, sickly man from his disgusting occupation. He was so saturated with the stench that, bathe as he might, he could not get rid of the sickening odor. In the street car people shied away from him as though he had the plague. For his dangerous and unhealthy work he received ten dollars a week and his helper got seven-fifty.

The machinery in these two plants was quite unprotected, and many workers were mangled and crippled. At Wyomissing there was an epileptic who should not have been permitted into such a plant, as he would collapse in a fit without a second's warning. But as he worked for almost nothing he was given a job. One day he had a sudden seizure and fell onto a whirling emory wheel. This ground half his face away before he could be rescued.

The most deadly menace to health in the fertilizer industry, however, was the terrible dust. The various grinding mills, mixers, conveyors, baggers and chutes, totally unequipped with ventilators, blowers, covers or other health-protection devices, constantly threw huge clouds of dust into the air. From a distance a plant often appeared to be on fire, with the volume of dust pouring out of the windows and doors. So dense was this dust at times, that, in daylight and with lanterns in our hands, we would stumble into posts and piles of stock while trying to make our way about. All the plants I worked in were very bad for dust, especially the big factory of Armour & Company in Jacksonville, then the largest in the South.

Most of the fertilizer dust consisted of chemicals highly injurious to health. One dust we particularly feared came from dry bones. The rapidly revolving mills threw out dense clouds of it, much of it doubtlessly germ-laden. It produced heavy chills in the men, and for hours after a bone-grinding they would shiver and shake. Another deadly dust arose from the milling of dry tobacco stems. This danger-out dust produced eye burning, sore throats and violent coughing. The Negro workers dreaded this most of all and called it "Old King Tobacco Dust."

We had no masks to protect ourselves. Some workers used hand-kerchiefs over their faces, but about the only effect was to incommode breathing. Nose, throat and lung troubles were widespread in the industry. Deaths from tuberculosis were common. After three years of it, I also began to develop tuberculosis. Fortunately, however, I took myself in hand in time. I quit the deadly fertilizer industry and went to sea. Three years of knocking over the world in windjammers finally put me back on my feet again. At the Kremlin hospital in Moscow, thirty years later, physicians X-raying me found traces of healed-over tuberculosis scars.

PEONAGE IN FLORIDA

In the winter of 1900 I pulled up stakes in Pennsylvania and worked my way to Havana, Cuba. The Spanish American war was just ended, and conditions for work were none too good; so, after a short stay, I returned to the States.

Arriving in Tampa broke, I aimed to get a job in the back country, to make a "road stake" before going North. Florida was (and still is) a tough country for workers. Wage rates were low and the employers used the police power and a system of peonage to get workers. Un-employed men were arrested and sentenced as vagrants and then farmed out in chain gangs to the turpentine camps and phosphate mines, where the greedy contractors mercilessly exploited them. The Negroes especially were victims of this persecution.

Conditions on the county prison farms and in the prison-operated turpentine and phosphate industries were terrible—brutal discipline, exhausting labor, garbage as food, unsanitary conditions. A man guilty of nothing but being out of work would be sentenced to work out a fine of say fifteen dollars at a few cents a day. This was bad enough, but from time to time he was furnished shoes, shirts, etc., at high prices and compelled to work out their cost at the regular rate. In consequence, it usually took a year or more before a man, often broken in health, finally succeeded in paying the State his original fine of a few dollars. A similar system prevailed in nearly all the Southern states.

I was soon to learn that Florida's "free" industries were not much better than her chain gangs and prison camps. I took a Seaboard Air Line freight out of Tampa and dropped off a few miles out at a place called Turkey Creek. There I got a job with a railroad grading outfit ten miles back in the woods. I arrived in camp just at supper time. There were about fifty workers, all whites. It was the night before the monthly pay day, and the men had just received their pay statements. Complaints and lamentations rose on all sides. Practically all the men were in debt to the contractor. Just as in the prison camps, they had been charged with various objects at high prices, and these were checked off against the wage of eighty cents a day. Only a few had any money coming, and these were local people.

I remember the plight of the donkey engine fireman. He was a youth with a broad Southern accent who had lived "away up north in Georgia." His wage was a dollar a day and he had twenty-one days' pay coming. But against his twenty-one dollars total wages, they had charged off, besides the regular board of three-fifty a week, a canthook, mattress, blanket, tobacco and doctor fee, amounting in all to twenty-seven dollars. Thus, after three weeks' hard work, the fireman was six dollars in debt, and nearly all the men were in the same boat.

I sounded out a few of the more discontented men about the possibility of a strike; but they were too badly demoralized to take any action. One told me that on the previous pay day, confronted by a similar payless situation, four men had quit. But when they reached Turkey Creek they were picked up by the police as "vags" and sent to prison camps. The bosses used the threat of imprisonment in the medieval Florida chain gangs to force the men to work practically for nothing. The line between "free" and prison labor was a thin one in the Florida backwoods.

Evidently I could not pick up my "road stake" at Turkey Creek; so I decided to "blow" in the morning. But I dared not tell the boss, as that would have invited a prison sentence. I ate breakfast after the rest, being delayed by the hiring-on process. The timekeeper directed me how to get to the "works." But at the forks of the road, where I should turn to the right, I went to the left instead and hot-footed the ten miles back to Turkey Creek. Fortunately the bosses did not check up on me until noon, and by that time I had already hit a freight and was gone. Otherwise I would have surely had a trip to the turpentine camps.

Still job hunting, I dropped off the freight train a few miles from Turkey Creek at a sawmill, owned by one Bramlitt. This man, a typical, rawboned Florida "cracker," immediately gave me a job with a partner felling trees. Our wages were a dollar a day, minus three dollars a week board, and we worked from daylight to dark.

Bramlitt had four sons, all yellow-faced and gaunt from constant quinine dosing in their never-ending war against malaria. There were eight white workers and half a dozen Negroes. The Negroes were Jim-Crowed in a nearby tumble-down shanty, while the whites bunked in a pine board shack. We were fed on the typical Southern workers' diet of sow-belly, beans, grits and corn pone.

One night the quiet air of our camp was broken by a medley of yells, pistol shots and the clatter of galloping horses. We whites piled out of the bunkhouse to learn what was up; but the Negroes, taught discretion by years of terrorism, fled into the nearby timber. About a dozen mounted men came riding boisterously into the mill yard.

It was a raid such as the "night-riders" and "white-caps" of that period often made in the Southern states. The raiders were armed, but did not wear masks or other regalia. Several were drunk and all displayed the traditional violent Ku Klux Klan spirit.

Bramlitt and the horsemen hailed each other in friendly fashion. But we workers were lined up, questioned singly and bawled out collectively. The leader informed me that in southern Florida "if a Yankee minds his own business he is almost as good as a dog."

Finally, the night-riders rode off, leaving us unmolested. Several complained loudly, however, because the "niggers" had escaped them. In talking about it later, the workers stated that such raids were not unusual and that their purpose was to terrorize the working crews. The frightened Negroes stayed out in the woods all night.

After two weeks' work at Bramlitt's mill I figured that, with all due allowance for commissary robbery, I should have at least three dollars for my "road stake." So I told Bramlitt one night that I was quitting and wanted my time. He "flew off the handle" and told me that I could not quit. I was astounded. He was actually trying to keep me on the job by force. All argument was fruitless. Bramlitt simply refused to pay me and warned me not to quit.

In the bunkhouse the men sympathized with me but said they could do nothing. My partner earnestly advised me not to go to the authorities with the matter. If I did, said he, I would be arrested as a vagrant. Anyhow, even if by some miracle I could force Bramlitt to pay, all I would get would be a typical statement showing me to be in debt to him. They told me to "beat it while my shoes were good," by hopping a north-bound freight train.

Next morning I refused to work. The Bramlitt clan were on hand to prevent my going into the dining-room. Bramlitt, violently angry, shouted that if I did not go to work he would have me arrested. The workers assured me it was no mere threat and they warned me I was heading for a turpentine camp. Nothing could be done about it; so that night I jumped a "rattler" into Jacksonville and saw no more of Bramlitt and his peonage camp.

THE NEW YORK STREET CARS

Returning from Florida, I worked several months in 1901 as a motorman on the Third Avenue lines in New York. The electric trolley car, now on its last legs, was then in its heyday. The old horse cars had almost died out, there were as yet no subways, the automobile was just being born, and the elevated trains were still being hauled by slow, chugging steam locomotives.

Our wages were only twenty-two cents per hour and we worked ten hours per day, seven days a week. The men were unorganized and the bosses ruled with an iron hand, abusing and discharging workers on the slightest pretext.

The motorman's work was hard and nerve-wracking. New York streets were then jammed with slow-moving, horse-drawn trucks, and to pilot a street car through this maze, and not fall behind, was a real task. We had no airbrakes, seats or vestibules. We had to stand up all day twisting heavy hand-brakes and being fully exposed to the weather. Many's the time I was soaked with driving rain and half frozen from cold. It was a man-killing job.

The workers thoroughly hated the company. As for the conductors, many of them helped themselves freely, with no twinges of conscience, to the fares they took in. There were no pay-as-you-enter cars, and with the conductors collecting in the densely packed cars even the army of company "spotters" could not keep tab on them. The "nickelers" and "short-arm artists," as they were called, were located mostly by bookkeeping methods. That is, when a run failed to bring in the regular average of receipts the conductor was fired forthwith for "nickeling."

We motormen deeply resented our unnecessarily hard work and exposure to severe weather conditions. We demanded airbrakes, seats and vestibules. But the company bosses and engineers assured us that these things, although in use elsewhere, were impossible in the dense traffic conditions of New York: the airbrakes would speedily wear out from incessant use, the seats would lessen our alertness, the vestibules would obscure our vision, and all three together would make for more accidents. But this was only a hypocritical, profit-grabbing defense. Years later the company was compelled to introduce these much-needed improvements, and the service was thereby greatly improved.

Determined to end the abuses from which we suffered, some of us younger workers began to organize. We set up groups of platform men in the several barns of the Third Avenue lines and also those of other companies. Then I contacted an A.F. of L. organizer, Herman Robinson. All he gave us was sympathy and a promise to "take in" the men if we would line them up. It was my first experience with A.F. of L. armchair organizing methods.

A few others and myself managed to become members of the union, and we were making considerable headway, when one day the half dozen of us in the 66th Street barn were called into the Super's office and given our walking papers. In those days of the brazen open shop the boss made no bones about telling us we were fired for union activity. He took a similar course the same day in the other barns, and our nascent union was killed. It was more than thirty years later when, after many fruitless struggles, New York's army of transport workers finally got organized into the C.I.O. Transport Workers Union.

TEXAN AMENITIES

Fired from the New York street cars, I decided to beat my way out West, and my first job en route was at Echo, Texas, on the Southern Pacific railroad, close to the Louisiana border. I worked there with a gang putting in a railroad yard. I started as a "flunkey" or waiter, but was soon promoted to second cook. This was no small advancement, let it be known for my reputation in the culinary art; because, although the Mexicans were fed on "garbage," the American boss elements got good fare and the cooks had to be expert.

Eastern Texas was a tough country. The whites settled their own quarrels with gun and knife, and dominated the Negroes and Mexicans by sheer terrorism. A few miles west of Echo was Beaumont, famous as the place where oil was first struck in the West. It was then perhaps the wildest town in the United States. Holdups were a daily occurrence, and in one week a dozen men were killed by gun-play.

The Mexicans at Echo worked under the usual system of semi-peonage. The most hard-boiled boss was "Lige" Gardner, timekeeper and gunman. Gardner, slight of build and dark-complexioned, came of an old aristocratic Southern family. His people had owned many slaves and a big plantation, but they lost everything in the Civil War. Gardner could not forget this and deeply hated Northerners.

Gardner's evil disposition was worsened because he suffered from Bright's disease, and the doctors had given him only a couple of years to live. He used to say, "If I've got to cash-in I might as well take along some of my enemies." And as good, or bad, as his word, Gardner had killed two white men and several Negroes; he was saved from prosecution by his aristocratic connections. He treated us in the kitchen with artificial politeness but, gun in hand, he terrorized the Mexican laborers.

It so happened that we cooks and flunkeys once developed a dispute over wages. Gardner did not interfere, but our head cook, Sam Frayne, opposed us, and also, to our surprise, boasted of being a strike-breaker. This embittered the other cook and myself, and we split completely with the scab "chef," Frayne.

Frayne, like Gardner, never wearied of boasting of his "good" family. His people were steel magnates in Pittsburgh and he, a Columbia graduate, bragged of having gone to school with Harry Thaw. Frayne had held high positions in the steel industry, his last, so he said, being general manager of a Midwest office of a big steel corporation; but he had lost out through drinking, gambling and general unreliability. So he became virtually a hobo, and for the past ten years had worked all over the South and West.

One day, Frayne, who had been drinking heavily, began shouting at the top of his voice about his great family. He compared his lineage with Gardner's, to the latter's disadvantage. Sneering at the old slave-holding Southern aristocracy, he gloried at their downfall in the Civil War. Then, growing bolder from the drink in him, he yelled: "These goddamned Southerners, you know why they're so dark—it's the 'nigger' blood in them!"

Gardner, sitting in the next car only a few feet away, heard this tirade. For a time he apparently paid no attention, but when Frayne uttered his last remark, which was about the deadliest insult that could be offered a Southern aristocrat, Gardner got up from his chair, checked his Colt 45 to see that it was loaded and walked into our cook car. As he entered with drawn gun, Frayne turned drunkenly to face him. Dashing at Frayne without a word, Gardner brought the heavy gun down on his head and dropped him like a poled ox. Then Gardner walked back to his car.

Frayne soon picked himself up from the floor. The whole side of his face was torn from the blow of the heavy revolver. Then in came Gardner again. Walking up to the scab cook, he said: "Frayne, you can consider yourself a lucky man to be alive. You will never be closer to death and not die than you were a few minutes ago. The only reason I didn't kill you was because the others in the cook car were in the line of fire and might be hit. Because of the insult you gave me I could have shot you down and never even been arrested for it. Now get out of camp. If I find you here after ten minutes I'll put a bullet in you."

Crestfallen, Frayne quickly packed his stuff and left. His plight awakened no indignation in the cook and myself. Frayne was just a scab and traitor, and his trouble with Gardner we looked upon as merely a fight between our enemies. We saw him go down the line without sympathy or regret.

TWENTIETH-CENTURY HOMESTEADING

In 1904, while living in Oregon, I decided to take up a homestead. The great wave of homesteaders, so basic in the settling of the West, was then wearing itself out. There was still much government free land, but the fertile prairies and valleys were long since taken. The homesteaders of the period were trying to win homes from stony, timbered uplands or parched deserts. They were the last of the pioneers, the rear-guard of their historic breed.

My "claim" was located at the juncture of Indian and Mosier Creeks in the foothill country on the east slope of the Cascade Mountains, about twelve miles south of the great Columbia River. It was at an elevation of two thousand feet in a rugged mountain country, a land of beautiful scenery. Great canyons gashed the country and in the background loomed magnificent Mount Hood. It was in this wild country that I took up my homestead of one hundred and sixty acres and a timber claim of equal size. My sister Anna, and her husband, George McVey, also had a homestead, adjoining mine.

At the time there was a rush of homesteaders into this Oregon foothill country. They hoped to carve apple orchards out of the dense wilderness. Only a few miles away was the famous Hood River Valley, where apple land was valued as high as a thousand dollars per acre, and experts declared that conditions in our district were similar to those in Hood River and should produce as good fruit.

I had little or no idea of making an apple orchard myself, but the lure of the back country attracted me enormously. At the most, I thought, I would secure a place that I could sell profitably; and at the least, it would be an interesting experience. Our locality was an inspiring country in which to spend a few months yearly in the spring and summer, which was all the homestead laws required. I earned my way by working in logging camps or on railroad jobs in the surrounding territory, and I had no idea of ceasing to be an industrial worker.

Our backwoods homestead community consisted of a couple of dozen families and bachelors. Many were ex-doctors, lawyers, preachers and petty-business men, trying for one reason or another to escape the city, and some were workers. A few were farmers, driven West by the exhaustion of their farms in the East and South. The community, mostly Protestant, was strongly fundamentalist, drinking, dancing and swearing being severely frowned upon. The youth were restive under these restrictions and at times came into sharp conflict with their parents. Two of us, Socialists and atheists, were social outlaws in this straight-laced neighborhood.

Old-time Western free hospitality prevailed. When a man traveling through the hills came upon an unoccupied homesteader's cabin he was free to help himself to food and shelter, but the custom provided that such a visitor should wash the dishes after eating, leave dry kindling wood handy and shut the cabin door so that animals could not get in.

The homesteaders' life was hard. The rocky land, dotted with great pines and firs, and covered with an almost impenetrable jungle of bowl-oak, willow, laurel and wild cherry, cost up to two hundred dollars per acre to clear. The settlers were poverty-stricken and they would work "outside" for a few months to get a small stake and then go back to clearing their homesteads. Few had horses and most of their houses, like my own, were built of logs cut on the spot.

Partial compensations for the homesteaders' hardships were the exhilarating mountain air, the splendid scenery, the excellent hunting and the healthful life generally. Of four-footed game were cougar, deer, bear, coyotes, rabbits and an occasional timber wolf. There were many rattlesnakes. There were also grouse and quail in profusion, and nobody ever troubled his head about the game laws. In the creeks fine mountain trout could be caught almost as fast as one cast his line. In winter the country was covered with a blanket of snow several feet deep and was almost a fairy land of beauty; but in summer it was practically rainless. Irrigation was a prime necessity for farming, but few had water.

After three summers of this homesteading life, I "proved up" on my claims and sold them for about half of what would have been wages for the time I spent on the homestead. Thus ended my interesting experience with the tail-end of the great wave of American homesteaders. This venture was the first and last time in my life that I ever attempted to gather together property of any kind: money, houses or land. What my whole homesteading period gave me was a considerable knowledge of the woodman's craft and a deep and abiding love of the mountains.

Our homestead district did not realize the rosy hopes of its belated pioneers. It never became an apple country. About this time a big over-planting of apple trees was taking place in all the Pacific Northwest states on irrigated, easily-cleared desert land. This soon created an overproduction of apples and made profitable apple growing impossible in places where land was so hard to clear as it was along the Mosier. Therefore, one by one the settlers in this backwoods country gave up the hopeless struggle. Eventually only a scattering of them were left, and they led a lonesome, poverty-stricken existence with no perspective. A new growth of pines and firs and jungle-like underbrush sprang up and reconquered most of our old hard-won clearings. The best timber land was grabbed by logging companies for almost nothing, and much of the rest reverted back to the government and to its old-time use as sheep and cattle range land. The Mosier homesteads were enterprises of primitive rugged individualism wrecked on the rocks of inhospitable economic conditions.

A SHEEPHERDER'S DOGS

Workers and farmers in the West always looked askance at sheepherders, who were considered just a little "off." The sheepherder, far back in the hills of Wyoming, Montana, Utah and other Western states, led a lonesome and vacant life. Often during the summer he saw no human being for months on end. With no companions but his dogs and the eternally bleating sheep, he developed habits of talking to himself and other idiosyncrasies. There were many stories about his practice of masturbation and his unnatural relations with the sheep. Popular belief had it that the insane asylums were filled with sheepherders, wrecked mentally by their life of isolation.

In 1907 I decided to have a couple of months' fling at sheepherding. It was during the lambing season, in early spring. At this time the sheep were usually brought in from the remote mountain ranges to the home ranches. There was no isolation at this period. That was why I chose it, for I wanted none of the months' long lonesomeness of the sheepherder's life.

The place where I worked was about thirty miles from The Dalles, Oregon, on the Deschutes River. The river ran in a great canyon about fifteen hundred feet deep and a couple of miles across at the top. From its brink the canyon was an awe-inspiring sight, with the river a thin silver ribbon far below. I remember the first time I saw it, it almost took my breath away. The sheep grazed upon the canyon slopes, which were so steep that if a stone (or man, or sheep) started rolling it would go to the bottom without stopping.

Lambing in a sheep camp is not a lovely job at best. But it was particularly revolting on those steep canyon sides. The ewes, feeding with the band, often would drop their lambs and then pass on nonchalantly, leaving the tottery lamblets to shift for themselves. But later they would sense that they had given birth and begin a frantic search for their missing lambs. They would tear through the band of three thousand sheep excitedly smelling the various lambs, for it is by smell that the mother ewe recognizes her young. As a frantic ewe rushed about sniffing the lambs she would give each one that was not her own a resounding butt. Often a lamb would thus be sent spinning to death down the steep canyon slopes, being nothing but a tangled bloody mass when it reached the bottom. At the end of the day there were always many lambs separated from their thick-headed, frenzied mothers, and the luckless sheepherders had the miserable job of gathering up all the stray lambs and carrying them off to the bedding ground, where they could be reunited with their distressed parents.

I took a violent dislike to sheepherding. Almost everything about the work nauseated me, except the sheep dogs. The dogs were real companions to the sheepherders. They were wonderfully intelligent and amazingly adapted to their work. The most remarkable dogs in our camp were a pair of Scotch collies, Jack and Pete, owned by Bill Simmons, an old-time sheepherder. Simmons treated his dogs as personal friends. He would not even speak sharply to the dogs, much less strike them. A central object in his life was the education of his beautiful collies. He talked to them as to human beings and was convinced they understood every word. He taught them no tricks, but he had trained them expertly for sheep work.

For the semi-trained, ordinary sheep dogs, herding on the canyon sides was killing work and their feet were torn and bleeding from constantly climbing over the rocks. But for Simmons' dogs it was all quite easy. Simmons worked his dogs on a different principle from the other herders. Instead of requiring them to make the hard trip all the way up and down the steep canyon side each time the sheep had to be turned, he had his dogs station themselves at strategic points far up on the hillside and work from there. After doing a job of turning the sheep, they simply went back and laid down again at their stations. They did their work with a fraction of the effort of the other dogs. Consequently, their feet were in excellent condition; they did not tire, and they never set the sheep in panic. They came down the canyon side only upon direct instruction by Simmons. To avoid confusion, the older one, Jack, was broken to work by whistle signals, while Pete, the younger, responded only to spoken commands. It was beautiful to watch these intelligent animals work. They were worth six ordinary dogs on the job and the whole camp admired them vastly.

A year previously these two splendid dogs saved Simmons' life. One evening, in early spring, while he was bringing his big band of sheep to the bedding ground, Simmons was overtaken by a sudden and fierce blizzard. In the blinding snow he fell over a high bluff and broke both pelvis bones. It was a remote place and he might have died there without anyone locating him. But Simmons had his intelligent dog friends to rely upon, and they did not fail him. He made Jack understand it was his task to round up the scattered sheep, while he dispatched Pete to the ranch house several miles off to bring assistance. And sure enough, a party of rescuers, following Pete, soon arrived on the scene of the accident. Simmons was laid up for six months in the hospital at The Dalles. I spoke to him a number of times about the whole affair, and marveled at his dogs; but Simmons took them for granted. He did not consider it at all remarkable that they should have understood just what he wanted of them in his dangerous situation. He had such a high opinion of their intelligence and loyalty that nothing they might do could surprise him.

HARD-LINE SKINNERS

In 1907, when the S.P. & S. railroad was being built along the north bank of the Columbia River from Spokane to Portland, I worked for a railroad grading outfit near White Salmon, Washington. The job was a typical Western layout, and the rockmen, muckers and skinners came from all over the West. In the towns along the line the sky was the limit in "entertainment"; they were full of gamblers, prostitutes and every other species that preyed upon Western workers.

The "working stiffs," totally unorganized, had to accept pretty much whatever wages, hours and working and living conditions the bosses decided upon. How little a worker's life was valued was illustrated one day when two rockmen, caught by a premature blast, were blown to bits. All we found of them was a shoe with a torn-off foot inside. The hard-boiled boss hefted this in his hand a moment, and remarking, "Well, I guess we can't have a funeral over that," threw the grisly object into the swirling Columbia River.

The "gippo" sub-contractor for whom I worked operated a number of "slips," "wheelers" and "fresnos," which are scrapers for grading work. The drivers were typical "hard-line" skinners, and hence among the most picturesque of all the migratory workers of the West. Homeless, familyless, drifting from one railroad grading camp to another, they were saturated with craft pride and looked down with contempt upon all "scissorbills" and "homeguards." For some reason which I was never able to fathom, many of them were "snowbirds"— cocaine users.

The hard-line skinners got their craft name from their dexterity in using their reins as whips. With a well-placed snap of the long "line" they would knock a patch of skin off a horse or mule. The flanks of these animals were usually white with scars from such cruel flecking. Most contractors strictly forbade the practice. I learned to perform this stunt, although I never used it on a horse or mule.

I drove a fresno, a scraper about seven feet wide, pulled by four mules abreast. I was a teamster of experience in logging and grading camps and in general hauling and ranch work. My driving philosophy was to make friends with my animals, and it worked well, horses and mules being quick to appreciate a considerate driver. So when I was given four mules, I applied my regular formula and everything went fine.

I had driven my team a few days when, to my surprise, I learned they had the worst reputation of any animals in the outfit. They had been "spoiled" by ignorant and cruel drivers, and no less than eight skinners had tried in vain to drive them during the week before I got them. Considering my success with this team, I began to flatter myself that I was a real skinner.

But the boss thought otherwise. One night, after I had driven the mules three weeks, I overheard him violently criticizing my driving. He said the mules had done as they pleased since "Slim" (that was me) got hold of them. What they needed, said he, was a damned good "tail-boning" (to be beaten over the tail-bone with a club), and by God he was going to see they got it. Now all this was a jolt to me, as I thought I was doing a very good job with the four "spoiled" mules.

Next day the stable-boss, equipped with a stout "sap," came up and had me turn over the "lines" to him. He would show me how mules should be driven. Now, mules have a great cunning, and skinners universally consider them uncannily intelligent. It is a never-failing source of wonder when, regularly as clock-work, grading camp mules set up an infernal braying a few minutes before noon knock-off time. They seem to know just what time it is. So no sooner had the boss, brandishing his club, taken hold of the lines then the intelligent mules sensed trouble in the air and prepared to fight.

We were working on a grade fill, and to unload our broad fresno scrapers two of the mules had to go over and down the side of the grade. One had to plow through the soft sliding earth knee-deep.

Usually the skinner stood on the solid ground as the mules went through the difficult dumping process; but the boss, club in hand, followed the off-mule over the side, viciously "tail-boning" the animal as it struggled desperately to clamber through the loose earth. The second time around the boss repeated his stunt. But this time, the off-mule suddenly stopped and lightning-like, lifted a hind leg and dealt him a crashing blow full in the face. Without even a moan the boss collapsed and rolled head over heels to the bottom of the fill. Half a dozen men scrambled down and picked him up, dead to the world. His face was all bashed in. The doctor said his skull was fractured but he would probably live. I never knew what finally became of him for, in accordance with good skinner tradition, I had quit my job the moment the boss took the lines from my hand to teach me to drive. But I thought that perhaps my system of skinning mules was the best after all.

THE CLASS POINT OF VIEW

The I.W.W. free speech fight in Spokane, Washington, in 1909, was just over. It had been a very bitter struggle, with hundreds of arrests and beatings, but it ended victoriously for the workers. Now our problem was to find jobs for those just released from jail. Harry Black had a suggestion.

Black had been through the fight and had conducted himself well. He was a Western floating worker, a ranch-hand, miner, logger, construction worker. Alive and energetic, he voiced the typical I.W.W. bitter hatred of the bosses.

Black's idea was this: A contractor had offered him some sewer digging on a sub-contracting basis. Black proposed that he take the sub-contract, which involved no financial outlay for him, and that we wobblies be his workers. As a good I.W.W., Black said he opposed exploitation of the workers, so he would make the sewer-digging job a "home" for us. He, himself, would be satisfied to make merely regular day wages. Nobody but wobblies would be given work.

We had nothing to lose, so we took it on. For a few days everything went fine. Black worked in the ditch with us; and we joked, smoked and talked of the revolution as we dug. This easy-going arrangement did not slow the job; if anything, we did more than a usual day's work.

Soon, however, Black began to change. He became impatient with our talk; he complained that it interfered with the work; he spent more and more time on the top, "looking down our collars" as we worked. In short, he started to "rawhide" us.

Black was fast taking on the typical employer's psychology. He was one of those who are quick to seek personal emancipation by climbing out of their class over the shoulders of their fellow workers. It is the type that gives birth to spies, strike-breakers and corrupt labor leaders. Lurking beneath his thin veneer of working-class revolutionary phrases had lain the seed of petty-bourgeois greed, planted there by his capitalist environment. Black was giving just one more illustration of the truth of Marx's great principle that the way people get their living determines their social outlook.

Black's progress capitalist-wards was swift. In the third week of our job he fired one of our gang for not doing enough work. Then he gave up eating dinner with us, and no more did he join in our revolutionary talk. He even complained against the union and hired two non-wobblies.

Meanwhile, we were boiling higher and higher with resentment. Things came to an open break when he took on the non-unionists. We struck. Whereupon Black denounced the union like any capitalist and called in the police to help smash our strike. He did not succeed, however, as the I.W.W. in Spokane was strong and militant. The general contractor, who had urgent need of the work, stepped in, eliminated the sub-contractor, Black, and reinstated the discharged workers. Then we returned to work. Thus ended Black's experiment at combining I.W.W.-ism and capitalism.

But Black had had a taste of exploiting workers. The capitalist tiger instinct in him was roused. No more working for wages, no more revolution, no more I.W.W. for him. He was now out to "get his."

Years later I ran across him, a non-union contractor in that haven of open-shoppers, Los Angeles. The capitalist class had recruited another bitter labor hater.

METAL MINING

In my varied experience as an industrial worker I never had much of a hankering for life underground. I always preferred to work in the daylight. The only spell I ever had at mining of any kind was in the Coeur d'Alene, Idaho, where I worked in the spring of 1909.

The I.W.W. in Spokane, Washington, of which I was a member, decided to organize the miners in the Coeur d'Alene district. It was a tough country. The body of miners were unorganized, the Western Federation of Miners having been smashed a dozen years before in one of the hardest fought strikes in the history of the West. The whole area was dominated by company gunmen, and typical open-shop conditions prevailed. Any miner known to be a union man was driven out of the community.

Several of us wobblies were delegated to go to the Coeur d'Alene, get jobs in the mines, and begin organization. We got not a cent for expense money. Sam Harrigan, a copper miner from Butte, and myself, were sent to Wardner, and after a day or so we got jobs in the Bunker Hill and Sullivan silver and lead mine, said to be the largest in the world.

Wardner was a typical Idaho mining camp, lost in a deep canyon of the Coeur d'Alene Mountains, a spur of the Bitter Root range. It was a collection of saloons, gambling joints, whore-houses and big rambling frame boarding shacks for miners.

We both went to work as muckers, or laborers. Sam was a miner, but could not tell the hiring agent so, as he would at once have been suspected of being a union man. The company hired its skilled workers mostly from the lead mines around Joplin, Missouri, the place where it recruited its scabs to break the big strike of years before.

I found mining very interesting. We worked in a stope several hundred feet underground. Before us the rich vein of ore, several inches thick, glistened diagonally in the face of the rock. Our job—miners, timbermen and muckers—was to blast out the ore and rock, and then shovel it all down a chute to the ore cars below. It was hard, unhealthy and dangerous work. In a nearby "glory hole"—an untimbered working thus named because so many men go to "glory" in such places— several workers had been killed a few weeks before by a heavy fall of rock.

Conditions were bad. Wages were about a dollar a day less than in Butte, nearby, which was a unionized copper mining town. The legal eight-hour day was grossly violated. The mine was dusty and un- healthy, many miners suffering from consumption. Safety conditions were wretched and accidents frequent. No one dared open his mouth, for the first complaint to the boss meant being fired, blacklisted and drilled out of camp.

Sam and I sized the situation up for about a week, before taking active steps. The men were discontented but terrorized by gunmen and the spy system. Finally, however, we located a miner who re- sponded to our broad hints. He was an old-timer, a hero of many brave fights of the old Western Federation of Miners in Rocky Moun- tain mining districts. By the fourth week we had lined up several more and things were going along swimmingly.

Then the blow fell. Sam and I were suddenly stopped one night in the middle of the shift and told to get our time. Several of our re- cruits were also fired. Evidently spies had reported us. At the time- keeper's office two gunmen tagged onto us and walked us over to our boarding shack, where we found that our meager belongings were already out on the wooden sidewalk. The gunmen warned us to leave Wardner immediately.

We stuck around town for a few days, however, sleeping in a hobo "jungle," as the hotels and lodging houses refused our money. We went on to Kellogg and Wallace, but gunmen were soon at our heels. Obviously, organizing work was out of the question for us, so we headed back to Spokane. There we learned that the other Coeur d'Alene delegates had had pretty much the same experience. The I.W.W. organizing campaign had failed.

This ended my short experience at mining. In after years I tried to "rustle" a job on several occasions "on the hill" in Butte, without success. That camp had also gone open shop and the Anaconda Copper Company had an elaborate blacklist system. They could spot "wobblies" from afar, and had no use for my services.

A TENT SHOW

My only experience in the theatrical business was in the summer of 1912, when I spent about three months with a wagon tent show. I served in the lowly capacity of canvasman. It was a repertoire show, playing small towns in southern Indiana and Illinois.

Our show was owned by Charlie Colton of Indianapolis. Colton's cousin, Earl G. Ford, was a friend of mine, and it was through him I got the job. Once Ford listed for me fifty-five of his relatives then in the show business—in circuses, stock companies, musical comedies, motion pictures, medicine shows and what not.

We made "jumps" of hardly more than thirty miles by wagon. Our repertoire consisted of several shows, a different one for each night of our usual week's stay. They were of the tear-jerking melodramatic type, including such old-timers as *Lena Rivers, Forget Me Not* and *East Lynne*. Between the acts the players doubled with song and dance numbers.

Everybody connected with the show, regardless of his job, was considered an actual or potential actor. When we put on a play demanding a larger cast, or if some of the troupe were sick or drunk, the boss and ticket-taker would be pressed into service on the stage. They even tried to induce me, the canvasman, to act. But I had other plans in mind than to become a Thespian. However, I did learn that many a well-known professional actor originally found his way onto the stage in a manner just as prosaic as that of a canvasman doubling for a regular player. Most of our actors had contempt for the public's artistic appreciation and they looked upon their own art as just so much work. They considered any good mechanical trade as hard to learn as acting. They averaged about twenty-five dollars per week in wages.

In the corn-belt towns where we played our shows went over big. The tent was crowded nearly every night. This was long before the radio, and motion pictures were just penetrating such rural districts. Rare also were road stock shows and circuses, and the people were starved for diversion. I never ceased to wonder at how the natives would accurately recall the previous visit of our show, often three or four years before, and recite in detail the plays and actors of the earlier visit. Another marvel to me was that although often some of our players went on the stage so drunk they could hardly "navigate," the rural audiences, although only a few feet away across the footlights, never noticed their intoxication. The public seemed quite unable to conceive of an actor being drunk while playing.

I had a fine experience with the tent show, driving through the beautiful corn country and meeting thousands of people in the various towns. But all this was secondary to me. I had taken the job so I could do some writing with Ford. He and I were pioneers in founding the Syndicalist League of North America, and we had to prepare its program and principles.

During those many weeks traveling with Colton's tent show, I wrote the pamphlet, *Syndicalism,* in consultation with Ford. This pamphlet later played a big role in the steel strike of 1919, when the employers, in order to picture the strike as a revolutionary attempt to overthrow the government, published and distributed free large quantities of the booklet. I hammered out the pamphlet during long hot afternoons in the empty tent, on the shaking wagons pounding over rough country roads, or while loafing in the beautiful fields and woods. When I was done writing the pamphlet my theatrical days were over. I quit my job and piled back into Chicago to put the pamphlet's principles into effect, by taking the initiative in launching the Syndicalist League of North America, forerunner of the Trade Union Educational League.

THE RAILROAD SPIRIT

Industrial workers as a whole react the same towards the basic problems that confront them in industry, yet they have considerable minor differences in psychology. The outlook of a needle worker is not like that of a steel worker, working in a huge plant amidst roaring machinery and elementary industrial processes and dominated by a powerful and ruthless trust. And, sailors, homeless and wandering over the face of the earth, have a considerably different point of view than packinghouse workers who work in crowds in the midst of blood and mass death.

The railroad worker also, especially in the running trades, has his own special psychology. His sense of control over the long trains, his feeling that he occupies a strategic position in industry, his meeting with many new scenes and people daily, his relative freedom on the road from the spying presence of the boss, his realization that he is a member of a strong labor union—all combine to give him a sense of sturdy independence. Despite efforts of the companies and conservative leaders to check it, he shows this spirit constantly in his daily life, and he has written many glorious pages in labor history, in the historic strike of 1877, the American Railway Union strike of 1894, the "outlaw" switchmen's strike of 1919, the national shopmen's strike of 1922, etc.

In the ten years that I spent as a railroader I got to know well and to admire the militant spirit of the railroad workers. Let me illustrate it by a simple story—the tale of a piece of apple pie—which at the time it happened tickled my sense of humor and class spirit.

I was working west out of Chicago as a brakeman on the Northwestern. We were held at a small place with a "meet order" and, while waiting for the train that had to pass us, we all went into the lone local restaurant to grab a bite to eat. In the crew there were five of us: the "hoghead" (engineer), the "con" (conductor), the "tallow-pot" (fireman) and two "shacks" (brakemen). We also had along with us the Division Superintendent, an officious bureaucrat.

The six of us sat down together. For dessert we had some particularly appetizing-looking apple pie. The one pie was cut in five pieces and on top sat an extra piece for the sixth man. As the waitress put the luscious pie on the table she remarked, "I was lucky to find the sixth piece, it's the last we've got."

As we ate, we workers chatted among ourselves, the "Super" eating without a word. He gobbled his food and was the first to reach the dessert stage. Whereupon he shoved his knife under the double-decked section of the pie, put the two pieces on his plate and began to wolf them.

I was amazed at this proceeding and so were the rest of the crew. What unspeakable gall. When the Super took the two pieces of pie he knew quite well that one of us would have to go pieless. I thought to myself, What a boss-hog, what a true representative of the North-western railroad company, in fact, of all the employing class.

The workers looked from one to another in rising contempt and anger. Finally, "Slim," our "boomer" hind-end brakeman, solved the situation in the traditional railroad workers' aggressive spirit. Quite unabashed by the Super's reputation as a bureaucratic tyrant, Slim called out to the waitress, "Say, sister, bring us five portions of tapioca pudding, there's only enough pie here for the Super."

All of us workers laughed loudly. The Super's face turned red and he left the table without finishing his pie. He also found some excuse for not traveling farther on our train. Within a couple of days the whole division was laughing over the incident. It was surprising how much class feeling could be evoked by just a piece of apple pie.

THE INTERCHANGE CAR INSPECTOR

For ten years, in various capacities, I worked as a railroader. I liked the work, but found it dangerous. Once, when a fireman on the O.R. &N. railroad in Portland, Oregon, an explosion on an oil-burner loco-motive seriously burned my face and might have destroyed my eyes. Another time I was nearly killed on the same road by a hostler start-ing a locomotive while I was underneath it. And again, I narrowly escaped gangrene from an injury received as a brakeman on the Chicago & Northwestern; I was laid up four months and lost my job. But my worst experience came at car inspecting.

When one railroad transfers cars to another, the receiving road has to make a close inspection of the cars as it accepts them. This is for self-protection, because the various railroads constantly seek to rob each other by smuggling through cars needing heavy repairs, with missing parts, or carrying wrong equipment. The men who do this inspection are called interchange car inspectors. It was my lot to work at this job for several years up to 1917, on a number of roads, mostly in the Chicago switching district.

The inspector had to be familiar with the innumerable parts of the hundreds of types of wooden freight cars in use upon scores of railroads. Besides, he had to know the equipment all these cars were supposed to carry, and he had to work so rapidly that he had to gauge at a glance the condition of the cars. If he made a mistake by failing to note that a car was carrying the wrong kind of wheels, airbrake or coupler, or that a pair of sills were broken, it cost his company considerable money and brought consequent "hell" down on himself.

The car inspector received from sixty-five to eighty dollars a month. For this wage he slaved twelve hours a day, seven days a week. As for myself, with the job an hour's street car ride distant, it used to be fourteen hours from the time I left home for work until I got back. There were no vacations and one had to put in as sick to get even a day's layoff. The car inspector's life was an eternal round of work and sleep, with no opportunity for education or relaxation.

In all kinds of weather the car inspectors could be found plugging along the trains, giving them a swift "once over." Even on the coldest nights we used to work without gloves, with record book in one hand and pencil in the other. But far worse than the overwork and inclement weather was the great eyestrain produced by the constant rapid glancing over the cars under all kinds of light conditions. Many an inspector ruined his eyes in this way.

It so happened that for me this eyestrain proved disastrous. The heavy pressure of the work upon my eyes was made worse by the fact that at the time, despite my long hours on the job, I was also acting as national secretary of the Syndicalist League of North America, and I devoted every available waking moment to reading and to writing letters. As a result, my eyes gave out and I had to give up my job on the C.&N.W. at Chicago.

My condition became so bad that for three years I hardly read a single newspaper or book. What correspondence I carried on as secretary of the S.L. of N.A. I actually wrote blindfolded. I could not look upon any kind of motion. When I rode in a street car I had to keep my eyes shut, the moving panorama outside the windows causing me acute agony. I also developed a photophobia, or sensitiveness to light. Any place brightly lighted was intolerable to me, and I had to blindfold myself against even heavily shaded electric lights at home. I thought I would go blind. For several months I was totally unemployed. When I finally returned to work I was forced to accept the cheapest laboring work. I did not receive a dime for my disability, the railroad company being in no way legally responsible. With no social security laws in effect and the union powerless, I was quite unprotected.

Meanwhile, I made every effort to gain relief from my eye condition. I was prescribed a dozen or two pairs of glasses of every imaginable character: green, amber, smoked, thick, thin, beveled and riffled, but without result; I was sent to the country in the hope that the green trees and grass would relieve my eyes; I underwent three agonizing and futile nasal operations on the theory that my trouble originated in nose-bone pressure upon the optic nerve; I fasted completely for ten days with the fruitless idea that an improvement in my general health might help my eyes; I stayed six weeks in a room kept black dark, on the supposition that complete eye rest was what I needed; yet I got no better.

So it went on for three years, until I was almost desperate. Then I found the solution: a Chicago physician, an advertising doctor who was a clever surgeon but known as a faker, operated on one of my eyes, slashing the muscles so that they would balance with those of the other eye. The cure was radical and immediate, after my three years of acute suffering. My eyes soon became strong again, and for the next dozen years I wore no glasses, although I did heavy secretarial work. I had finally escaped disaster, but I never did another's day's work at car inspecting.

PIECE-WORK

Piece-work is a bane to the working class. It means the most destructive speed-up and exploitation. The workers in the railroad industry, especially in the car works and locomotive repair shops, suffered greatly from this evil up to the time of the World War, when the unions succeeded largely in abolishing it.

In the several pre-war years that I worked in the railroad car department—as car inspector, car carpenter, airbrakeman and laborer on various railroads—I had much experience with piece-work. It was particularly vicious in the numerous car shops in the Chicago district, and was so general there that even laborers who gathered up the scrap lumber and iron were paid on the piece basis.

Repairing the wooden railroad cars of those days was very heavy work, but when paid by the piece it was simply man-killing. In my time I have done much hard labor, but none so exhausting as piece-work car-repairing. The working day was ten hours and the pace grueling. The workers were mostly Poles, Lithuanians and other Slavs—a husky bunch indeed. Americans, English and Irish were as scarce as hen's teeth at this hard and ill-paid work. The car repairers worked at a speed that literally burned them up, but few could earn over fifteen to twenty dollars a week. An ordinary worker would starve at the job, and the average work life of the powerful immigrant piece-work car repairers did not exceed ten years.

Straight piece-work was bad enough, but when bonus systems were injected into it then it became real hell. Take, for example, the time-bonus system in the car shops and on the "rip" tracks of the C.&E.I. railroad. The immigrant workers looked upon this as an invention of the devil. Besides driving them to the limit of endurance, it was so complicated that none could understand it. Two elements, the basic piece price and the time it took to do the work, entered into the final calculation of what a worker was paid for a given job. As an illustration: replacing a few boards on a car had a basic rate of, say, twenty cents, with a time allowance of twenty minutes; thus if you finished the job in twenty minutes you got twenty cents for it. Simple enough so far; but if it took twenty-five minutes you got only eighteen cents or, if you could conclude the job within fifteen minutes you would get twenty-two cents.

This complicated system created confusion worst confounded. No worker knew how much he was earning, for there were hundreds of parts and combinations of parts in the old wooden cars, and only the timekeeper knew the exact time consumed and the ultimate piece price arrived at on each operation. The general result was that the men speeded themselves desperately. They had no protection against being robbed shamelessly by the company lickspittle piece-work checkers. On pay day the men, almost entirely unorganized, took whatever was handed to them, helpless to make a re-check of their many piece jobs of the previous two weeks. Small wonder that the railroad companies defended the piece-work plan as the apple of their eye, and that the railroad unions made it the center of their attack.

Piece-work car repairing not only destroyed the workers by excessive toil, it also often brought them terrible injuries, and sudden death. The following was an all-too-common occurrence. Mike Kovecs was a truck-hand at Swift's refrigerator car shops in the Chicago stockyards, where I worked as an airbrake repairman. Now, even at regular rates, work on car trucks—the wheels and the heavy steel framework about them—is very hard and dangerous work, but when it is done on a piece basis it is truly murderous. On Swift's repair track the company had formerly had a special crew of day-work men to jack up the cars so that the piece-work truck hands could work under them. This gave the latter a measure of protection, for the jacking up of the cars was done by experts. But the company, for economy's sake, abolished the jacking crew and threw upon the piece-working truck hands the task of jacking up their own cars.

This change meant, as the company well understood, exposing the truck hands to terrible danger, for in the usual rush of piece-work they could not use the necessary care in jacking up the heavy cars. Soon the inevitable "accident" happened. Mike and his partner had hurriedly jacked up a heavily loaded refrigerator car. But in their haste they had failed properly to place the blocking for the jack, setting it on too soft ground. They got the car raised, but hardly had Mike crawled under it than the treacherous blocking collapsed and the loaded car fell full upon him. His body was crushed flat, almost cut in two, between the car sills and the wheel, and he died instantly without uttering a sound. I saw the whole tragedy from where I was working nearby.

Mike was just another of the nameless thousands of workers slaughtered yearly for profit's sake. After the death of Mike, Swift & Company, with cynical hypocrisy, put up many snappy "Safety First" signs; but they refused to give the truck hands back their jacking crew.

The deadly menace of piece-work car repairing extended beyond the car department. It was also a threat to the life and limb of the train service workers and to the traveling public. This I saw tragically illustrated one night in the killing of a young switchman in the Woods Street (Chicago) yards of the C.&N.W. railroad, where I was employed as a car inspector.

Near our car shanty a switching crew were breaking up a "cut" of cars. They uncoupled a big steel hopper car loaded with fifty tons of coal, and gave it a sharp kick down the track. A switchman leaped (they were overspeeded also) to brake down the hopper before it should crash into a string of box cars farther along. Clambering hastily up the head-end side-ladder, he grabbed for the handwheel to screw up the brakes. The handwheel, on top of the brakestaff, is supposed to be kept in place by a single nut. But this car had just come from the piece-work repair track, and in the hurry of the work the all-important brake-nut had not been properly tightened.

So, when the switchman grabbed the handwheel and threw his weight into a twisting grasp to put on the brakes, the handwheel came loose, and with a wild shriek the switchman pitched forward beneath the wheels of the heavy car. Both trucks passed over him. His head was cut off completely. His body was carried home to his widow and three young children, who were left to meet life without a breadwinner and practically penniless. But the Juggernaut of the railroad piece-work system went right on, undisturbed by this proletarian tragedy and hundreds of others like it.

CHAPTER II . . . SAILING SHIP DAYS

The period from 1901 to 1904 I spent going to sea in old square-rigged sailing ships. I sailed one and one-half times around the world, twice doubling Cape Horn and once the Cape of Good Hope. Counting considerable stays on the coasts of Africa, Australia and South America, my journey lasted nearly three years and covered some fifty thousand miles. I sailed in four British merchant ships: the Pegasus, Black Prince, Alliance and County of Cardigan. I became an able seaman and was qualified to do a sailor's work, from making a ratline on a spinning jenny to stepping a mast. The following are a few true, undecorated pictures of the life of the deep-water sailor during those years in the square-riggers, which have now almost completely disappeared from the seas.

A GALE OFF CAPE HORN

We were in the four-masted bark, *Pegasus,* Captain Moulton, of Liverpool, bound from Portland, Oregon, to Capetown, South Africa, in 1901. The *Pegasus* was a fast sailer, but because of alternating headwinds and calms it was three and a half months before we reached the latitude of Cape Horn, usually a two-months' run. We found ourselves far out in the Pacific, about fifteen hundred miles west of the Horn. A strong wind sprang up from the southwest, and the *Pegasus* made rapid headway.

Hourly the gale grew stronger; it whistled through the rigging and the seas mounted rapidly. Gradually we reduced sail and the *Pegasus* raced before the storm. She logged as much as eighteen knots per hour, the speed of a seven-day transatlantic liner. The storm grew steadily worse. Right from the Antarctic, it howled and shrieked as the seas piled higher and higher. The *Pegasus* dashed onward under nothing but lower topsails and a goose-winged foresail.

It was the third night of the storm, and it was our watch on deck. Another young sailor and myself were standing under the fo'c's'le head, speculating whether our ship could ride out the storm. We had to shout in each other's ears to be heard above the roar of the wind. To make one's way along the decks was difficult, even with the stretched life-lines. Suddenly the ship received an awful blow and shook all over as though she were going to pieces. We realized at once she had shipped a great sea astern.

We started aft, and as we passed the midships bridge the mate bawled out the dreaded, "All hands on deck." The after part of the ship was a chaos. The big sea that had boarded us smashed two boats and the after wheel-house, carried away a long section of the fore-and-aft bridge, wrecked the large harness cask (the slate vat used for soaking out salt meat) and obliterated the big teakwood chicken coop and its dozen occupants. The deck was awash and waist deep with water. As the ship rolled in the heavy seas, the water dashed from side to side; the men were in great danger of being crushed by the surging wreckage or swept overboard. Old Captain Moulton lost his head and Collins, the second mate, took practical control. Under his direction we managed to lasso all the careening wreckage and heave it overboard.

It was a rough moment, but still there was humor in it. We sailors were glad to see the big chicken coop go to smash, and we joked about it in the midst of the storm's roar. We hated the chickens, which used to lay eggs for the officers while we lived on starvation food. But now the miserable "fowls" were gone, and we laughed despite the confusion and danger. Then a Swede got the happy thought that perhaps, somewhere in the chaos, we might locate the chickens. Finally, by good luck, we found the rooster, in the port scupper, drowned and sadly bedraggled. But the manner of his demise nor the condition of his remains did not disturb us. With special satisfaction, in close conspiracy with the cook, we ate him that very night.

The following morning the storm continued to rage on. It was our watch below from four to eight. The fo'c's'le was awash with icy water and everything we had, bunks, clothes and all, was soaked through. Suddenly we heard a great sea come roaring aboard. As it crashed on the deck over our heads, the hundreds of tons of water seemed about to smash through the heavy planking and drown us like rats.

Above the roar of the storm we could hear shouts and heavy tramping on the deck. We knew something serious had happened. Soon the upper half of the iron fo'c's'le door was flung open and two men crawled in. They pulled after them another, screaming in pain. It was Fred Wolfe, with a broken leg. He had been hit by the sea she had just shipped, and had almost gone over the side in the backwash.

The fifth day of the blow started gray and menacing. The wind roared and screamed louder than ever. Never before or since have I seen such seas. Great gray-black mountains of water lashed white with foam, they raced ahead with twice the speed of the flying *Pegasus,* lifting her like a cork. Once in a while a snow squall raced past frantically, the flying scud lashing our faces like a whip. We were cold, water-soaked and depressed, and we got only a slight relief from the only ration of grog served us on the whole trip. It seemed the terrific sou'wester would never stop. Our one consolation was that it was a fair wind, and the *Pegasus* was making the best of it. Already, in four days, she had logged off the fifteen hundred miles of easting and was now abreast of Cape Horn.

On this never-to-be-forgotten day it was my watch on deck from four to eight A.M. Seven bells (7:20 A.M.) had just struck and we were preparing to go below for breakfast and four hours' rest. The second mate yelled out to us above the storm to "sweat the lee braces." Now, to explain this order a bit: the braces are the rigging by which the yards are hauled around and held to the wind, and to "sweat" them meant to take up on the lee side the slack that had developed from the mad tossing of the ship during the night. So we lined up at the lee fore brace for a pull. Our whole watch, including the idlers (carpenters, sailmakers, donkeymen and cook) numbered eighteen. Mickey O'Brien, our chantey man, was first on the line, and singing out as best he could in the storm's roaring. After him came Ole, the Norwegian, then Dawson, then myself and next "Frenchy," with the rest of the watch strung out along the brace.

Just as we were about to pull and Mickey had struck up "A Long Time Ago," the man at the wheel, Wilson, a Lowestoft fisherman and an excellent sailor, on the orders of the second mate put down his helm and brought the ship up a point or two into the wind. The purpose of this was to put more wind pressure upon the weather side of the yards, so we could take in the slack on the lee side. But it was a bad maneuver in such a terrific gale and it might easily have foundered the ship.

Hardly had the ship come up a bit than she lost the swing of the swell and a monster sea boarded her weather side just opposite where we were working. With a roar the sea crashed across the deck full tilt at us. We could see it coming—a deadly avalanche of green-gray water. To the shout of "Look out, here she comes!," everyone grabbed what he could for safety. I dropped into the scupper and wrapped myself around an iron bulwark stanchion. The heavy sea struck us and poured over the lee side of the ship like a Niagara. I still have a vivid recollection of how the tremendous lift of the water, as it went over the side, almost tore me loose and dragged me overboard with it.

As the *Pegasus* righted herself I got up, half strangled with the brine I had swallowed and wet to the skin. I stood waist deep in water. Soon the ship shook herself free of the water on deck and we finished sweating the lee fore braces. We then went aft to the mainmast to repeat the process there. But suddenly the second mate, from the weather side of the deck, looked sharply at us, crossed over and yelled out above the storm, "Where's the watch?" We began to count ourselves. One was missing. It was Ole the Norwegian, who had stood just in front of me as we hauled in the fore brace. Something sharp and chill struck my heart. At once I knew that death had passed by my elbow. The second mate ordered me to the fo'c's'le to look for Ole. But we knew it was useless. We knew he had gone over the side in the great sea we had shipped just a while ago.

The watch below stopped eating when I asked for Ole, for they realized what had happened. In the meantime our watch on deck had counted themselves again and found still another missing! It was "Frenchy," who had stood exactly behind me. He from one side of me, and Ole from the other side, had been carried overboard. And no one had seen or heard them go! They had simply vanished, swallowed by the rush of the sea and washed over the side without sight or sound.

The skipper and the two mates talked together a minute or two as to what should be done. They told us an attempt to heave the ship to (bring her to a stop) or to put her about (turn her around) would founder her and send us all to the bottom. Also it would be utterly impossible for a ship's boat to live in such a sea, even if we could launch one. Besides, twenty minutes had elapsed since Ole and "Frenchy" had been swept overboard, and as the *Pegasus* was logging sixteen knots, the lost sailors were already five or six miles astern and probably drowned by then or slashed to death by the huge beaks of hungry albatrosses. So the Captain declared nothing could be done. We of the crew made no answer, but later among ourselves in the fo'c's'le we agreed that any attempt to rescue the two men would have been suicidal.

The *Pegasus* sailed right on with the furious storm behind her. Powerless to assist them, we left poor Ole and "Frenchy" to their fate "off the pitch of the Horn." Later, according to the time-honored custom, we divided their few things amongst us.

Who they were, where they lived, or whether they had families we never knew, and I doubt it the ship's officers did either. They were just two more sailors, unknown and unsung, lost off that great graveyard of deep-water ships and men, Cape Horn.

PARADISE

Towards the end of 1903 we were aboard the three-masted British bark *County of Cardigan,* laying in Talcahuano Bay, Chile, loading wheat for Queenstown, Ireland. Talcahuano, not far from Patagonia, is one of the southernmost ports in the world. Fierce gales suddenly develop there, and often ships are driven ashore and wrecked. There were no docks in this port, the windjammers lying out in the bay to load their cargoes from lighters. In view of the grave danger from storms, the ships had to be ready to stand out to sea at a moment's notice. So shore leave for the crews was highly restricted, our ship allowing only two men to go ashore each Saturday night, for a twenty-four hours' stay.

This limited shore leave was a great grief to our crew who, after long months of ship life, were thoroughly sex-starved and land-hungry. But we had to make the best of it. Each Saturday night we drew lots to decide upon the two men to go ashore. The first winners were Ned Lyndon and Jim Macklin.

Ned and Jim duly went ashore, while the crew impatiently awaited their return on Sunday to learn their experiences. When the two got back aboard it was an alluring story they told, while the crew in the dingy fo'c's'le sat about, enraptured. Through Saturday night, they said, they had been royally entertained by Chilean girls in a swell establishment frequented mostly by Chilean army and navy officers. The girls were beautiful black-eyed, long-tressed houris, overflowing with spontaneous affection and passion for the two eager sailors. It was indeed a paradise, and the woman-starved crew listened hungrily while Ned and Jim recounted their thrilling adventures.

Saturday slowly rolled around once again and, according to the rule, also the shore-leave lottery. Ned and Jim gave the two lucky winners detailed instructions on how to locate the house with the lovely girls, upon whose beauty and tenderness they had not ceased to expand during the whole week. Noting down the directions carefully, the two sailors, with five Childean dollars apiece, went ashore for a night's gaiety.

Next day they came back disappointed and angry. Several hours the previous night they had spent looking for Ned's and Jim's paradise. But in vain. They bawled out Ned and Jim for giving them wrong information. This only stimulated the latter to enlarge still more upon the golden charms of their girl friends. And so it went week after week, with sailors going ashore and not finding the place, and with Ned and Jim pretty thoroughly discredited but still sticking to the story of their voluptuous adventures.

Finally "Cockney" Veal and I drew the lucky lots and we went ashore, also resolved to prove or disprove the existence of the now almost legendary paradise of Ned and Jim. We duly went to Manchester Kate's and followed the other minute directions we had received aboard ship from Ned Lyndon. But we, too, found nothing, although we branched out in our search, frisking the whole town, which was not a large one.

We went into a dozen houses, usually terrible in their squalor and filth. One, I recall, was an especially tough-looking joint. The "reception" room was a small dance hall. The floors were of earth, and as it was the rainy season they were slippery and wet. In the middle of the hall was a dingy coal oil lamp, hung high to keep it out of the way of the frequent fights. In one corner sat an old, weazened woman picking at a guitar. The "girls," mostly from forty upwards, were dirty and unkempt. Their naked legs were thickly spattered with mud, and all were maudlin drunk. Half a dozen drunken soldiers surged about the place.

"Cockney" and I were no sooner in this den than we wished ourselves outside. But the "girls" objected to our going, and the several soldiers were also in a belligerent mood, resenting our evident lack of enthusiasm for their lady friends. It looked as though there would be knife play, but we managed to get out with whole skins. After this we gave up in disgust our hunt for Ned's and Jim's gentle houris. But these two worthies were not impressed by our failure any more than they had been by that of the others. They still clung to their original story.

So the matter seemed slated to remain, with Ned and Jim the butt of a ship full of scoffers. But it so happened we had a strike, or refusal of duty aboard our ship. The officers promptly had us all arrested and, while awaiting trial before the British consul, we had a few hours free to wander about the beach. Then it occurred to me this would be a good time for Ned and Jim to lead us in person to their palace of joy. They agreed with alacrity, evidently glad at last for a chance to justify themselves.

Soon, under their guidance, we were in a familiar-looking street. "Cockney" and I began to laugh. For the two had led us to the terrible den where my mate and I got such a shock. Both Ned and Jim seemed astonished at the kind of a dive they now found themselves in. But they agreed it was the right place, while the crew gave them the horse-laugh. They, their houris and their paradise were the stock joke of the crew all the way around Cape Horn.

Ned and Jim were not so wrong after all. They had really told the truth as they saw it. Their finding so much joy and beauty in the miserable girls and their wretched hovel was only the reaction of sex-starved sailors freed from the artificial life of a ship's fo'c's'le and generously warmed by women and an alcohol long denied them. Had those sailors who criticized them lingered a bit longer at Manchester Kate's "pub," instead of rushing off so hastily to find the fabled paradise, they too might have seen beauty in it. Many a deep-water sailor, ashore from his ship after a long voyage, has built himself a night's paradise out of even less promising material than Ned's and Jim's.

HUNGER AFLOAT

One of the greatest hardships on British square-rigged vessels was the abominable food. The rich shipping companies exploited the seamen through beggarly wages, by undermanning the ships, and also by a vicious system of "belly-robbing." The food on the ships was insufficient in quantity and wretched in quality.

Many ships were actually lost in earlier years because of scurvy conditions. The ship insurance companies finally objected and the Board of Trade worked out its notorious "whack," or minimum rations for seamen. This "whack," which was figured as low as possible, was in force upon most British windjammers.

Our breakfast aboard ship consisted of coffee and hardtack; dinner for three days a week was a small slice of salt beef and a single bread roll, and for the other three work days, salt pork and pea soup; supper comprised only tea and hardtack, with sometimes "dog-body," "dandy-funk," or some other doubtful dish made from dinner leftovers which, incredibly enough, the sailors managed to save.

This was the steady diet at sea, and we seldom had a chance to add to it by fish caught over the side. In port the grub was almost as bad and we sailors used to conveniently visit the steamers at neighboring docks in time to eat; the steamer men, situated more strategically and possessing some rudiments of organization, were able to insist upon better food than we had.

The ship used to rob us also on the food measure. I never saw a pound of meat or bread so tiny as on a windjammer. Our daily pound of sea biscuit consisted of only four hardtacks. On the worst ships the crew had a man present at the weighing of the meat, after which it was placed in a small locked cage-like affair, where it remained locked during the cooking to prevent its being stolen. Often the ship supplies ran short and then it was real hell. Once, on the *County of Cardigan,* a hungry Welsh ship, we ran entirely out of white flour, salt pork, sugar and tobacco. The crew smoked tea leaves and rope yarn, cutting up their old pipes to lend at least a savor of tobacco to the strange smoking mixtures.

Worst of all was the water. We were allowed only three quarts each per day. This, often full of wrigglers, had to suffice for all purposes. Morning coffee and evening tea took one-and-a-half quarts; another quart went to the galley, most of which was stolen by the officers. In the tropics, unless we were fortunate enough to collect a little brackish rain water off the deck houses, we actually went thirsty. To wash our clothes was a real holiday and it could only be done when we had rain water.

For baths and face washing we had to depend on salt water, but without salt water soap it did not cut the grease, tar, paint and oil with which sailors work. Dirty beyond description, we used to scrub each other's necks with kerosene in order to be "presentable" for shore leave.

The salt meat was incredibly tough and indigestible. Often it had been twenty years or more in the casks and was in a state of decomposition. Many times we would take the rotten meat aft, protest to the skipper and then throw the foul mess overboard. The sailors religiously believed the salt beef to be salt horse. On Sundays our meat consisted of a half pound of "fresh" canned beef, called Harriet Lane, in memory of a woman murdered many years before and sold to shipping companies as tinned "beef" by her butcher husband, like the Chicago sausage maker, Lutgert, who also got rid of his wife by working her up for the trade.

A real grief was the hardtack, or sea biscuit, the main staff of our diet. Sailing vessels leaving England usually took a three years' supply. At the end of a year or two of hot summer weather in the tropics this biscuit ordinarily became a crawling mass of weevils. But it was either eat it or starve. Cleaning out the weevils as best we could, we would devour the hardtack, knowing it was still tenanted and making sour jokes about the advantage of fresh meat in our meals. Oldtime sailors developed a technique of splitting the sea biscuits with their knife so as to avoid crushing the weevils inside. Then they would scrape away the weevils and their filth. At supper we used to break sea biscuits into the tea, skim off the weevils that came to the top, and trust to luck for the rest.

Our coffee, called "crew coffee," was not even chicory. The tea, of course, had never seen China; the salt was plain rock salt; the peas could have served as buckshot; the jam was made of fruit scraps, and had such an evil reputation that many hard-boiled sailors refused to eat it. Once, in Chile, our captain, to placate the crew's demands for food, bought two barrels of honey. Imagine our disgust when it turned out to be dregs from honey vats—a mess of bees' legs, wings, etc., in a thick, waxy liquid. But we ate it just the same.

Of course, human beings could not live healthily on such garbage, which lacked the minerals and vitamins of a sound diet. So, to avoid a complete breakdown in the men's health and the ensuing danger to the ships, the British shipowners served a glass of lime-juice, an antiscorbutic, twice a week to each man. The lime juice was dosed with saltpeter to check the men's sexual appetites, though it was hardly necessary on such a diet. This was how British ships came to be known as "lime-juicers."

The only reason for such a wretched diet was, of course, the desire of the shipowners for more profits. It was not because of the competition of the steamers, as the shipowners said; for the starvation diet was traditional in the windjammers. There were likewise no serious technical reasons why the old sailing vessels could not have had good food and pure water. The employers were greedy and the sailors were unorganized; so our starvation diet, low wages and generally bad conditions resulted as a matter of course.

HELL ABOARD SHIP

In the old windjammers many harrowing experiences occurred as a result of their carrying no doctors. The captains, with no medical training and little equipment, were supposed to care for the men's health. Hence, if a man had an accident or fell acutely sick, he either died or got well as best as he could; or if someone came aboard with gonorrhea or some other chronic contagious disease, it ran its course unchecked.

Some of the most terrible of all sea tragedies have to do with sailors who, incapacitated by various causes, literally rotted and died in their bunks. The following incident is typical of such terrors in the life of the deep-water sailor. It all happened to Fred Wolfe, a young Canadian sailor on the *Pegasus,* who broke his leg in a storm off Cape Horn.

Wolfe was hit by a heavy sea and thrown violently against an iron stanchion. Like a pipe-stem his right leg snapped. Several of the crew seized him before he was washed overboard, though we often thought later it would have been an act of mercy to let the sea have him. Screaming in agony, he was brought into the fo'c's'le. This place was in a bad condition from the storm. Several inches of icy cold water was on the deck, and as the ship pitched and rolled the water raced from side to side, and as it encountered obstructions on the deck it cascaded high into the air, soaking the bunks and their occupants.

We stripped the oilskins and other clothes from the lower part of Wolfe's body, and as the injured, groaning lad lay on the deck, the water, shuttling back and forth with the wild heavings of the ship, repeatedly drenched him. Meanwhile the captain arrived and pronounced it a case of a broken leg. After much delay, while Wolfe was half frozen from the cold sea water, the skipper clumsily put on a splint and bandages. But he placed them between the knee and the ankle, whereas even we sailors could see that the leg was broken above the knee.

Wolfe protested frantically at the captain's ministrations, cursing wildly and tearing off the dressing. The captain bawled him out and warned him he would not be responsible for any bad effects upon his leg. Wolfe denounced the captain for his criminal incompetence, and we then lifted the miserable lad into his water-soaked bunk. He was almost delirious with pain. After the captain left we men talked it over and sent a couple of sailors aft to demand treatment for Wolfe. The captain replied he could do nothing more as he was no doctor. He blamed Wolfe for removing the splint and bandages. So the care of the injured man fell entirely to us.

We wanted to try to set Wolfe's leg, but he stridently objected, arguing that the trouble was a pulled tendon, and all the while whining with pain. We bound up his leg as best we could. But Wolfe's pain got unbearable and he made us take off the dressing. From then on he lay in his bunk with his broken leg without any bandaging whatever until we reached Capetown over two months later. All we could do to relieve him was to apply hot wet cloths.

The fracture of the bone was diagonal. This made Wolfe's pain more severe than if it had been a horizontal break. At times the torture was so great from the rolling of the ship that he became delirious. His agony appeared to be due to the action of the muscles pulling the broken parts past each other, so that the sharp points of the broken bone ripped their way through the flesh on both sides of the break until finally they almost broke out through the skin. The captain used to visit Wolfe for form's sake once a week, taking care, however, to keep beyond the reach of the frantic youth, who shouted that he would stick a knife into the captain's heart once he was able to stand on his feet.

From the time of the accident until we dropped anchor in Table Bay, Capetown, it was just ten weeks. For seven of these weeks Wolfe's agony endured. Then the pain gradually ceased, the break having evidently knitted. How the leg bones grew together under such conditions always seemed a bit of a miracle to me. Had Wolfe been an older man he probably would have died of blood poisoning or gone crazy from the exquisite pain.

When Wolfe was put on crutches to go ashore at Capetown his right leg was three or four inches shorter than the left. This showed how far the sharp points of the broken bones, under the pull of the leg muscles, had dug into his flesh during those horrible weeks of suffering. Even if Wolfe lives to be a hundred he will surely never forget the horrors of that awful journey from Cape Horn to Capetown. Nor will his shipmates.

In Capetown we investigated the possibilities of Wolfe's taking action against the captain and the ship. But we got nowhere; the companies and ship's officers were quite protected legally. The best we could do was to make them pay Wolfe's passage back to Montreal. The last I saw of him he was hobbling along a hospital walk in Capetown, a tragic example of the greed of the shipowners, one of the great army of workers destroyed yearly by the capitalist industrial Juggernaut.

SHANGHAIED

In the old days shanghaing men on board windjammers was an everyday occurrence. Conditions on the ships were so bad—with low wages, garbage as food and the officers' tyranny—that it was difficult to recruit crews, especially in places where deep-water sailors could find jobs if they jumped ship. In such ports the ship captains frequently shanghaied men with the assistance of local boarding house crimps, who got so much per head for each sailor furnished. The American coasts were notorious for this criminal practice.

Every old sailor could recall scores of cases of shanghaing. Even in my day as a sailor it was still very common, but I knew of only two shanghai incidents at first hand, both on the same ship. Let me relate one of them here.

I had just shipped on the *Pegasus*, bound from Portland, Oregon, to Capetown, South Africa. We took on most of the crew at Portland. We were then towed down to Astoria, a few miles from the open Pacific, where we shipped half a dozen additional men.

For some reason the arrival of the expected sailors was delayed. Impatiently the captain stalked up and down the poop. Darkness fell, and still no men. Finally they arrived, a boatload in charge of a notorious crimp. With loud swearing they clambered over the ship's rail. Two were so drunk they had to be hauled aboard and carried forward to the fo'c's'le, where they were dumped into a couple of filthy bunks to sleep it off. We weighed anchor, the tug towed us down the river and cast us off for our long, long trip around Cape Horn to South Africa.

Next morning everybody "turned-to" (went to work) except one, and a sick-looking crowd they were. The missing man lay in his bunk, too befuddled to get up and evidently not knowing where he was. He had a big gash in his head, all clotted with dried blood, and we treated it as best we could. Evidently knowing what was up, the mates made no special effort to force the sick sailor to work. Meanwhile, the *Pegasus*, with a strong wind behind her, dashed south at about twelve knots per hour.

On the morning of our second day at sea the injured man clambered out of his bunk. He was seasick and still shaky from the blow on his head. His face was full of amazement and confusion when he found he was at sea on a windjammer. When we told him what ship it was and where she was bound, he threw himself in his bunk and sobbed violently.

Recovering a bit, the sick man told us his story. His name was Erickson and he had worked as a logger in a camp not far from

Astoria. In a nearby Washington town he had a wife and three children. He had been in a waterfront saloon drinking with a couple of casual friends when suddenly things went black, and he remembered nothing until he woke up on board the *Pegasus*. It was a case of knockout drops, organized by the crimp who needed one more man on short notice for our ship. Where or how Erickson received the gash in his head he did not know; probably the crimp had given it to him "to make assurance doubly sure."

Erickson begged the skipper to put him ashore in some California port. But the latter wouldn't listen to his pleadings in behalf of his wife and children. To the skipper it was only another case of a shanghaied sailor, one of many he had seen in his long sea experience. He said nothing could be done; Erickson's name was on the ship's articles and there was no recourse but to go on to Capetown.

So Erickson was sentenced to the mental hell of a long trip in that windjammer. And as worse luck would have it, the *Pegasus'* passage was a slow one, lasting six months instead of the customary four months or less. All that time Erickson grieved and worried over his family. When the ship was becalmed or held back by contrary head winds, he was beside himself with anxiety and restlessness. I often feared he would go mad. Only when the *Pegasus* was scudding away before a fair wind did his spirits rise a little. Not once did we "speak" a ship, so that Erickson's whereabouts might be made known to his family.

Finally, the *Pegasus* arrived at Capetown. Landed at last, Erickson hurried to the cable office and, with a good part of his meager wages, sent a long wire to his wife. In a few days he got an answer that she had been prostrated by his disappearance and had finally given him up for dead.

How was he to get home now, ten thousand miles away? The American consul in Capetown refused him help. But he finally succeeded in shipping on a steamer bound for Liverpool, where we hoped that eventually he would find his way home again to his family.

Just a typical case of being shanghaied, and it might have been much worse.

A SAILOR'S WORK

On my first day aboard the *Pegasus* the mate lined us all up and ordered those who had never been to sea before to stand aside. A few stepped out, but not I. I was determined to be a sailor from the start. The mate, however, was quite wise to me and shouted, "Hey you, go aloft and work with those men on the main skysail yard."

I felt a stab of fear; for the skysail was the highest of all, except on ships that carried sails called, suggestively enough, "angels' footstools." I took to the rigging as the mate watched me from the deck. Up I went past the main, lower-topsail, upper-topsail, top-gallant and royal yards, until I finally climbed the swaying "Jacob's Ladder" up to the dizzy skysail yard. At the "futtock" rigging, where for about eight feet one actually climbs upside down, I thought I was a goner. But I made it. The men on the skysail yard laughed and told me to just hang on while they did the work. After that I had no further trouble about climbing.

The sailor's work aloft was very dangerous. Often the ratlines upon which he stepped were rotten and gave way. On the yards he stood on a foot rope that was always slack and slippery and which frequently broke under his weight. He might also be thrown from the yards by the wild pitching of the ship, the motion aloft being much greater than on deck. Or he could be dragged off the yards by the wind while he was making sail fast during a storm. Perhaps as many were killed by falls as were washed overboard. Aboard one ship that I was on, an apprentice, on the previous voyage, had his back broken by a fall from aloft. In the rigging the sailor's motto was, "One hand for the ship and one hand for myself."

The crew of a square-rigger was divided into two shifts or "watches," called "starboard" and "port," directed by the mate and second mate, respectively. The watches worked alternately four hours on and four hours off, which meant twelve hours a day for each. These four-hour shifts were also called "watches." Thus one would say that the port watch has the watch on deck. Between four and eight P.M. the watches, known as the "dog-watches," were only two hours long. This difference was to change the hours about; so that if the starboard watch had the watch below from twelve to four P.M. today, it would have the watch on deck the same hours tomorrow.

The working hours on deck were from five-thirty A.M. to six P.M. except on Sundays, holidays and in bad weather. If not working the ship, the sailors were kept busy at painting, sewing sails, holystoning decks, making small ropes, cleaning paint work, splicing cables and ropes and a hundred other tasks. The mates could always find some job to keep the men busy, as it was almost a religion with them never to let the men idle about.

The able seamen took turns of two hours each at the wheel and, after dusk, at the lookout on the forecastle head. Much of the rest of the daytime they spent aloft bending and unbending sails, reeving new rigging or at other jobs constantly needed to keep the vessel "ship-shape and Bristol fashion." Ordinarily the watch on deck could do the work alone of "making or reducing" sail, but if the ship had to "wear" (turn around with the wind) or "put about" (turn against the wind) the watch below were called on deck to help.

The square-rigger sailor had to know many knots, hitches and bends. There was also considerable "fancy work" aboard the wind-jammers, including Turks' heads, bucket ropes, bell lanyards, rope mats, cork fenders, grummets, sinnots, etc. The men also made many curios for their families and friends at "home."

The rigging of a tall windjammer seems a maze of ropes and cables. But it is all quite simple. To begin with, the ropes (nearly all called "lines") are identical on each of the masts. Likewise, the ropes on each of the several yards on a given mast are, with minor exceptions, the same. Then, the ropes on either side of the same yard are identical. Thus the whole "tangle" of rigging reduces itself very largely to learning the ropes for one side of one yard, plus a few others. So orderly are the ropes arranged that even on the darkest night and in the midst of the worst storm the sailor can locate them without diffi-culty.

For me sea life had a great fascination. I planned to study navigation on a three years' voyage to China I had in mind. But I reconsidered the matter, as it took me too far from the acute phases of the class struggle, in which I was deeply interested. So I gave it all up and became a landsman again. But it was a good dozen years before I finally reconciled myself to quitting the sea and its ships and men.

CHANTEYS

Sea chanteys are work songs. Their purpose was to organize the pulling on ropes and chains which constituted so much of a sailor's work. When work was in progress, if the men themselves did not start a chantey the officer on deck would call for one. Bad off, indeed, was the ship that had no capable chanteyman among its crew.

Deep sea chanteys were of several types. First, for light and rapid, hand-over-hand pulling on buntlines, clewlines, leechlines, etc., there were weird chants, a continuous stream of musical notes without words. These were the most difficult chanteys to sing.

Then, for heavier and regular pulling (sheets, braces) there was another type of wordless chantey, consisting only of "Yo-ho's," "Ho-he's," etc., also hard to sing. They were always rendered in a manner quite distinctive with each singer.

When the pulling became really heavy (hoisting yards) the chanteys first broke into actual words. These were the "halyards" chanteys, and the tempo of the work and the songs was much slower. The chantey singer would sing a line while the men rested; then the men would join in with a one-line chorus, giving two heavy pulls as they sang it. The chantey would thus ramble on indefinitely, until the job in hand was completed. There were many chanteys of this type, including such famous ones as "Whiskey Johnny," "Blow the Man Down," "Old Horse," "Jean Francois," "Ranzo Was No Sailor," "I Wonder What She Meant." Many had rollicking tunes. I even tried my hand at writing one. The words of the same chantey usually differed from ship to ship and from singer to singer.

"Whiskey Johnny" was characteristic of the halyard chanteys. The following gives an idea of it:

>Oh, whiskey is the life of man;
>>(*chorus*) Whiskey, Johnny;
>Oh, I'll get whiskey when I can;
>>(*chorus*) Whiskey for my Johnny;
>Oh, whiskey killed my poor old dad;
>>(*chorus*) Whiskey, Johnny;
>Oh, whiskey drove my mother mad;
>>(*chorus*) Whiskey for my Johnny.

For the heaviest work, such as weighing anchor, the capstan (a vertical windlass operated by man power) was used and "capstan chanteys" sung. As the men walked around the capstan, the chantey-man sang the verses, and the men joined in the relatively long choruses. There were numerous capstan chanteys, many with beautiful music. A very famous one was "Rolling Home," of which the first verse and chorus were:

>Call all hands to man the capstan,
>>See the cable run down clear,
>Heave away and with a will, boys,
>>For old England we will steer;
>And we'll sing in jolly chorus
>>In the watches of the night,
>And we'll sight the shores of England
>>When the gray dawn brings the light.

>(Chorus)

>Rolling home, rolling home,
>>Rolling home across the sea;
>Rolling home to dear old England,
>>Rolling home, fair land, to thee.

The chanteys were built from the lives of the sailors. The men sang of their homes, of their wretched ship's food and low wages, of the officers' brutality, of their work, of shipwrecks, of races between noted ships. In many chanteys the note was one of discontent and revolt. Very few expressed religious or patriotic sentiments. Reflecting the sex hunger on the ships, the favorite theme was of "love," that is, the "love" the deep-water sailor usually knew—his adventures with prostitutes. Scores of chanteys told of such adventures in full detail, and characteristically ended with the hero being robbed, shanghaied and infected with venereal disease. These chanteys were frank to the point of completeness. "The Maid of Amsterdam" was such a capstan chantey. Here are a few of its earlier verses, before the song becomes unprintable:

> In Amsterdam there dwelt a maid,
>   Mark well what I do say;
> In Amsterdam there dwelt a maid
>   And she was mistress of her trade;
> I'll go no more a-roving with you, fair maid.

(Chorus)

> A-roving, a-roving,
>   Since roving's been my ruin,
> I'll go not more a-roving
>   With you, fair maid.

> I put my hand upon her knee,
>   She said, "Young man, you're rather free."
> I put my hand upon her knee,
>   She said, "Young man, you're rather free."
> I'll go no more a-roving with you, fair maid.

(Chorus)

> I put my hand upon her thigh,
>   She said, "Young man, you're rather high."
> I put my hand upon her thigh,
>   She said, "Young man, you're rather high."
> No more I'll go a-roving with you, fair maid.

Often the chanteys were full of tradition. "Jean Francois," for example, dated back to the Napoleonic era. The first verse of this old-timer was:

> Bony (Bonaparte) was a warrior,
>   Hay, hi, ho;
> A warrior, a terrier,
>   Jean Francois.

Some hailed from American clipper ship days. One that we sang dealt with the 1849 gold rush to California:

> Blow, bully boys, blow,
>   For Cal-i-for-ni-o,
> For there's lots of gold,
>   So I've been told
> On the banks of the Sac-ra-men-to.

Many of the chanteys were rich in sentiment and beautiful in tune. And the sailors sang them well, accustomed as they were to constant group singing in the open air. It was indeed a stirring scene when, in some remote port, the sailors on a ship just weighing anchor for Europe began walking around the fo'c's'le head capstan, singing the beautiful, "We're homeward bound around Cape Horn," or "We're bound for Rio Grande"; while the home-sick crews of dozens of windjammers in the harbor gathered along their ships' sides to listen and to long for the day when they, too, would be homeward bound.

RANZO

In the old square-riggers the most pitiful figures were the "ranzoes." These were landsmen who, although totally unfitted for the life of a sailor, found themselves, usually by being shanghaied, on board windjammers. Such unfortunates were the victims of paralyzing fears: they were mortally afraid of the sea, with its storms and dangers, and they were terrified by the high, spidery rigging of the ship. Worse than useless for the working of the ship, they were like trapped wild animals, the whole life about them being strange, hostile, overwhelming. One or more of such ranzoes was to be found on nearly every deepwater ship.

The ranzoes became the ship's scapegoats, the butt of every ridicule, abuse and tyranny. Not only did the officers pick on these unfortunates, but many of the older sailors also made life a hell for them. This attitude of the sailors was mostly due to the under-manned condition of the ships, each ranzo aboard adding to the work of the real sailors and also endangering the crew's lives.

For ranzoes, a voyage of six months to a year on a windjammer, with never a sight of land, was an awful experience. Their terror of the sea, of the ship's high rigging, of the crew's abuse, of the narrow fo'c's'le life, often proved too much for them. Many went insane and committed suicide or ran amuck. Old sailors told horrible stories of ranzoes leaping overboard, setting fire to the ship or slitting the throats of the crew as they slept in their bunks.

Old "Chips," the carpenter on the *Alliance,* told of a ranzo he had once sailed with. It was in a tough ship, a Nova-Scotiaman, and the "buckaroo" mate ordered the ranzo lashed into a "boatswain's chair" and hauled up to the mast-head, to stay there until cured of his rigging fear. But the unfortunate man, stricken with fright, actually cut himself loose with his sheath knife, fell to the deck a hundred feet below and was killed.

Jack Callahan, a demoted mate serving as a sailor before the mast on the *Pegasus,* related an even more harrowing experience. There were two ranzoes, American hoboes, on a ship bound from San Francisco to Liverpool. The ranzos were obsessed with the usual fears and developed into the ship's scapegoats. They stood it for a month, until the ship was well below the equator, when finally their desperation broke bonds.

One evening, when only four others were on deck, the two ranzoes suddenly pulled guns (which they had brought aboard with them) and, driving the four men before them, locked the officers in their quarters and captured the ship. They then announced they were going to make their way ashore.

Unable to launch a boat because the ship was bowling along at a dozen knots, they contrived a small raft of hatch-covers. Gathering up whatever little food there was in the galley, together with a few quarts of water, they launched the crazy raft and cut themselves adrift in the darkness. As their raft slipped past the stern the ranzoes sang out, "Hooray for the United States!" Nothing more was seen of them. The officers hove the ship to and put out a boat, but they could not be found in the tropical darkness. Next day there was not a sign of them on the empty horizon. Their fate can be imagined: the ship was seven hundred miles off the South American coast and they had hardly a chance of making such a distance or being picked up by another ship in that vacant sea. Their food and water would last a few days; then would come hunger and maddening thirst, and the final end of their insane act would be in the bellies of voracious sharks.

In my sailing experience I met with several ranzoes. One aboard the *Pegasus* was an Englishman about forty years old, an office worker of some education. He had been doped and shanghaied aboard at Astoria, Oregon. The only name I ever knew for him was Ranzo, and he was the true type. Incapable of learning even the simplest tasks of a sailor, he was obsessed with the characteristic fear of the sea. The approach of a storm prostrated him, and the lofty rigging was a wild terror for him. During six months not a foot would he climb from the deck, regardless of the officers' threats and the men's ridicule.

For a while Ranzo made no resistance to the officers' tyranny and the abuse of the men. His was indeed a dog's life. As the weeks wore on, he developed a morose and belligerent attitude. The older sailors declared he was approaching the typical desperation point. We younger men, I especially, tried to win his confidence. But it was no use, he spoke friendly to no one. He was too overwhelmed with the fear that the sea, the ship and the crew were his mortal enemies.

Ranzo's whole aspect was ominous. The crew grew afraid of him and their abuse stopped. A hundred stories of butcheries of sleeping sailors by crazed ranzoes were bandied about. By the time we reached the tropics, the crew refused to allow Ranzo to sleep in the fo'c's'le, so thereafter he bunked on deck. They also delegated two men in each watch to keep him under observation day and night. They took away his sheath knife so he could not cut their throats while they slept, and they deprived him of matches, for fear he might set fire to the ship.

Thus it went on for weeks. Ranzo became so solitary and sullen that I thought he was going insane. He did little or no work, being "all thumbs" at a sailor's tasks. Always two sailors kept their eyes on him. He became a sort of menacing specter, wandering about the ship, sinister and alone. Eventually we began to reach the cold Southern latitudes and the older men proposed to Ranzo that he make his bed in the fo'c's'le under guard. But he refused. So he actually went around Cape Horn, in wild and bitterly cold weather, making his "home" in the cupboard-like paint locker, which was both watersoaked and heatless. Nor could he be cajoled into leaving it. I was amazed that he did not die of pneumonia.

At last, after six months, the *Pegasus* arrived at Capetown. Ranzo must have been happy to be free from the torture of the ship and the sea life; but he said nothing. When our ship dropped anchor he was the first to pile over the side to go ashore. I never saw him again.

PASTIMES AT SEA

Passengers on modern liners are always so bored by the sea and each other that they have to be entertained with dances, deck games, radio, movies, gambling, horse racing, swimming pools, gymnasiums, ship papers and what not. The sailor aboard the old windjammer had none of these diversions; yet, he never knew boredom even on trips that lasted as long as a year or more.

Card-playing was the deep-water man's greatest diversion, and cribbage was the favorite game on English ships. The men literally played it day and night. For weeks at a time the game would go on, the watch coming below always relieving the watch going on deck. But, strangely enough, I never saw any gambling.

The next greatest pastime was just conversation. In fine weather the men walked the deck together for hours, talking mostly about their past history. After months of this one came to know the life stories of his particular friends almost as well as his own.

The special social time aboard ship was the second dog-watch, from six to eight P.M. At this time both watches were below and no one was sleeping. But the men seldom organized any social affairs. Once in a while some storyteller would hold forth, but he had to be good to attract attention away from the eternal cribbage game. Occasionally, on a Christmas or some other gala occasion, the men held a typical English "sing-song," when every man had to either tell a story or sing a song.

Music played little part in the crew's life aboard ship. This was because of the narrow living quarters and the fact that nearly always someone was sleeping. I never saw a deep-water sailor carrying a musical instrument of any kind. The only time our crews would break out into "music" was on some Saturday night in port, with a tin pan band, the "instruments" for which had been mostly collected in the ship's galley.

Reading was a favorite pastime and many of the men were very well read. We were just going around the Cape of Good Hope when I first read *Les Miserables*. But usually books were scarce. The ships carried no libraries for the crews and, of course, it would be against the dignity of the officers to lend the men any books. What stuff the sailors' missions might put aboard was pretty much trash, and the sailors seldom read it.

A restricted life such as that aboard a windjammer seemed to provoke the spirit of the practical joker. Usually the "jokes" were plenty rough. The lookout man, leading his lonely vigil on the fo'c's'le-head, was a favorite target. On one ship a greenhorn was on the lookout during a dark night when suddenly a stuffed figure tumbled from aloft upon him. He was so frightened that from then on he refused point blank to do his turn on the lookout.

"Crossing the Line" (the equator) was an occasion when the spirit of devilment cut loose. All first timers across had to be initiated. This ceremony was barbarous. First, the victim was forced to swallow an unmentionable pill made from the pig-pen offal, next he was lathered thick all over the face with ship's tar and then "shaved" with a barrel hoop, and finally he was stood on his head in a cask of sea water until he nearly drowned.

Of sports there were but few. Once in a while in fine weather the men would cook up a boxing match. If there was any fighting it was usually in earnest. Occasionally, when becalmed in the tropics, there would be swimming over the ship's side, while we kept a very sharp lookout for sharks. And sometimes there was very good fishing.

One thing that struck me about the deep-water man's life aboard ship was the absence of sexual abnormalities. Where men are congregated together, such vices usually flourish. In all prisons, for example, they are rampant, and the men I sailed with also used to tell amazing stories of mis-relationships between men and boys in the British Navy. But I saw absolutely nothing of the kind aboard windjammers. Perhaps the fresh open air and the low quality of the saltpetered diet had something to do with this.

Aboard ship the square-rigger sailor lived a sedate, virtuous life. But when he came to port—whew!—he let go with a bang. He went in for wine, women and song in a big way—as long as his few pounds, shillings and pence lasted. This wild roistering ashore gave him the reputation of being a drunkard and a general tough-nut, but actually, in his true life aboard ship, he was sober and calm, quite a normal person.

DEEP-WATER FISHING

Sailors on the old square-rigged ships had frequent opportunities for fishing at sea. When the ship was becalmed we put lines over the side, and often in the warm latitudes we displayed lanterns at night to lure the tasty flying-fish to fling themselves on deck. But the best sport was fishing for bonito and albacor in the tropics. This was simply wonderful.

These powerful and voracious fish, weighing up to fifty pounds apiece, constantly prey upon the tens of thousands of flying-fish, which skim swiftly through the air like miniature airplanes, actually covering several hundred yards in one flight. Closely pursuing them, tearing along like "greased lightning," the finned tigers leap far out of the water to capture these flying-fish on the wing.

To fish for bonito and albacor we would station ourselves at the end of the bowsprit or jibboom, a dizzy perch. Our fishing gear was a strong line and a heavy hook, with a small piece of white cloth as "bait." With the ship bowling along through the trade winds, we dangled the hook until it just touched the water. As the ship lurched forward our hooked cloth was sent flying through the air, dipping into the water every fifty feet or so. To the albacor and bonito the dancing white rag was a flying-fish, and soon half a dozen of them would rush with express speed for our lure, the "lucky" one often catching it on the fly. Then came the dangerous job of hauling the powerful fish aboard. It was a thrilling but risky sport; and many were the fo'c's'le stories of sailors being toppled overboard from the jibboom by the hooked fish and devoured by sharks.

The bonito and albacor were good eating, but one drawback was that nearly all were afflicted with parasitic maggots which bored through the stomach walls and lodged throughout the flesh of the fish. This detail was a small matter, however, to hungry windjammer sailors. We picked out whatever worms were to be found easily and ate the fish on our usual principle that "what the eye don't see the mind don't believe."

Fishing for shark was also a favorite with us. But this was purely sport, full-grown sharks being inedible. For shark-fishing we used to bait a great hook with a big lump of salt pork and, leading the line through a strong outrigging, trail it along in the water. Soon a shark would take after it, and then his pilot fish would go into action. I know that most naturalists dispute sailors' stories about the pilot fish being a guide and protector to the slow-witted shark, but I relate simply what I have seen take place.

The pilot fish, a beautiful creature somewhat larger than a mackerel, would swim just above the shark's head. Active and alert, his suspicions would be at once aroused by our pork, hook and line. He would, therefore, apparently make efforts to draw the shark away from our trap, dashing to one side and then the other. But usually to no avail; the hungry shark would be lured by the pork. Many sea fish and birds are greatly fascinated by pork, especially the shark, which acts towards pork like a cat with catnip. Many's the time I saw one caress our pork bait and rub himself all over it, until finally his hunger got the best of his fears and he grabbed it with one ferocious bite.

Once hooked, the shark is not game and makes little fight. We used to hoist the monsters aboard methodically. Sailors, for obvious reasons, hate the shark. Often they actually tortured him while he lay helpless on the deck. One of their special joys was to let him try his needle-like teeth on wooden capstan bars; and how he would make the splinters fly. Finally, the sailors would cut off his tail and nail it to the jibboom, where it stayed until the ship reached port.

Another very interesting form of "fishing" was for albatross. The albatross is the greatest and most famous of all sea birds. Found only in the cold latitudes of the Southern hemisphere, a full-grown specimen will measure as much as seventeen feet from tip to tip of his wings. The albatross is a wonderful flyer, gliding and soaring indefinitely, even in the heaviest storms, without flapping its wings. Windjammer sailors hated the albatross, for if a man fell overboard this gigantic bird (so they believed) would slash him to pieces with its great shear-like beak. But the sailors feared to kill the albatross; for the traditional sea superstition, made famous by Coleridge in his *Ancient Mariner,* that the souls of lost sailors became albatrosses and that on pain of shipwreck the albatross must not be killed, still lingered in my day.

Fishing for albatross was thrilling. A small triangular float, attached to a thin, stout line, was put out over the ship's stern. In the center of this float was a small hole, across which, suspended on wire, was a sizable piece of pork. Soon the albatross, with the magic lure of pork drawing him on, would make a dash at the bait. His beak is a great hook, and as he grabbed the bait the curved beak would go through the hole and get caught in the float. Alarmed, the great albatross would then quickly take to the air, dragging the float with him, and flying wildly in every direction. This was great sport for the sailors, and gradually they hauled the huge bird down on deck. Once there, the albatross comically enough proved he was no sailor by getting seasick and emptying his stomach. The men were always very cautious to keep beyond reach of the huge bird's murderous beak, claws and wings. Eventually, they would cut the "fishing" line and the albatross, shaking himself loose from the float, soon resumed his endless dipping and soaring over the wastes of his watery home.

LURE OF THE SEA

Although their work was dangerous, their food atrocious, their pay small, their discipline brutal and their sex life abnormal, sailors on the old square-riggers were fascinated by sea life. The seaman, while he habitually swore that every voyage was his last, found it very difficult to quit the sea, even in the unlikely event of his achieving a favorable job ashore.

Much of this lure of the sea came from the reckless life of adventure the men led: an endless panorama of far-away ports with curious customs, exotic women, hilarious sprees and strange ships and men. But much, also, of the fascination grew out of the life on the sea itself.

The windjammer sailors, far more than steamer seamen or modern ocean travelers, came to know the sea most intimately. Spending many months at a time on its broad bosom in a small ship and rarely sighting land, they became literally saturated with its magic influence. In spite of all the bitter hardships of their life they grew insensibly to love the sea, which profoundly shaped their psychology and their whole outlook on life.

Landsmen often dread the sea, but true deep-water sailors, even in the midst of a dangerous storm, seemed quite immune to fear. The windjammer sailors always found the sea itself interesting, even on passages as long as six to twelve months. Sometimes the sea was oily and smooth and glassy, or covered with lovely whitecaps or lashed with a fierce storm. Now it was gray, or green, or the bluest of blues. The sea has a hundred moods.

The deep-water sailor was also profoundly affected by and interested in the natural phenomena of climate and wind and rain and fog and clouds and sun and stars. His work was dictated by their condition; often his very life was menaced by their vagaries. He came to know them far better than any landsman ever does, but their complicated operation remained mysterious to him and hence his notorious superstition. These natural factors brought spice and labor and danger into his life. One week he was sweltering in the windless doldrums of the equatorial zones; a couple of weeks later he was bowling along through sub-tropical white-capped seas, pushed on by the balmy trades winds and watching night after night the most brilliant and lovely of all constellations, the Southern Cross, climbing higher and higher as his ship worked her way down into Southerly latitudes; and a few weeks later he was off Cape Horn, or "Cape Stiff," as he called it, fighting against snow and ice and howling storms.

Glorious sunsets and sunrises were everyday sights for the sailor, and often he saw fearsome waterspouts. One of the most interesting things I ever saw was the famed "St. Elmo's fire." We were on the *Pegasus,* just south of the equator in the Pacific Ocean. The night was pitch black; a tropical storm was blowing, and three of us younger sailors were on deck, huddled behind the galley. Suddenly one of the men grabbed my arm and, pointing to the main yard, yelled in my ear, "Look!" There it was, the St. Elmo's fire I had heard and read so much about. Several pale, greenish-blue lights danced along the main yard. They seemed to originate at the throat of the yard (at the mast) and then tinkled off to the lee end, where they disappeared. The whole thing lasted only a couple of minutes. Excitedly we told a couple of older sailors about it, but they took it all very calmly, saying they had seen St. Elmo's fire many times.

The life with which the sea teems, especially in the tropics, also did much to dispel monotony from the sailor's life. The endless shoals of herring, the vicious albacor, the shimmering flying-fish, the playful porpoises and seals, the leaping tuna, the lazy sea-turtle, the sinister shark, the fearsome squid, the majestic whale and the deadly and spectacular battles for existence among them were all intimate parts of the deep-water man's daily life. And also the Mother Carey's chickens, the lovely little cape pigeons, the gulls and goonies, the huge pelicans and especially the king of them all, the great Southern albatross.

Then there was for the sailor the strong attraction of the ships themselves. Even the landsman recognized beauty in the old square-riggers; the old-time sailor himself was far more sensitive to this beauty. While he always hated, with a healthy class spirit, the ship's tyrannical officers and her belly-robbing owners, his ship had to be a poor tub indeed if he did not have a soft spot, a sort of masculine regard, in his heart for her. The ship was always "she" to him. The square-rigger sailor also had a craftsman's pride in his ship. He knew her "from truck to keelson," and her graceful rigging, to a landsman only a tangled maze, was to him simple and orderly even on the darkest night and in the most terrific gale. His ship was his home, a home that carried him through storm and stress, through joys and sorrows and dangers, for months and years together. I have seen old sailors, just paid off, go back for a last lingering look at the beautiful ship they had quit, a veritable "hell-ship" perhaps, but which they nevertheless loved for her beauty and human associations.

Another alluring factor in the old deep-water sailor's life was the many intimate bonds of friendship it set up. Some men, cooped up for months in a tiny forecastle, were inclined to become sensitive and quarrelsome, but others developed the warmest friendships. These friendships were intensified because in the dangerous tasks of working the ship the men carried each other's lives in their hands. No group of men, unless it be war veterans, know the degree of intimacy expressed by the term "shipmate."

The deep-water sailor was indeed deeply influenced by the lure of the sea; yet he remained a land animal at heart. Throughout his long voyages he never ceased speculating about what he would do when he set foot on solid green earth again. Dana expresses this well in his

Two Years Before the Mast. Every old sailor cherished the dream that, when worn out at last as a seaman, he should spend his declining years in some home close by the shore, near his mistress, the sea. But this idyllic "snug harbor" dream of the sailor before the mast seldom came true; usually his tragic finish was to meet sudden death at sea or to come to a lingering end, friendless and penniless, in some miserable poorhouse.

THE WIDE, WIDE SEA

In these days of fast steamers travelers never get a sense of the vastness of the sea such as the old windjammer sailors had. Often the latter were as much as a year between ports, with never a sight of land or vessel, and they became overwhelmed by the immensity of the sea and the tininess of their little world, the ship. It seemed as though the whole universe were water. In *Moby Dick* Melville caught this spirit of the vast distances and emptiness of the sea that the old-time sailor felt in his very bones.

On long trips it was a joy to sight a ship, or maybe to speak her. Clear cut in my memory is a ship we sighted once in the middle of the South Atlantic. We were five months out of Portland, bound for Capetown, and had seen no land whatever and only two ships. But one bright morning, just as day broke, there stood a square-rigged ship far away on the horizon, just off our starboard bow and as small as a toy ship, right on the sharp rim between sky and water. How we guessed who she was, where she hailed from and whither she was bound. For a week she remained in sight, always in about the same position. But one morning our now familiar neighbor was no longer to be seen. It was as though the sea had swallowed her up. Evidently during the night she had gone off on another tack and left us again to solitude.

The overwhelming vastness of the sea was impressed deeply upon the consciousness of the deep-water sailor but also, upon occasion, the sea became fatally cramped and narrow for him—when his storm-driven ship wrecked itself upon a lee shore, when it piled up upon some uncharted rock isle or when it collided with another ship unexpectedly looming up out of the darkness. I had an experience of the latter kind that I shall never forget.

I was an able seaman aboard the three-masted bark *Alliance,* loaded with coal and bound from Newcastle, Australia, to Callao, Peru. We had been a month at sea and were in mid-South Pacific. Roughly, we were about two thousand miles east of New Zealand; the coast of Peru was at least four thousand miles west; to the northward of us probably eight hundred miles was the famous Pitcairn Island and some three thousand miles southward, Antarctica. We were in the middle of nowhere, a tiny speck of a ship in a wide watery universe. Not a single sail had we sighted since we weighed anchor. It seemed as though we were the only ship in all that great world of water.

On the memorable night in question it blew hard from the southwest and we were bowling along at a dozen knots an hour. It was a dirty night; there were no moon or stars, we were enmeshed in low flying clouds and the man on the lookout kept the hand-operated foghorn growling every few moments.

It was our watch and six bells (eleven P.M.) had just "gone." I had the trick at the wheel and we were running almost directly before the wind. The ship was steering badly and it was hard to keep her on the course. The second mate, the officer of our watch, tramped back and forth across the poop, smoking his pipe and mooning to himself, while the rest of the watch loafed about the decks, seeking shelter and "forty winks" of sleep.

Suddenly the second mate and I were thrown to the alert by a frantic ringing of the ship's bell and a cry of the lookout man, heard only faintly through the noise of the gathering storm. "Light on the starboard bow!" And there, of all things in that empty ocean, was the red port light of a ship hardly more than half a mile away, and we were bearing right down upon her. We could barely see the dull outlines of the ship. She was a big one, on the port tack, and steering a course which, intersecting ours at a right angle, would bring us smash into each other in a few minutes.

The second mate and I were both momentarily paralyzed with surprise at this apparition—a ship in these deserted seas. But quickly recovering his wits, the officer, a good seaman, stamped heavily on the deck to attract the attention of the officers below and yelled to me, "Starboard your helm, steer east-southeast!" I jammed the wheel down and pulled her up into the wind. By this time the captain and mate, half dressed, had arrived on deck, and the crew were already hauling the yards around for our new course.

Meanwhile, the other ship apparently had sighted us about the same time and also veered off her course two or three points. This shift in the ships' courses prevented an otherwise certain collision. As it was, there was hardly two hundred feet of open water between the two ships as they passed each other. We were left dizzy with astonishment and excitement.

The other ship was a big four-master, full-rigged and, like us, running under upper topsails. As she crossed our bow we saw her binnacle light and the man at the wheel. We could also see men on her decks, but could not hear whatever they may have shouted. In the murky darkness the name on her stern was illegible. But we figured her a German, just around Cape Horn and bound China-wards.

Had the two ships crashed together, doubtless all hands would have been lost. It all would have meant just two more windjammers added to the long list of "ships that never returned." All the way to Callao we never ceased yarning about the mysterious "ship that passed in the night" and the chance in a million that almost brought us together in a death crash in those trackless wastes of water. Believe me, on the rest of the passage both officers and men kept a wide-awake lookout.

A STRIKE ABOARD SHIP

It was aboard the *County of Cardigan* in Talcahuano, a small port near the lower end of Chile, where we had arrived from Tumbez, Peru, and were loading wheat for Ireland. The crew were thoroughly discontented with conditions aboard this hungry Welsh ship and matters soon came to a strike, or "refusal of duty," as it was called.

The cause of the strike was this: Men aboard the old deep-water British ships had to sign up for a voyage of three years, or until they reached a North European port. Wages equaled seventeen dollars per month for able seamen and twelve dollars for ordinary seamen. During the three-year period the men had no right to any wages. This hold-up of wages was made worse by the fact that if a man deserted his ship he lost all the wages he had standing plus whatever wages he might earn upon other ships during the three year period.

The shipowners and officers would starve and bullyrag the men, practically forcing them to desert their ships, often to leave a year or two's wages behind them. They would also be on hand (advised by the elaborate world blacklist system of ship captains, boarding-house crimps and British consuls) when the "deserters" returned to England on other ships, and they would confiscate their wages on the pretext that the first ship had been caused expense by the desertions. Many a man, after three years of hard life in windjammers, received not a pound sterling when he was finally "paid off" in England.

Our crew, without exception, had all deserted British ships in one port or another, and in doing so had abandoned many months' wages. Most of us were sailing under false names (mine was Tom Donahoe), but we knew of the blacklist system of the ship owners and British consuls; and we realized that when we hit a British port each of us would be confronted with an agent of our previous ship who would take away every shilling we had coming to us as wages on the *County of Cardigan*. Our only hope to beat this robbery was to get paid off in Talcahuano, go to Valparaiso and, under new names, sign on other ships.

So we demanded our pay and discharge. I was chosen spokesman (I was an "able" seaman by this time). The captain, who had fortified himself with a few drinks for our "conference," violently rejected our demands. It was unheard of, doubly impossible, a mutiny, said he. So we decided to quit work. We refused to "turn to" at our task of loading grain from lighters. The captain stormed at us, told the cook not to give us breakfast, and then went ashore for help.

Under the medieval British shipping laws we had no "right" to strike. By quitting work in port we were guilty of the penal offense of "refusing duty." Such a strike at sea would be called "mutiny" and be punishable by long imprisonment. Soon the captain returned with a boatload of barefooted Chilean soldiers, who took the sixteen of us ashore and marched us to the office of the British consul.

Now, in the innocence of my youth, I thought we would be given a trial under the laws of Chile. But the British consul handled the whole business himself. Before giving us a chance to say a word, he shouted at us that we must either return to work or go to jail. We demanded to be paid off. Whereupon he ordered the soldiers to march us away to jail. The consul told us we would be kept there until we decided to resume our "duty." As the soldiers escorted us along the street, prostitutes from their windows sang out after us, "In jail, plenty louse."

The jail was a horrible affair. It was a large former residence; the regular calaboose had recently collapsed in an earthquake, killing forty prisoners. The place was indescribably dirty and lousy. Several prisoners had syphilitic sores. All were hungry and penniless. At night the jail filled up until there was no space on the filth-covered floors to sleep. The first night, Saturday, two drunks began to fight. One pulled a knife and there was pandemonium in the crowded room. Suddenly a soldier flung open the door and flattened the armed man with a smash in the forehead from the butt of his rifle. They carried out the prostrate man, dead to the world from a fractured skull.

Evidently, our case was not unusual, as there were many wind-jammers and lots of discontented sailors in the port. On the second day of our jail stay, a soldier, with many meaningful smiles, led us to a room adjoining ours. There, on the doorpost, under the caption, "Mutineers of the *Haddon Hall*," was sketched a rough picture of a full-rigged ship, a skull and cross bones, signed by a dozen names. We could easily figure out that situation.

The consul kept us two days in this hell-hole. Not a taste of food of any kind did we receive. We began to wonder if they were going to actually starve us into submission. Finally, on the third day, the consul sent us a message that the British Minister to Chile was in that part of the country and would hear our case. Then they served us a cup of coffee and a bun apiece to brighten us up a bit for our appearance before the high official.

He was a big fat, dignified fellow. We were lined up in a wide semi-circle in front of him. Our skipper said nothing but the consul acted as prosecuting attorney. As spokesman, I stated our demand for a pay-off, complained about the ship's miserable food, protested at our imprisonment and demanded our immediate release. The consul cut me off in the midst of my remarks with a storm of abuse about our "unheard-of" demands. Then he "laid-out" in turn each man around the semi-circle, giving him his record since the time he had last shipped from England. I was amazed at the thoroughness of the blacklist system.

The British Minister told us curtly we could not be paid off. It was against the law and the Board of Trade would not permit it. The consul threatened to send us back to jail again until we agreed to work. But sailors in square-rigged ships were toughened to hard conditions, and this wretched jail did not have us licked so soon. We stood pat on our demands.

Then the Minister, the consul and the skipper put their heads together. We learned afterward they were afraid of our fight spreading to the many other ships in the harbor, and they made us the following proposal: the skipper declared that none of us would lose our wages in England, and that the ship would lay in some new provisions. The consul also assured us that later on those of us who wanted to would be transferred to other ships; because, he let it slip out, all the crews in the port were as sick of their ships as we were and would be glad of a change.

These proposals did not meet our demands, but they were the best we could do. So we accepted them and went back to work. None of us, however, were transferred to other ships, all making the trip around the Horn in the *County of Cardigan,* and she remained as hungry as ever. But at least the captain did not turn us in as "deserters" and none of us lost our wages in England. Thus we won our main point after all.

One day, however, as we were far along on our way homeward bound, the mate told a man at the wheel we had been hoodwinked in Talcahuano. He said the British "Minister" was not in reality the high government official the consul had led us to believe, but an imposter. He was a British minister all right—the local Protestant missionary preacher, not a government representative. We were plenty sore at this news but were not surprised at such close working together of the captain, the consul and the preacher. On the long journey back to England we dumped many a hearty curse on the head of the contemptible sky pilot who had played us this scurvy trick.

THE FLEET'S IN

In 1903 I was on the beach in Callao, Peru, when half a dozen American warships, including a couple of Dewey's old battle-of-Manilla fleet, paid the town a visit. The ships had been stationed at Panama, the United States then being engaged in the early stages of accomplishing that imperialistic master stroke, the Panama Canal. Because of yellow fever locally, no shore leave had been allowed the enlisted men in the Central American ports for six months past. The warships came to Callao to give the men a chance to go ashore "for their health's sake," as it was phrased.

To me it did not seem that Callao could put forth any convincing claims as a health resort. It was then in the midst of an epidemic of bubonic plague. The whole town was in a scare. Posters were plastered all around warning the people how to avoid the plague and what to do if attacked by it. The President of the country had conveniently seized upon a mission to a far corner of Peru. The day before I saw a man, very sick, sitting on a park bench, and someone raised a cry of the plague. The crowd would not come nearer than fifty feet of the stricken man. Eventually a decrepit ambulance arrived and the doctors, gloved and masked, wrapped him in sheets and carted him away. The bench he had been sitting upon was burned, the ground all about disinfected and even the nearby trees sprayed.

Nevertheless the American warships came to Callao "for the men's health," and soon a couple of thousand blue jackets were turned loose on the town with two-days' leave, most of them with several months' wages in their pockets. They at once proceeded to give Callao a taste of high life that it would not soon forget.

As the many launches loaded with enlisted men drew up to the quay, there awaiting them was an unofficial reception committee of practically every dance hall runner, pimp, gambler and prostitute in town. Here were some two thousand young men who had been cooped up in the warships for six months without shore leave, bullyragged by tyrannical officers, sex-starved and generally repressed. So now that they were ashore, temporarily free of their unnatural life, they let go with a loud bang. Soon there was a wild orgy on all fronts. The blue jackets took complete charge of the town. In the harbor were lying a British and a French warship, but their commanders discreetly cancelled all shore leave while the Americans were having their fling.

It was a rich harvest for the shore parasites. They robbed the blue jackets right and left. The native drink, *pisco,* drove the sailors half crazy. Fist fights took place all over the city, among the Navy men themselves and between them and the townspeople. I even saw sailors, wild with *pisco,* standing on the docks casting silver coins into the bay, trying to hit the fish. Others gathered crowds about them and flung money broadcast to see the people scramble for it.

At this pace it did not take long to "clean" the blue jackets. When their forty-eight hours' leave of absence expired only about half went back aboard ship, the other thousand overstaying their leave. Two to three hundred actually deserted. Callao and Lima were full of stray sailors. Many deserters scattered up country, going as far as the Cerro de Pasco mines in the mountains, while others went to various points along the coast.

The warships were crippled by this wholesale desertion and overstaying of leave. In Callao itself there was the devil to pay. The A.W. O.L. blue jackets, broke and still whiskey-crazed, traveled in bands of a dozen or so, invading restaurants, saloons and houses of prostitution and helping themselves freely to food, drink and women. As a result, these places closed up all over town. Many sailors were sleeping on the beach. In the roofless, furnitureless shack where my shipmate and I slept nightly on newspapers, we had a blue jacket for a co-lodger, a certain "Tin Can" Kelly of Brooklyn.

The Navy officers, on the fourth day, got out patrols which worked with the local authorities to round up the stragglers. At the end of two weeks, it was estimated that there were a hundred or more of the sailors still scattered about the country. It was all just a little visit of Uncle Sam's warships, "for health's sake," to Callao.

ON TO PANAMA

Jack Harris and I were on the *Alliance,* then at Callao, Peru, discharging Australian coal. We had fallen in with two other young sailors ashore, Fred Leight, a Penobscot Indian, and Carl Hanson, a Swede; and the four of us decided that instead of going round Cape Horn to Europe in a windjammer we would go overland to Panama. Once there we would decide whether to go to New York or San Francisco.

This was before the time of the Canal. We calculated the distance to be about fifteen hundred miles, taking us across the equator. Our route lay along the Pacific coast, via Tumbez and Guyaquil. An old prospector assured us there were banana and other plantations along the way, and this was alluring to us. Hanson, the only one of us who had anything, sold his sea outfit and bought a few pounds of bread and sausage for the road. As for Harris and me, we had to walk off our ship with just what we wore on our backs.

On the morning when we were to "jump" the *Alliance,* I was suddenly awakened at five o'clock by a violent shaking of the ship. At first I thought that she, being almost empty, was "turning turtle." I lost no time in hopping on deck. The ship was quite upright, but still quivering. Over the city was a strange moaning noise. Dogs were barking and the cries of frightened people rang out. It was an earth-quake, and a heavy one. Great cracks were made in the streets, many houses were overthrown and a number of people killed. But the center of the disturbance was far away in the Andes, where the mountains were tossed about considerably.

However, our Panama expedition got started; not even an earth-quake could disrupt our preparations. A few hours' walk brought us to Lima, the capital of Peru. Next evening we arrived at a small coast village called Ancon. A few miles before coming into town the countryside became a sandy waste, and scattered about were hundreds of skeletons. It was an old battlefield, the scene of the last battle between Chile and Peru. We were a sensation as we walked down the street of Ancon. The whole population turned out to see us, for few foreigners ever came to this place. The citizens gave us a good welcome and we had three invitations to supper.

It was an auspicious beginning. But we didn't know that we were entering the thousand mile desert on the slopes of the Andes Mountains that skirts the ocean north of Callao. Our growing suspicions were offset by the faith we had in the banana plantations that were to come. So we plugged out of town the following morning. No one in Ancon seemed to know exactly how far the next town might be. Estimates ranged from four to eight leagues to the next stop. The village people told us that everybody traveled by boat, for the country between was a roadless waste of sand.

This did not sound so good, but we started anyhow. The equatorial heat was terrific. We sank to our ankles in the fine sand. To avoid getting lost we had to keep in sight of the sea, following all the indentations of the coast and going up one sand dune and down the other. Along the way we saw an occasional skeleton of man or horse, sinister warnings.

At the next village the people were astounded to see us. They advised us not to go on, as the whole coast was a barren desert. It often went years, they said, without rain falling. As in Ancon, the local people could not tell us even approximately the distance to the next town as they, too, always traveled by water. By this time we were pretty well disillusioned. Our dream of drifting peacefully along through a paradise of fruit plantations had evaporated. We cursed the lying prospector who had misled us in Callao.

But we plugged on. It was too hot to walk in the day, the fierce tropical sun literally roasting us. So we adopted night traveling. We went barefoot, for it was impossible to walk in the fine sand with shoes. But this barefoot business was very dangerous, there being large numbers of scorpions, whose bite is often fatal. By this time we had used up all our scanty provisions and were reduced to beggary. A night's journey brought us to another small town. Nearly the whole population were Indians. They were having a big religious festival when we arrived, and in the procession about a hundred men were carrying a great image of Christ on an enormous float. It looked like a throwback to the Middle Ages. They paid little attention to us.

We kept up our journey for a couple of days more. The country was nothing but sand, sand, sand. Then we came to a jump of sixteen leagues, or forty-eight miles, to the next town, with no road and no fresh water on the way. We calculated to make it in two days. We gathered water cans, begged food and started out in face of the natives' warnings. We walked two whole nights, and as the third day broke we could still see nothing ahead of us but sand. Our water and food were completely gone. We feared that by following the sea line we had wandered out into some cape or other, had missed the town and were lost. But just as we were beginning to be alarmed, we spotted a couple of men with burros. They were bound for salt mines some fifteen miles away. They told us that had we gone a few steps farther before making camp we could have seen the houses of the town. Up to this point we had made a hundred and seventy-five miles and were on the road a week.

In this town they informed us that the next village was fifty leagues ahead. This meant no road and no fresh water for a hundred and fifty miles, a week's walk even without counting the lost mileage by our system of following the coast indentations. Such a jump without water was impossible. We decided to stay in town, secure jobs and equip ourselves to make the big trip ahead of us. But only two jobs were available—in the salt mines, and these merely for a week's time. Harris and I took them, while the other two remained on the beach, living as best they could.

The mines were big salt springs, which were allowed to flow far out over the flats. As the water evaporated, a layer of salt was gradually deposited. When the salt became eight or ten inches thick, it was cut into great blocks and shipped. Harris and I juggled these two two hundred and fifty pound cakes of salt under the tropical sun twelve hours a day and received a Peruvian dollar a day minus twenty-five cents for our beans and rice. Indians made up the working crew, and it was evident that some sort of peonage system existed in the camp; the discipline was brutal and the living conditions barbaric.

When, at the end of our week's work, we got back to the town, Leight and Hanson were gone. They had shipped on a little coaster down to Callao, so we did the same. Thus ended our expedition to Panama.

For a long time I felt we could have got through afoot to Panama had we stuck it out; but this notion was knocked out of me when, long afterward, I read Tschiffely's interesting story of his famous ten-thousand mile horseback ride from Buenos Aires to Washington twenty-five years later. Tschiffely ran into many hardships, but he said the road from Lima to Guyaquil was the worst of all. In his book, *Southern Cross to Polar Star,* he wrote:

"Journeys through such deserts are trying in the extreme. At first the body suffers, then everything becomes abstract. Later on the brain becomes dull and the thoughts mixed, and only the will to arrive and keep awake is left.... Dante's Inferno is a creation of stupendous imagination, but the Peruvian deserts are real, very real."

A LOST DINNER

Harris and I formed the crew on the little sloop, *Juanita,* bound south along the coast of Peru to Callao. We had aboard four passengers, a big crate of chickens and a hold full of hogs. It was a week's run and the passage was very rough. The trade wind came on to blow sharply and the sloop danced dizzily among the high seas.

I counted myself a good sailor and quite immune to seasickness, but this situation made my stomach quite squeamish. The wild pitching of the sloop was bad enough, and the stench from the hogs, many of them sick, was horrible. The passengers and even the chickens got seasick. On the evening of the first day out one of the sick chickens gave up the ghost and passed on to the happy hunting ground of barnyard fowl. And thereby hangs my tale.

Next day the blow was still worse. The seas ran higher; the sloop tossed dizzier; the hogs stank louder; the passengers were sicker. As for myself, I cared not how soon we reached Callao. Pedro, the cook, himself sick, announced dinner. The captain, the cook and myself lined up to eat. Jack said he was not hungry; he was evidently seasick, but with a sailor's reluctance to admit it. With a shock, I learned that for dinner we had chicken stew. It was manifestly made of the defunct chicken of yesterday.

Now when the *Juanita's* crew ate chicken they ate chicken—all of it, much on the principle that one eats oysters. They let the tail go with the hide, so to speak. About the only part abstracted from the defunct bird were the largest feathers. As an experienced sailor, I had learned not to be finicky about my eating, yet this combination, the seasickness, the stinking hogs, the deceased chicken, seemed carrying things a bit too far.

Without delay the cook began to ladle out the stew. He served the skipper first; and together with some feather-flecked soup, the captain got a whole chicken leg, claws and all. I gasped when I saw that awful looking chicken foot, encrusted with scabs. But to these hardy sailors this was evidently quite all right. With the stench of the sick hogs in the hold permeating everything, the cook, business-like, turned to fill his own plate. I held my breath in anticipation of what he should draw from the kettle. And lo, his portion contained the chicken's head—blue swollen eyes, bedraggled comb and all. He took this tid-bit in the most matter of fact way. I turned faint as I specu-lated on what shocking part of the chicken I should get.

Again the cook applied himself to the stew pot. When he turned back to me with my plate, I was no longer there to see what fresh horror he had brought forth from the chicken's remains. To my disgrace as a deep-water sailor I had lost my appetite and passed up my dinner, the first and only one I ever missed at sea.

THE LOUSE

My friend Harris and I were in Callao. We had been up country and were now "on the beach." During our wanderings Jack had got himself lousy and spread his uncomfortable tenants to me. Under the equatorial sun they thrived, and soon we were "as lousy as pet coons."

What to do to get rid of our unwelcome guests was a problem. From time to time we "read our shirts" diligently, but such crude handwork could not cope with our prolific boarders, who multiplied on a mass production basis. Evidently drastic measures were necessary. So we located an empty Standard Oil can and hied ourselves out to the suburbs for a boil-up. And what a boil-up. We stewed our shirts, pants, socks and caps. We scrubbed each other vigorously. Then, rid of our living hair shirt, we felt fine and clean.

Jack soon left for up country again, and I decided it was time to get a ship. The only way to do this was through the Royal Oak sailors' boarding house. This place operated upon the usual robbery basis. The sailor was furnished a bunk and vile food for a week or two until a windjammer was leaving, when he had to sign a month's pay over to the boarding house shark. The ship captains got a "cut" of this "blood money" as the sailors called it, in return for which they refused to hire men any other way than through the boarding houses. The boarding house crimps, tools of the shipowners, were a convenient means of blacklisting militant sailors. In Callao, old Townsend, the Royal Oak boarding house crimp, had a monopoly. Many a sailor who had fallen foul of him for one cause or another had lain for months on the beach and eventually been forced to stow away or make his way overland to Iquiqu or other ports.

Townsend, quite conscious of his power, was a petty tyrant. He treated the sailors like dogs. For such a dictatorial role he had been well trained in the British Navy, where he had served many years as a boatswain's mate. Townsend had his joint all rigged up like a ship's fo'c's'le. One of his fads was cleanliness. Though he fed the men garbage and forced them to live in tier bunks, he made them holystone the floors as he had long ago learned on British warships.

When I asked old Townsend for a berth in his outfit he excoriated deep-water sailors in general as dirty beachcombers who came in and loused up his place. With special fury he swore the direst vengeance upon any man in his house upon whom he should find a louse. Such a man, he declared, would never get a ship out of Callao, but would leave his bones to bleach on the west coast.

Now as I listened to Townsend his remarks had only an academic interest for me. Secure in the memory of my yesterday's boil-up, I felt quite immune to his criticism. But just then I happened to look down at my coat lapel, and my heart stood still. There, streaking it along, was a large, prosperous-looking, well-nourished louse, evidently upon urgent business bent. Bold, brazen and unafraid, he had sallied forth from the dark recesses of his habitat adventurously into the light of the sun. How he escaped the holocaust of the Standard Oil can of yesterday was a mystery to me. But there he was in all his lousy majesty, so to speak. As he hurried along, carefree and self-confident, he seemed quite oblivious of the great danger he carried for my prospects in life.

Through my mind flashed visions of the miserable fate of the legendary sailors blacklisted by Townsend and forced to live the rest of their days on the bleak west coast of South America. Was I doomed, too, to leave my bones to bleach in Peru, as Townsend had so vigorously threatened? Was I to be denied the "opportunity" to starve my way around Cape Horn in some hungry British ship? Quickly, with as much nonchalance as I could muster, I covered the louse with my hand and deftly removed him. The danger passed. The half-blind Townsend had not noticed the recklessly promenading louse, nor my seizure of him. The near-tragedy had a happy ending after all. The boarding house crimp secured his month's blood money, I got my ship, bound 'round Cape Horn, and the hero of my story, the louse, received his just desserts.

NELLIE OF THE CLARENDON

Nellie was a barmaid at the Clarendon public house, or bar, in Newcastle, Australia. She was famous among deep-water sailors of a generation ago. On ships, in sailors' boarding houses, in saloons all over the world, whenever these men discussed Australia, sooner or later Nellie would be mentioned. The sailors all had a good word, a soft spot in their hearts for her. At the time she was perhaps the most widely-known personality in the whole world marine industry.

I got to meet Nellie in 1902. Newcastle was on the regular path of the old windjammers on their beaten track around the world. Hundreds of such ships went there in ballast from Africa and loaded coal for the west coast of South America, after which they proceeded on to Europe with cargoes of wheat or nitrates. I was aboard the three-masted full-rigged British ship, *Black Prince,* and we were following just that route.

Nellie was quite an ordinary-looking person and seemed to carry her wide fame very modestly. A regular working barmaid, she was a young married woman in her early thirties. She was a jolly, hail-fellow-well-met sort. Naturally, my mate and I had the honor of being served a glass of ale by Nellie.

What was the secret of the amazing popularity of this plain barmaid? So far as I could learn its main basis was that Nellie was a square shooter with the sailors. She had a sterling reputation among them for honesty, and they trusted her implicitly. The deep-sea sailor of those days, even more so than his steamer brother of today, was, while on shore, preyed upon by a host of parasites. He was robbed right and left by crooked saloon keepers, boarding-house bosses and prostitutes. In the midst of this maze of treachery and robbery, an honest figure like Nellie stood out like a lighthouse on a perilous coast.

She was a point of reliance in the territory of the enemy for these homeless, friendless, unorganized workers, and they made the most of her. Of course, in every port there were honest barmaids in sailors' saloons, but none of them succeeded in so deeply impressing the sailors with a sense of their integrity as did the famous Nellie.

Nellie carried on no political work for the sailors, nor did she try to save their "souls." She was just an all-around friend of the seamen. She acted as a voluntary banker to many of them. Much as the floating workers in the American West used to make a banker out of some trusted barkeeper, gambler or prostitute, the deep-water men, when they came ashore, often turned their money over to Nellie, and she kept a check on their spending. Nor could any waterfront crook find a way to the money in her care. The sailors saw no selfish motives in her attitude, though she was a drawing card and a profit-maker for the owner of the Clarendon.

This was about all there was at the bottom of her world-wide popularity. But apparently it was quite enough. The sailors sang Nellie's praises in hundreds of fo'c's'les, in every port in the world. Despite all their roughness and devil-may-care spirit, deep-water sailors were pretty simple and naïve, and a striking manifestation of it was this idealization of their curious proletarian heroine, Nellie of the Clarendon.

JORGENSEN: DEEP-WATER SAILOR

Jorgensen was a tall, black-haired Dane of about thirty. He had been going to sea since he was fifteen years old. We were shipmates in the *County of Cardigan,* which we joined in Peru. Jorgensen was of a sullen, quarrelsome disposition. For the most part we were not good friends, and once we came to blows. We were off the Chilean coast, and so motionless was our ship at the time that small cape pigeons, most tame of sea birds, swam leisurely alongside looking for bits of bread and meat. Jorgensen began "fishing" for these beautiful and friendly birds by baiting a hook with pork and hauling them aboard once they swallowed it. The pigeons being inedible, he would then release them, with their tongues badly lacerated or torn out. I objected to this cruel sport. Jorgensen promptly told me to mind my own business and we went to the deck fighting.

But it was only in calms or fair weather that Jorgensen and I did not hitch well together. When gales began to blow we became friends, and our friendship lasted as long as the bad weather. Jorgensen was a good sailor and I was young, strong and agile, and we liked to work together when the going was hard. When it came to making sail fast in the howling storms of Cape Horn latitudes, we always found ourselves working side-by-side on the weather end of the lower yards. This was the post of hard work and danger, for on the lee side and the higher yards the wind and peril are less and the sails not so heavy.

Jorgensen had the attitude typical of seamen on windjammers. Although a prisoner of the fascination and entanglements of sea life, he nevertheless declared that he hated the sea and all its works: the homelessness, the starvation, the low wages, the brutality and the other hardships of windjammer existence. Like so many others, he swore by all the gods this was to be his very last trip. He wanted to live like a human being. Henceforth, he was determined to have a home, a wife and children, like other men. He planned, immediately upon the end of this miserable voyage, to head for Iowa, where he had a prosperous brother, a farmer. Iowa was the end of the rainbow for him. In that magic place awaited joy, peace and comfort, such as only a deep-water sailor could long for.

All the way around Cape Horn and up through the tropics to the temperate latitudes to England, a three and one-half months' trip, Jorgensen dreamed and talked of Iowa. Scrupulously he saved his meager wages. Throughout the voyage he would not spend so much as a shilling for anything at the ship's "slop chest." He bought no soap, nor clothes, and he put patch upon patch on his dungarees. He even gave up smoking, a real hardship for a deep-water sailor. It was Iowa or bust. I marveled at his great determination, but the hard-boiled old sailors smiled cynically and said he would never reach Iowa. He belonged, they said, to the sea and would not be able to quit it.

They knew all too well how difficult it was to escape from the trap of a deep-water sailor's life.

Finally, we reached North Shields to be paid off. Jorgensen was happy and talked much of his trip to Iowa. That evening the captain gave us a sovereign apiece to go ashore with, while awaiting our pay day on the morrow. Jorgensen and I were on the "outs" at the time, as we had had several weeks of fine weather, so I did not go with him, nor did I know what his adventures ashore were that night. But evidently they were plenty.

Next morning we were paid off. Jorgensen was there, half drunk, and he had a black eye. With him were a tough-looking girl and her plug-ugly friend. They hovered about Jorgensen, waiting at the ship's gangway while he was drawing his wages for the voyage. Then Jorgensen walked over and counted out no less than six gold sovereigns to the man. Thus went three-fourths of his savings at one swoop. We figured it was some kind of a badger game and proposed to stop it by force. But the half-drunken Jorgensen belligerently scorned our help and advice.

The rest of Jorgensen's scanty wages went to hell in the next two days in the usual sailor manner. Saloon keepers, prostitutes and other shore sharks soon picked him clean. Jorgensen's hopes and plans for Iowa and a home evaporated with his wages. He was learning again, as he had done so many times before, that it was next to impossible to escape from the sea. In a week, broke and sick, he had signed on another windjammer and was outward-bound, around Cape Horn to Shanghai, China, a ten to twelve months' trip each way. And I have no doubt that, sailor-like, as soon as he recovered from his debauch and despair and felt the stimulating effect of the fresh sea air, he made a new set of vows that this was to be his very last voyage, and once more began to save diligently for his will-o'-the-wisp home and wife in Iowa.

THE END OF THE ROAD

I first met old Jim Ward aboard the British ship *Black Prince,* bound from Capetown to Newcastle, Australia. Jim was an American, a man of about seventy. He had a most interesting history and was a wonderful storyteller. We younger sailors sat entranced through many a second dog watch while old Jim drew upon his rich fund of experience. And it may surprise many to learn that deep-water sailors were simple, honest and straightforward in their stories. Their tales might sound "tall" to shore-folk, but to sailors they were commonplace; nor could they deceive each other with their stories.

Old Jim got a sort of a story-book start at sea life. He was born in Salem, Mass. When about nineteen he fell in love, but the girl jilted him, "gave him the mitten," as he said. Disgusted, Jim picked up and went to sea. Then followed fifty years before the mast, wandering all over the globe, always in square-riggers, for old Jim had only contempt for steamers. He served under Farragut in the Civil War. More than twenty times he doubled Cape Horn and he circled the world a dozen times. He sailed every sea and was intimately familiar with almost every important port. But never did old Jim go back to Salem.

The high point of Jim's adventures he had reached a generation before, when he was wrecked three times in three different oceans within two years, and each time was cast away among savages. The first time was when his ship, during the Italian-Zulu war, foundered off the African coast and its crew were taken by the cannibalistic Zulus. But these natives, although they were being slaughtered in a hopeless war, armed only with spears against a European enemy equipped with the most modern weapons, treated the castaway sailors well, and soon Jim was in Zanzibar looking for a ship. He got one, and a few months later she was wrecked on a wild coast of Borneo. Again savages, again good treatment and again a new ship, this time out of Manila.

This last ship was a whaler and, Jim's wreck-jinx being actively at work, she eventually piled herself up on the Alaskan coast, to the north of Point Barrow, everybody being lost except Jim and another sailor. There, being completely isolated, they "went native," living seven months with the Esquimaux. Old Jim's description of these seven months was the most interesting adventure story I ever heard. Finally the two were picked up by an American naval vessel. Jim's simplicity and earnestness lent an air of conviction to everything he said, and like many deep-water sailors he had enriched his mind by wide reading.

Old Jim, when I met him aboard the *Black Prince,* had passed his best sailoring time. Yet he was well-preserved for his age and still quite agile. But the shipping masters of those days, like the employers of today, did not like old workers; they wanted fresh young slaves. They had hired old Jim for the trip to Australia only because there was no one else available.

Jim Ward was paid off in Newcastle, but not my mate Jack Harris and I. We were under the usual clause by which we had no wages coming for three years. But we jumped the hungry *Black Prince* and went "up country." We knocked around Sydney for ten days and conceived the bright idea of walking to Melbourne, a distance of several hundred miles. Putting our "swags" (bundles) upon our backs, we started off "on the wallaby" (on the tramp). But it was no go. After a week's walking, hobnobbing with "sundowners" (wayfarers who make a practice of arriving at a "station," or ranch house, just in time for supper), Harris was overcome by the heat, it being December and midsummer. So we made our way back to Newcastle, where we signed on the *Alliance,* loaded with coal for the west coast of South America.

The night before we were to go aboard I ran into old Jim Ward. He was on the beach, hungry and broke. All his attempts to get a ship had failed. There were plenty of able-bodied seamen in Newcastle and he was not wanted. Old Jim was up against the fate of the aged sailor, sentenced to the scrap heap. His half century of labor and hardship on ships all over the world counted for precisely nothing with the shipowners now that he was old and worn out. He was friendless and homeless and quite unfitted for work ashore. When he went to the American consul for assistance, the latter, with customary consular brutality towards sailors, put Jim out of his office; and there was no union for him to turn to for help. Old Jim faced the hard alternative of an Australian poor house or a wretched end on the beach. Beyond giving him our few remaining shillings, we couldn't help him.

Next day Jim was on hand when we rowed out to the *Alliance*, which lay in the stream. He gave us a cheery good-by, though he felt pretty bad. It was not long until, to the tune of a capstan chantey, we had weighed anchor and were being towed down the river. Our old sailor friend sat on the dock and watched us go, and we looked sadly back at him. His fifty years of wandering, adventure and work had at last come to a close. For poor old Jim it was the end of the road.

CHAPTER III . . . . . ON THE HOBO

From 1900 to 1916 I "beat my way" about thirty-five thousand miles on American railroads. Besides many shorter trips, my hoboing consisted of seven runs from coast to coast, and two run-offs from Chicago to the Pacific. These transcontinental trips took me over the main lines of the Pennsylvania, Baltimore & Ohio and Erie in the East, and the Milwaukee, Great Northern, Northern Pacific, Chicago & Northwestern, Burlington, Southern Pacific, Union Pacific, Rock Island, Oregon Short Line, Denver & Rio Grande and Canadian Pacific in the West. To some extent my aim in this extensive hoboing was the not unusual worker's desire to find work and to see the country at the same time. But mostly my hobo travels were for revolutionary agitational purposes, in my work in the Socialist Party, the Industrial Workers of the World, the Syndicalist League of North America and the International Trade Union Educational League.

HOBOING IN THE WEST

During the years in which I made my hobo trips the conditions for hoboing varied greatly in different sections of the country. In the East and South things were bad enough, but the West was the really hard section. There the hobo met with the heaviest hardships. Seasoned hoboes of that time did not consider a man a real hobo unless he had beaten his way over the "big hump," the Rocky Mountain continental divide.

In the West, because the country was thinly populated, and the climate severe in many sections, it toughened up everything for the hobo. The towns were small and far between, and it was difficult to eat on the way. The country was overrun with hungry hoboes; along desert stretches of the Southern Pacific I have seen, in the "jungles" at a railroad division point, one-third as many hoboes as there were inhabitants in the town. Such circumstances made the hobo-plagued towns very "hostile." Their usual answer to the hobo problem was the policeman's club and the "hoosegow." Because of these conditions large numbers of hoboes were literally half starved as they beat their way through the West.

In the East, with railroads closer together and trains more frequent, it was no calamity to a hobo to be "ditched" from a train. He usually could eat in the surrounding populated country, and all he had to do was to wait an hour or two until the next train came along, or maybe he would just hop over to some other road and catch a train. The railroad bulls and train crews bothered him little, the Eastern hobo usually riding openly on the trains.

But in the sparsely populated West it was quite a different matter. Through the wide deserts and mountains the railroads were few and trains ran seldom. Hence a hobo ditched off a train might have to stick around a day or two waiting for another, probably with nothing to eat while doing so. And of course, in those days automobile roads were practically unknown in the West and hitch-hiking was still a thing of the future.

Many Western railroad "shacks" (brakemen) utilized these conditions to prey upon the armies of worker-hoboes. Their method was to charge "fares" of a dollar to two dollars per division of one hundred to two hundred and fifty miles. It was a case of "pay or hit the grit." Sometimes these grafters let a man ride if he had a union card, but their customary answer was, "I can't eat that; pay or unload!" Such shacks almost always went armed. Their usual technique was to give no attention to the hoboes as the train pulled out, but when it reached some isolated stopping point ten to fifty miles out, Mr. Shack would show up, gun in hand, to make his collections. Those who had money paid, rather than face a wait of possibly days before another train halted in the god-forsaken place. If it was a desert siding, with no water for miles in either direction, or on some bleak and freezing mountain top, it was all the more a favorite spot with the shacks to rob the hoboes. Those who did not pay were left behind, unless they were skillful enough to ride the train in spite of all efforts of the train crew to ditch them.

Another method of the shacks was to go over the top of a train while it was in motion. When they came to a car in which there were hoboes (and the shacks seemed to know this by some sort of sixth sense) they would climb into the car and, pulling their guns, begin their regular dollar apiece stickup. Those failing to pay were often forced to leap from the speeding train, a practice which cost many a hobo his life.

Brakemen frequently made hundreds of dollars a month from this robbery. I have seen a dozen hoboes in a single car pay a dollar each, and there were many more hoboes on the same train. The pickings were especially rich when large numbers of workers, coming from the harvest or some big construction job, were beating their way back to their "home" territory.

The dollar graft reached such dimensions that it affected the companies' passenger revenues, and they made desultory efforts to check it. Often they sent out agents who, posing as hoboes, would pay a shack a dollar and then turn him in to be discharged. A brakeman so fired was said to have "taken a hot dollar."

These hard conditions—few towns, few trains, long stretches of mountains and deserts, fierce cold and burning heat, hostile police, grafting shacks—made hoboing toughest in the West in those days; and consequently developed the art of hoboing to greater heights there than anywhere else in the country. The most skilled hoboes refused to pay the shack's dollar (even if they had it), and they learned a thousand tricks to beat the road in spite of all efforts of police and train crews to unload them. As for the less skilled hoboes, broke and persecuted by police and shacks, they made their way slowly over the Western roads in misery and hardship; that is, if they did not leave their bones along the way.

The hoboes of the time, 1900 to 1916, the great army of men perpetually beating back and forth over the Western railroads, were chiefly the so-called "floating workers," the real builders of the West. Into this category I fitted for about a dozen years. They were the construction gangs on the great railroads, the builders of roads and irrigation canals, the ranch-hands who operated the immense agricultural industry, the lumber workers of the giant forests of the Northwest, the metal and coal miners of the Rocky Mountain country, the boomer railroad men and building-trades workers, the sheepherders and cowhands. For the most part their work was seasonal. They worked in the summer and were unemployed in the winter, when they congregated in great numbers in every Western city. Back and forth they went, a restless wandering mass, "following the harvest" all over the West, or beating their way to and from construction jobs and industries in remote sections of the country. Periodically their numbers were swollen by the recurring industrial crises.

The floating Western workers usually had no homes or families, and often no religion. They were voteless and took little or no part in the political and social life of the cities, where during the winter months they crowded the lodging houses in the "slave markets" and "skid-roads." They were inclined to be syndicalistic. Their whole life tended to make them militant fighters, and the heroic strikes of Western metal miners, lumber workers and farm-hands wrote many of the most glorious pages in American labor history.

The Industrial Workers of the World, from 1905 on, was the true organization of the floating workers, the hoboes of the West. Such bodies as Eads Howe's and Jeff Davis' Brotherhood Welfare Association were mere pretenders. The I.W.W. was bone of the bone and flesh of the flesh of the floating workers. It shared their utter contempt for the home-guard, the politician and the preacher. Its famous songs, "Hallelujah I'm a Bum," "Long-Haired Preacher" and dozens of others reflected the joys and miseries of the floating worker's life.

The I.W.W. made its red card respected throughout the West by police, crooked shacks and traveling yeggmen. Many a time, in I.W.W. territory, some armed shack bounced into a box car intent upon dollar-robbing the hoboes, only to find himself disarmed and kicked through the car door into the ditch, river or whatever happened to be the scenery at that particular spot.

The decline of the I.W.W. as an organization kept pace with the diminishing role of the floating workers in the West through the introduction of farm machinery, the completion of the building of the railroads, the tendency of the workers to "settle down" in the lumber industry, etc.

Many I.W.W. militants were skilled hoboes. For them to make the jump from Chicago to the Pacific coast in four or five days, enduring great hardships and exposure en route, was a small matter. When the I.W.W. held its convention in Chicago in 1912, at which I was a delegate, characteristically most of the delegates from the Pacific coast received no expense money from their locals. Without a dime, they had to beat their way over some five thousand miles of hostile railroads and spend about three weeks in Chicago, and nobody thought anything unusual of it. Such was the spirit of the floating workers of the West.

A NARROW SQUEAK

The first of my seven hobo trips, from coast to coast, was in the winter of 1901. I worked my way from New York to Galveston, Texas, as a deckhand on a tramp steamer, and then beat the Southern Pacific railroad three thousand miles from that city into Portland, Oregon, via Los Angeles and San Francisco.

Road conditions were very tough. Armies of " 'boes" were all along the line, driven south by cold weather. Many were on the verge of starvation. It was almost impossible to beg anything in the little desert towns, and there was no work. Bands of foragers robbed the chicken coops of the ranchers, and others systematically bummed the residents. Sometimes a man would "hit" all the houses in town and even go over them a second time before he got a "lump" to eat.

It was extremely hard to ride the trains, especially on the twelve hundred mile stretch of desert west of San Antonio. The passenger trains were manned by armed guards who clubbed the hoboes and kicked them off. On the freight trains the shacks, all armed, demanded a "fare" of two dollars for each railroad division. Whoever did not pay was thrown off. Sometimes ditched hoboes remained for days without food or water at remote desert points until freight trains chanced to stop. To cover the road by walking was out of the question; for sometimes water tanks were as much as a hundred miles apart, the trains carrying their water with them in special cars. Only in large gangs could the 'boes overawe the shacks and stay on the trains.

The bulls were exceedingly hostile. In San Antonio, El Paso, Yuma and other large towns they were rounding up big bunches of the 'boes and giving them six months apiece in the notorious chain gangs. The sheriffs made a double rake-off, stealing on the rate allowed the prisoners for food and also getting a fee for each hobo arrested. In the smaller places the 'boes, camped beside fires of railroad coal, seemed almost to outnumber the resident population, and the local police were helpless to handle them.

As for myself, I had plenty of difficulty getting across the desert, what with dodging shacks and bulls. My A.F. of L. union card helped me with one or two shacks, but as for the bulls I had to duck them at all costs. I had no relish for a Southern "hell" county farm, and it was in trying to evade arrest that I had a narrow escape.

It happened on the division between Yuma and Los Angeles. I was riding in the ice-box of an empty "freezer" fruit car, and we had stopped at a desert siding when two 'boes piled into the car. They were ex-soldiers, recently discharged from service in the Philippines. Paid off in Los Angeles and soon broke, they had started to beat their way East, but had been ditched on the desert. For four days they remained at the siding without food and with only such water as dripped from the high water tank. No trains, freight or passenger, had stopped. The ex-soldiers could not cross the uninhabited desert afoot, and they dared not flag a train, as that would mean six months in jail, or possibly being shot as stickup men. So they decided to go West again on our train.

The 'boes warned me that Colton, just east of Los Angeles, was a very hostile town, as its police were frisking every train and giving six months apiece to every hobo they caught. I resolved that they should not get me, and planned to drop off the train before it got into the Colton railroad yards, make my way through the town (a small one), and then pick the train up again on the fly as it pulled out for "L.A."

My plan seemed to work fine. It was late at night. I duly "unloaded" outside Colton while the train was going so fast it threw me off my feet into the ditch. Then I circled through the town's streets outside the railroad yards and came to the railroad tracks again on the west end. There I was fortunate, or thought I was, in finding a point where another railroad crossed the S.P. "Good," I concluded, "this means that the S.P. train will have to stop for the crossing, so I'll go along a few hundred yards beyond the railroad crossing and grab her as she picks up speed pulling westward." I made this calculation as a railroad worker and an experienced hobo, but it lacked reality and it almost finished me.

The night was pitch black, and I carefully walked over the ground upon which I would later have to run in "making" the train. A skilled hobo always does this to avoid the grave danger of stumbling into a switch standard, trestle or some other unseen obstacle in the dark, while running for his train. Many a poor hobo, failing to take such precautions, has been picked up along the right-of-way, a bloody, mangled mass.

My inspection of the runway I expected to cover completed, I sat down to wait for the train. Soon it "toot-tooted" and started to pull out from the yards. But to my surprise and consternation the train did not stop at the railroad crossing as I had calculated, but pounded over it, picking up speed rapidly as she came towards me. Having no desire to stay in hostile Colton, I determined to make the train anyhow. I was young and agile; I had been a brakeman and considered myself a hobo of parts; but my decision to jump the now fast-speeding train was foolish, and it came perilously near ending my life.

I made a wild run for the train, dashing along the right-of-way in the black dark. It was going so fast that my running took me far beyond the stretch I had previously inspected for obstacles. Finally, I seized a grab-iron on a box-car, but was yanked clear off my feet by the speed of the train. Then, just in the same split second, my swaying body slammed into a cattleguard (a fence-like arrangement placed upon both sides of a railroad wagon road crossing to prevent cattle from straying onto the tracks) at a wagon road crossing which I had not seen before. Miraculously, the impact did not break my hold on the grab-iron, but the inward slope of the cattleguard threw my legs across the rails and I could feel them slipping on the smooth steel as I dragged along, hanging from the side-ladder. I was within inches of the wheels.

I hadn't time to be frightened. One thought flashed through my mind, dictated instantaneously by my railroad experience. Quicker than I can write it, I realized that on the farther side of the wagon road, just a few feet away was another cattleguard, and if I bumped into it, dragging as I was, I would surely be killed. So happening in that very moment to sway clear of the rails, I let go my hold of the side-ladder—just in time. I rolled over on the dirt road and smashed into the second cattle-guard. But I was safely away from the train, the rails and the grinding wheels.

The wind was knocked out of me, but I was not seriously hurt. And so, clambering over the cattleguard, I again grabbed the freight, which by this time had slowed down. Only when I was safely ensconced in the ice-box of a refrigerator car and we began chugging up a long, hard grade did I realize how close I had been to death, and I trembled from head to foot. I figured out then why the train did not stop at the crossing as I had expected. It was because, there being a heavy grade on the S.P. just beyond the crossing, the S.P. trains had the right-of-way so they might pick up all possible speed to make the grade. Ignorance of the fact had almost cost me my life. But, after all, the experience was only one of many hazards of the road, and I soon forgot my fright in congratulating myself that I had outwitted the hostile Colton bulls.

KAMELA

Between Western hoboes and dollar-collecting shacks there existed a deep and abiding hostility; but towards the engineers and firemen ("hogheads" and "tallow-pots"), who usually had a craft feud against the cons and shacks, the 'boes had a better feeling. Once while I was a fireman on the O.R.&N. railroad out of Portland, Oregon, in 1907, I saw this feudism illustrated interestingly.

Our freight train had pulled into a siding at Deschutes to meet the passenger train "Number Five." The head-end shack had ditched a hobo who could not pay and was bawling him out, when the latter turned on him. "It's easy for you to talk big," he said. "You've got a gun, and the law and the train crew are on your side. But at that if I had a good meal under my belt I'd punch you all over the right-of-way." The engineer, who had his craft's usual contempt for brake-men, heard this and said to the hobo, "Here, 'bo, take these four bits, go up to the hotel and get yourself a meal, and then if you'll tie into that shack I'll see you get a square shake." The hobo got his feed and then thoroughly trimmed the brakeman, all before "Number Five" arrived. To me, an ex-hobo, this example of poetic justice was enor-mously gratifying.

One of the many experiences I had with dollar-hunting shacks was in the winter of 1904 as I was beating my way from New York to The Dalles, Oregon. The going had been extremely hard all the way, and I was flat broke and exhausted by the hardships of the long trip. From Omaha to Pocatello the temperature had ranged from twenty to thirty-five degrees below zero. On the O.S.L. and O.R.&N. the passenger trains were loaded with guards, so unwillingly I had to take a freight out of La Grande, Oregon. My "accommodations" were poor indeed, riding in a cattle car loaded with railroad steel. It was extremely cold, with the wind sweeping through the open stock car, and soon my feet were nearly frozen from standing on the icy steel rails.

The train slowly slogged up the heavy grade west of La Grande and came to a halt at Kamela, twenty miles out and four thou-sand feet high, on top of the Blue Mountains. There was only a scat-tering of buildings, the weather was far below zero, and the ground was blanketed with four feet of snow—an ideal place for a crooked shack to rob or ditch a hobo.

And, sure enough, as the train stood on the siding the head-end shack climbed into my car and saluted me with the traditional, "Hey, 'bo, what are you riding on?" I showed him my union card—I was a member of the Atlantic Coast Seamen's Union. But he gruffly rejected it, with the usual, "I can't eat that. Shell out a dollar or hit the grit." When I did not pay he drove me out of the car with a stout club, such as brakemen carried on the mountain divisions to screw up hand brakes.

Now I simply had to make that train out of Kamela. There would not be another along for many hours and if left behind I might freeze. As the train pulled out, the shack rode on top and leaned over to see if I jumped on. I let several cars pass me and then grabbed another stock car loaded with steel.

I knew I might now expect the worst from the shack; so before getting aboard I had picked up a heavy iron bolt about eighteen inches long. Soon the end top door was flung open and the shack piled in with a lantern in one hand (it was night time) and his brake club in the other. Advancing menacingly towards me, he yelled, "You son-of-a-bitch, I thought I told you to unload! Here's where you hit the grit plenty hard." His plan was to make me jump off as the train was speeding down the heavy grade; this might have killed me.

I resolved to make a battle for it. I was only twenty-three years old, had just been toughened by three years at sea, and although starved and worn out from my long hobo trip, I still had a fight left in me. Seeing that the brakeman was brandishing his brake club, I concluded he had no gun. Setting his lantern down, the shack advanced upon me, not noticing in the semi-dark car the long bolt which I held behind me. He made a vicious swing at me with his club, but I countered it with a blow of my bolt. He howled with pain and his club flew out of his hand, away over in one corner. I think I broke one of his fingers. At this unexpected resistance the shack retreated quickly to the other end of the car. Then, swearing vengeance, he picked up his lantern and, with difficulty from his injured hand, climbed out on top of the fast running train.

I knew now that I was really in for it. The shack was bound to come back with reinforcements, probably armed, and I would be in serious danger if they caught me. So I, too, got out on top, and as I made my way towards the head-end of the train I could see the brakeman going to the hind-end to get help. Fortunately, the train stopped at a siding soon afterward, and I could scurry away behind a nearby shanty.

Shortly the train crew came looking for me. They did it in the classical manner, one man on top of the train and one on either side, frisking each car, top, bottom and inside, as they went along. But it was a very black night (moonlight nights are bad for hoboing), and I was able to evade them. Circling around the searching trainmen, I made my way ahead of the train and caught her on the fly, unseen by them, as she pulled out. But I did not dare ride inside the cattle cars. Instead I rode the "rods" (body rods under the cars). Here I was safe while the train was in motion, but chilled to the marrow of my bones from the severe cold.

Evidently I had hurt the shack, and the train crew were plenty sore. They repeatedly searched the train for me, both while it was in motion and at the various stops. But, with darkness on my side and by dint of my skill as a hobo, I managed to elude them. Finally they gave it up as a bad job, not catching sight of me and probably concluding that I had been ditched somewhere along the line. So, dodging the hostile train crew all night, I reached the next division town, Umatilla, Oregon.

DANGERS ON THE ROAD

Railroading in those years was very dangerous for train and engine crews, but incomparably more so for hoboes. Besides hunger and cold, the hobo was confronted with a maze of perils. Death laid in wait for him at every turn. The hobo might dash his brains out or be cut to pieces while jumping on or off a rapidly moving train; he might fall from the top of a swaying box-car or be swept off by a low bridge of whose presence he was unaware; he might have his head torn off by a car or railroad structure that was not "in the clear"; he might be crushed between telescoping cars or mangled in wrecks. Broken bodies of hoboes were constantly picked up along the railroad right-of-way, and hurried off to nameless graves in local Potters' Fields.

Experienced hoboes, wise to the ways of the road, like veteran soldiers in war, were able to shield themselves somewhat from the thickly-strewn hazards. But green hoboes, "gay cats," walked into these dangers blindly and were mowed down in hundreds. The latter exposed themselves to disaster especially in their frantic efforts to hide from trainmen and bulls.

One of the deadliest and prolific sources of death to hoboes was the shifting of loads in cars. Often, by rough switching in yards or by a heavy application of the airbrakes on the road, the cars were so violently jerked as to literally catapult their loads against the car ends, smashing them out. Worst of all cargoes in this respect was lumber, especially planed lumber. Expert 'boes were always very careful about riding in cars with loads liable to shift, and especially to keep away from the chief danger spot, the forward-end of the car. But greenhorn hoboes were frequently killed or badly injured.

Once in Avery, Idaho, while beating my way over the Milwaukee, I was walking through the local yards when I noticed a knot of railroad men gathered around a freight car in a train that had just arrived from the West. I went over and found a horrible sight. It was a box-car loaded with planed lumber, and on the heavy grades in the Bitterroot Mountains the slippery, treacherous load had shifted so hard as to break out the whole forward-end of the car. A hobo had been killed in the shift. His bones were crushed like pipe-stems and his flesh was smeared against the shattered car-end. I shuddered and passed by as they gathered up what they could of the shapeless mass and put it into a wheelbarrow.

Low bridges also killed many hoboes. Trainmen knew where these fatal obstacles were located, but even they often got caught. To a hobo who did not even know of their existence such bridges were a deadly menace, especially in the dark. One night, while I was beating my way east through Maryland over the Baltimore & Ohio railroad, a hobo was riding several cars ahead of me. He wanted to cross over a couple of cars to an open gondola where the riding would be easier. But hardly had he climbed to the top of the box-car when he crashed into a low wagon-road bridge and was instantly killed.

A special horror that all expert hoboes constantly bore in mind was the danger of being locked in a car and left at some isolated point to starve. Railroad annals record many cases where this occurred. It could easily happen. A trainman or yard-bull going along a train finds a box-car door unlocked and locks it. The green hobo inside, afraid of being arrested or ditched, keeps still. Then on the road the train crew sets out this particular car on a siding because of a "hot-box," a pulled "lung" (wrecked coupling) or for some other reason. The hobo locked inside, not knowing what all the switching is about, is careful to make no noise that might attract the train crew. Finally, however, when he hears the train whistle he becomes alarmed and tries to get out. If the car is at some frequented spot he is not so bad off; the worst that will happen to him is to be slugged or thrown in jail. But if the car happens to be at some desert siding, maybe miles from the nearest house, then this unfortunate hobo faces the prospect of dying from hunger and thirst. Many's the time trainmen and car inspectors have opened foul-smelling box-cars and discovered dead hoboes, starved to death.

RIDING THE TRUCKS

Much skill was needed in hoboing, especially in the mountain and desert regions of the West. As a rule the best hoboes were native-born Americans. They possessed a knowledge of the railroads and the country which gave them a self-confidence such as the foreign-born hobo seldom acquired.

There were many methods of beating one's way over the railroads. First, there were those slick elements who—through faked passes, stolen hat checks and other devices—"rode the cushions." But the bulk of the hoboes did not know how to work these dodges, and rode the freight and passenger trains.

On a freight train there were many places to ride—inside box-cars and gondolas, in ice-boxes of refrigerator cars, on body rods under the cars, on the locomotive tenders, etc. Only greenhorns rode the "bump-ers" between the cars, because here they were most exposd to shacks, police and accidents. From one hundred to three hundred miles of road was a day's run for a 'bo by freight.

But "fast" hoboes scorned freights and rode passenger trains when-ever possible. On passenger trains, or "rattlers," they rode the "blinds," the "rods," the side-boxes on Pullman diners, vestibules, the steps, the men's washrooms and the car tops. They also rode the locomotive pilots, or "cow-catchers," and even the engine brakebeams.

But when it came to really getting over the road in a hurry, the expert hobo made for the trucks, or wheel structure under the pas-senger coaches. There, hidden in a maze of axles, wheels and springs, it was difficult for police or trainmen to find him. He could ride day and night and make long "jumps." I remember once how Frank Little, one of the fastest hoboes in the I.W.W., and a brave fighter who was lynched in Butte during the war while leading a miners' strike, held down the trucks of the Overland Limited from Chicago without a break all the way to Ogden, Utah. There, hungry and exhausted, he got off, ate and slept, caught the Limited twenty-four hours later and rode her right into Oakland, California.

Riding the trucks was something that only experienced hoboes ven-tured. It was packed full of danger. One had to know precisely what he was about, or face disaster. Even with all his skill he might easily be cut to pieces. When a 'bo crawled into the trucks he usually had only a minute or two to do so, and if, once inside, he found he had made a mistake and there was no place for him to ride in that par-ticular kind of truck, he was a good candidate for Potter's Field, as he would hardly have time to get out before the train started.

My first ride on the trucks was on the Northern Pacific, between Missoula and Butte, Montana, on my way to New York. I'll never forget the experience. I had made two coast-to-coast trips already and considered myself an expert hobo, before I finally ventured upon trying the trucks, my favorite riding place on rattlers being the tops.

Missoula was a tough town at the time, with hostile shacks and bulls, and there was no chance to ride a freight or the tops of a rattler. So I decided to hit the trucks. It was about a three-hour run to Butte. But just how to get into the trucks was not altogether clear. I had no time to lose, as the passenger train was about to pull out. Selecting a rear car, I crawled over the brakebeam and across the axle. I was now in the very heart of the truck. I had to figure out instantly how to place myself in order to ride, for the train began to move. To get out alive from the truck would now have been impossible.

The way I rode was as follows: There was a brakerod, or bottom rod, connecting the two brakebeams of the truck. It was so low it cleared the rails by only a few inches. Upon this slender rod I had to sit. There I balanced myself by bracing my shoulders against the truck frame on one side and my feet against the truck frame on the opposite side. This left me riding sidewise to the direction of the train, with my feet raised as high as my head. The thin rod cut into my seat, the whirling axle was within three or four inches of my elbow, and the roaring wheels were even closer to my shoulders and feet. It was a cramped, uncomfortable and dangerous position, but a good one for knocking off the miles, and this was all that counted.

As the train rapidly gained headway, the one-inch brakerod I was sitting on sagged heavily under my weight. The car rumbled over a switch, and the rod cleared the rails by hardly more than an inch or two. My heart "popped into my mouth." I shivered at such a narrow margin and tried not to think of what would happen to me if the brakerod should come loose, bend down more or break outright, or if we should run across one of those pieces of wire that are frequently to be found snagged in the ballast between the tracks. In any of these cases I should be instantaneously cut to pieces, as hundreds of hoboes had been before me.

In my narrow quarters, I had nothing between me and sudden death but the slender brakerod. I had difficulty in balancing myself on my precarious perch, with the jerking and bouncing of the truck. The roar of the train was so deafening that I could not even "hear myself think." I was pelted with stones and half smothered with dust, picked up by the rushing train. Many a hobo has been knocked off the trucks by such stones or actually suffocated while crossing long sections of dusty roadbed. And an even greater danger, I was peppered with hot coals dropped by the locomotive. Fortunately I knew enough not to ride too close to the head-end of the train, because there hoboes are sometimes badly burned by the spray of blazing coals, and even forced to let go their hold and fall beneath the wheels.

The first stop out of Missoula was Garrison, a one-and-a-half-hours' run. I did not think I could stick it out that far. My situation was alarming. But as time went on I began to get a little used to the terrific roar, the cramped quarters, the unnatural and painful position of my body, the precariousness of my brakerod seat and the acute sense of danger; so that when we reached Garrison I decided to ride it out to Butte, and I did. Arrived there, I felt that now I was indeed a real hobo.

After that I made dozens of divisions on the trucks of rattlers. The trucks became my favorite place to ride, and so accustomed to all their inconveniences did I become that I eventually had to watch out for a special danger of the experienced hobo, that of falling asleep on the trucks and tumbling beneath the wheels. I later made many a long and hard trip on the trucks, but I never had such a thrilling ride as that first one from Missoula to Butte.

DEATH AT MY FEET

On the railroads sudden death grasps at the hobo from most unexpected quarters. I had scores of narrow escapes. A day's riding that did not contain some deadly peril was exceptional. And usually the danger situation developed so swiftly that one hardly had time to think before it was all over.

How unexpectedly a hobo may get into mortal difficulty was illustrated to me one night in The Dalles, Oregon. I was just finishing a transcontinental trip from Galveston, Texas, and The Dalles was my destination. It was a very hostile town, and they were sentencing hoboes to four months in jail. I had heard this, so I rode on the top (roof) of a passenger coach several cars back from the engine, in order not to be "glommed" by the bulls in the depot.

The train pulled into the station, and I could see the police giving her the once-over at both ends and along the sides. What was I to do? I simply had to get off at The Dalles, as the next stop was many miles away. Evidently I couldn't go to either the head- or hind-end of the train, so I decided to leap to a string of box-cars on the next track. It was a difficult jump, as there was a gap of several feet and I had a very bad take-off from the rounded passenger car-roof, which was covered with ice.

I waited until the train started to pull out and then rose to jump. Just then a 'bo beside me shouted, "For Christ's sake, don't jump, you'll be killed," and he clutched at my coat-tail. He got enough of a grip to check my jump. But I managed to light on the very edge of the box-car. There I teetered precariously for a moment or two on the verge of falling between the moving cars, which would have been certain death. Fortunately, I caught my balance and righted myself. Quickly I clambered down from the box-car and disappeared in the yards, evading the police. In spite of the cold night I was covered with sweat. It was just an everyday incident in the life of a hobo.

Many times, while hoboing, I found myself in similarly dangerous situations, but my most agonizing experience occurred while I was beating my way over the Great Northern. I was eastbound and had just hopped a freight train leaving Havre, Montana. The yards were full of bulls, so I couldn't look her over and find an inside place to ride, but had caught her on the fly. I grabbed the first thing that came along, a gondola loaded with coal. It was a bitterly cold night, far below zero, and I had to locate a better place, so, although it was extremely hazardous for a 'bo to wander over a train top at night, I decided to do it in the hope of finding an open end-door or top-door of a box-car.

I started forward on the swaying, surging train, and I had crossed a few box-cars when I struck another gondola. It was here that I nearly came to grief, trying to climb from this gondola to the roof of the adjoining box-car. Ordinarily it was not difficult to stand on a gondola-end, throw myself over to the box-car end and elbow up onto the running board on the box-car roof. I had often done it before. But this time, as I was trying to get my elbows upon the roof running-board, the box car gave a big lurch that broke my grip, and in a fraction of a second I found myself hanging at arm's length from the roof running-board.

This put me in a strange position. Hanging from the box-car roof, I had no footing beneath me. A couple of feet below were the narrow, swaying couplers. To let go and drop down upon the jiggling couplers would mean almost certainly to fall beneath the wheels. For there was hardly a chance that I could maintain my balance on the couplers, leaping and dancing as they were, long enough to spring back upon the gondola-end. If I were to let go death would be the result.

Evidently to get out of my predicament I had to climb up onto the box-car roof. But how? The box-car end was quite flat and smooth, with no toe-hold anywhere. There was no brakestaff or end-door upon which to get a purchase for my foot. I tried several times to "chin" myself up to the roof running-board and then clamber up onto the roof. But with my exhaustion from hard riding, the wild swaying of the box-car, with my hands in gloves, and my poor grip on the roof running-board, I simply could not make it. After many fruitless attempts, I dropped back to my old position of hanging at arm's length from the roof flat against the smooth car-end.

Things began to look black. I did not dare to drop down upon the couplers and I could not climb onto the roof; I had no idea when the train would stop, and there was no way to notify the train crew of my difficulty. Besides, it was desperately cold. I did not know what to do. I felt I was facing death. But I was more angry than frightened; angry that I, an expert hobo, had allowed myself to get into such a jam.

I realized that sooner or later I would be forced to let go. The strain was so great I felt my arms were being pulled from their sockets.

My fingers seemed to be paralyzed, or frozen. I became truly alarmed. The hungry-looking wheels appeared to be reaching up for me. I finally resolved upon a plan. I would hang on as long as I could, but if I reached the end of my endurance before the train halted, I would let go, drop onto the swaying couplers and then, practically with the same motion, try to leap clear of the speeding train.

It was a desperate expedient, with only a faint hope for success. I tried not to think of where my flying leap from the rapidly moving train might land me, even if I escaped falling beneath the wheels. But my plan offered a better chance for me than to drop onto the swaying couplers and try to balance myself there even long enough to grab the top of the gondola. I was certain that if I tried the latter I would be thrown beneath the wheels and ground to pieces.

With my desperate plan in mind, I hung on to the roof running-board. How long I don't know. I felt it was an hour or more. My arms were numb, my strength was rapidly failing and my mind was in torture. The agony seemed endless. Suddenly I heard the engine "whistle in" to a station. A quick flash of relief passed over me. The pain seemed to leave my arms and I grew stronger. Now I really did hang on for dear life. The train slowed down and stopped. I dropped on the coupler and got off the train. I was almost in a state of collapse, but our stopping place was only a desert siding and I had to keep going. I managed to find a satisfactory place on the train and rode out the division. For two weeks afterward my sore arms and three frozen fingers were constant reminders of how I almost left my bones along Jim Hill's railroad, and to my dying day I shall not forget this odd adventure.

RAILROAD BULLS

The hobo was constantly harassed by an army of "bulls," city and railroad police. They jailed and abused him at their pleasure. The usual charges against him were vagrancy and trespass; but he was always an easy victim when some local crime had taken place. Many were the poor 'boes railroaded to the penitentiary for crimes they never committed.

Throughout the South conditions were very bad. Every hobo ran grave danger of being picked up and sent to turpentine camps, phosphate mines or county farms, then to spend six months to three years slaving for conscienceless prison contractors. The West also was tough on the hobo. Everywhere he was slugged and jailed. A favorite stunt of the local police was to round up the hoboes in the local "jungles" and "drill" them out of town into the desert—with the next stop probably a water tank thirty miles away and not a single house there or anywhere in between.

The railroad bulls were even worse than the city police. They seemed to take a sadistic delight in maltreating hoboes. Numerous railroads were notorious among hoboes all over the country because of their ferocious railroad police. Many stirring tales heard in the jungles recited how hoboes "laid for" some such police tyrant in the dark of a railroad yard and finished him off.

The railroad police often rode the trains and slugged the hoboes off them. If a hobo were found killed along the railroad right-of-way no official troubled his head over the detail of whether the dead man fell off or was thrown from a train. Once I stood in a railroad yard in a Texas division town and watched the bulls shooting at hoboes riding the rods as a freight pulled out. And I was in Southern California when a couple of railroad bulls clubbed to death one of two boys they found on the head-end blind of a passenger train. This incident attracted much attention only because the boys were sons of well-to-do people, on a hoboing trip for adventure. Hundreds of hoboes have met death at the hands of railroad bulls.

A murderous trick was that of the railroad police on the Southern Pacific railroad. When a freight train gets well into motion it is difficult for the bulls to reach hoboes riding the rods underneath; so the S.P. police worked out the following brutal device. Stationing themselves on top at the end of a car under which men were riding, they would lower some heavy iron object made fast to a stout line. As the train sped along it would send the iron bumping upon the ties and flying wildly about. If it hit a hobo riding the rods underneath, ten chances to one he was done for. To protect themselves the hoboes would try to seize the hurtling missile and give it a turn around a body rod, so that it no longer bounced from the ties and the bulls could not haul it up again.

One night I saw a hobo killed by railroad bulls. Several of us were waiting to make a train west out of the Southern Pacific yards in El Paso, Texas. Just as she got under way two railroad police appeared and began to shoot at us. We all rushed wildly for the train. But in the semi-darkness one man ran full tilt into a switch-standard beside the track. The impact threw him against the moving train and in an instant he was dragged under the wheels and cut to pieces. It happened so suddenly that he never even screamed.

The hind-end brakeman "pulled the air" and brought the train to a standstill, the police rounded us up and we gathered together the gory remnants of the hobo that were scattered along the track. Of course, nothing was done about the matter, as it was only an "accident." Heaping abuse on us as "no-good sons-of-bitches," the bulls loaded us all on a train going east, which was precisely the direction we did not want to go.

A NEGRO HOBO DIES

In the latter part of 1900 I hoboed my way into Jacksonville, Florida, from Tampa. I had been in Havana, Cuba. Some time before, in the North, a doctor told me I had contracted tuberculosis as a result of my several years' work in a type foundry and various fertilizer plants. So I pulled up stakes and hit the road, determined not to die without a fight for health. I went steerage to Havana and knocked around there a couple of weeks until my few dollars were gone. No job was to be had and I worked my way by steamer to Tampa. From there I beat the railroad the length of the state up into Jacksonville. I found it hard going, and part of the distance I helped the Negro fireman load cord wood for the wheezy old wood-burning locomotive.

I found work in Jacksonville, which at the time was a very tough town. Some months before it had suffered a huge fire, nearly half the city being destroyed. A great rebuilding boom was on, attracting thousands of building-trades workers from all over the country. And, like harpies, there came also a drove of gamblers, crooks, prostitutes and pimps to enjoy the easy pickings. Robbery and murder were daily occurrences.

One night, going home to my boarding-house, I was crossing a rather deserted railroad viaduct when I heard a voice calling faintly for help. The sound came from down among the maze of railroad tracks in the black darkness. At once my suspicions were aroused. I thought to myself, It's only a trick to get me down under the viaduct, where I'll be knocked on the head and robbed.

But I found it impossible to ignore the persistent, plaintive calls for help. Unsheathing a sizable jackknife that I carried, I went down the stairs and out onto the railroad tracks. By the sound of the voice, now grown more distinct, I cautiously made my way, knife in hand, to where a Negro lay all bunched up beside a track. He had been run over and horribly injured. But he was still conscious, and in a few words he told me his story.

He was a hobo, heading for Mississippi where his people lived. He had grabbed a freight that was pulling out, and, hanging on the side-ladder of a car, he was wiped off and swept under the wheels by some timber-work that was not "in the clear." Two cars and the caboose passed over him. His right arm was cut off completely at the elbow, while his left leg, horribly smashed above the knee, was still hanging by a bloody shred of flesh and cloth.

The accident had apparently happened twenty or thirty minutes before. The train crew, not noticing the accident, had gone on. The Negro had already lost much blood and was rapidly bleeding to death. Amazingly he was still conscious and apparently felt little pain. He complained only of being cold, and actually held up his terribly crushed leg for me to look at.

I didn't know what to do to help him. Not a soul could be seen above on the viaduct and I had no idea where to find a yard office or switch shanty to secure aid. Finally I spied a light in a freight house, some distance away. Running there, I knocked on the big sliding door. Without opening the door, a watchman inside asked what I wanted. I told him a hobo had been run over and asked him to telephone for an ambulance, and would he help me carry the man to shelter? Being finally assured I was not a hold-up man, the watchman began to unbolt the door. But suddenly he stopped and asked, "Is he a white man?" I was dumbfounded at such a question. "What's that got to do with it?" I said. "He's a human being and bleeding to death. We must get him to a hospital at once." But the watchman slipped the bolt back into its slot and, despite my insistence, refused to open the door.

I was amazed and revolted and I swore all over the place. In the South I had seen many manifestations of the brutal Jim-Crow practice, but this cold-hearted act exposed in all its rotten nakedness the system which robs the Negroes of their rights and treats them as though they were sub-human beings.

Cursing the watchman, I went back to the injured Negro. Just as I got there a Negro switchman, lantern in hand, happened by. While I stayed with the injured man, the switchman hurried to the yard-master's office to telephone the hospital and to bring the emergency stretcher which was always kept on hand to gather up what was left of the many railroad workers constantly mutilated in the big yards.

We carefully lifted the crushed Negro onto the stretcher, placing his cut-off arm beside him. He did not even groan. As they started off with him he called to the stretcher bearers, "Where's my hat? Get my hat." They went back and picked it up, a torn and dirty cap.

Next day the Negro switchman told me the injured man died during the night. That same morning I went to the freight-house to protest against the watchman who refused to open the door and help the Negro 'bo. The boss listened, but from his cynical manner I was convinced his promised investigation would never take place. After that I went to a local paper and gave my story to the editor, but not a line of it appeared in print.

A COLD RIDE

One of the real hardships of the transcontinental hobo was the fierce cold in the northern and mountain states. I had a full share of cold, because practically all my hoboing was done in the winter. There were several reasons for this. In winter there were fewer hoboes along the roads and train riding was easier; the danger of arrest was not so great, and it was not so hard to eat along the line. The shacks, bulls and "citizens" were not so hostile as during the warmer months.

During the winter of 1911-12 I made a hobo trip from Chicago to the Pacific coast and back. It took me north to Vancouver, B.C., and as far south as Los Angeles, or about six thousand miles in all. The purpose of the trip was agitation: I was trying to win the I.W.W. from its traditional policy of dual unionism to one of working within the conservative trade unions.

I experienced many hardships, especially from cold weather. I was almost broke starting, and I averaged about one meal a day for the entire trip. I slept in box-cars, "bird-cage flop houses," "honkey-tonks," etc. According to my usual routine, I kept pretty well away from the "jungles," for in the hobo camps one ran a variety of perils, among them being robbed, getting loused up, having clothes burned around campfires and being arrested by local bulls.

My greatest difficulty was that all through the Middle West and Rocky Mountain regions, both coming and going, it was as cold as the devil. When I left Chicago westbound on the head-end of a fast C.&A. rattler, it was fourteen degrees below zero. After seven hours of this, when I got to St. Louis both my feet were badly frosted. Next day each heel had a blister on it as big as a dollar. But the worst cold was while crossing western Nebraska and eastern Colorado, where it ran down to thirty below zero. Even the sheepskin coat and "thousand mile shirt" (blue flannel) I wore were quite inadequate in the arctic-like temperatures.

On the division between McCook, Nebraska, and Akron, Colorado, on the Burlington road, I nearly met my Waterloo. I already had made a division that morning on a rattler, but was ditched at McCook by ultra-alert shacks. It had been a very cold ride, facing an icy blast on the first blind of the train, but I had stood it fairly well, because I had breakfast that morning and slept in a bed the night before. I was thoroughly chilled, but it was still early and I hated to loaf around McCook until a train left next day. So I decided to make the division of one hundred and fifty miles to Akron, Colorado.

A freight was just about to pull out. The box cars were sealed shut throughout the train, and the only thing I could find rideable at all was a gondola loaded with bridge steel. I had no appetite for that in the bitter weather, so I asked the fireman if I might pass coal for him. This meant to push down coal from the rear of the tender so that he could reach it for shoveling into the firebox. It was an expedient which experienced hoboes seldom adopted because it ruined their clothes, and they also objected to "working for nothing." The fireman was willing, but the master mechanic was along that trip, and I lost my chance to ride the division in the warm cab of the locomotive. So I hopped on the gondola full of bridge steel.

From McCook to Akron a blizzard raged the whole way. I learned later it was thirty-five below zero. From the outset I suffered intensely from the cold, especially as I was hungry and exhausted by hard riding when I started. But I decided to stick it out, having confidence in my ability to withstand extreme cold.

The trip lasted about ten hours, but it seemed endless to me. After a few hours the cold began to get me. I grew dazed and confused. I felt an intense desire to sleep, and the acute discomfort of the cold left me. I had sense enough left, however, to realize I was in danger of freezing to death. I said to myself, "If you sit down you'll freeze and days later someone will find your body in this car corner."

I flailed my arms, I stamped energetically, I climbed around through the steel and out over the adjoining coal cars in the teeth of the biting wind. When the train halted I ran up and down on the right-of-way to get my blood in circulation. But I kept out of sight of the trainmen for fear of being ditched. I was in a strange struggle with myself. I felt only a sort of abstract interest in my efforts to keep from freezing. All

I wanted was to sit down and sleep. I was weary to the bone. My whole situation on the train became vague and filmy. But my reason kept urging me not to sleep. I had no idea of how much farther it was to the division point. I even forgot the name of that place. The last couple of hours were the worst. The train made no stops and the cold wind blew fiercely. I could not have notified the train crew then had I tried to. Night had long since fallen.

After what seemed ages, the train stopped. I looked over the gondola side and ahead electric lights glittered brightly in the clear night. "This must be the place," I thought. So I unloaded and staggered along the tracks toward the lights. Even then I was still persecuted with the strange desire to lie down and sleep. Near the station I found a small lunch room and I went in and bought myself a bowl of *chili con carne*. After a few spoonfuls of this hot stuff I began to wake up a bit. At the other end of the counter sat the fireman and the head-end shack. The fireman recognized me from our talk at McCook. Both were amazed and incredulous when I told them I had ridden that open car of bridge steel. They thought I had broken a seal and gotten inside some box-car. The hind-end shack, coming in, announced that he and the conductor had almost frozen in the caboose, despite their big hot stove.

After devouring my *chili,* I went to a two-bit flop house across the street. I checked up on myself and was surprised to find that my only damages were a frosting of my nose and one cheek. Fortunately, my feet, which I had frozen on my ride from Chicago to St. Louis, had somehow escaped. By bathing the frosted parts with ice-cold water I managed to take the chill out of them. Then I laid down and slept eighteen hours, the longest spell of sleeping in my whole adult life. Next day I made the division into Denver. During the five-thousand-mile journey ahead of me I had several other bad experiences with cold weather, but none so bad as that ride from McCook to Akron.

I LEARN TO BEG

A worker who has to do any considerable hoboing is forced sooner or later to "panhandle" or beg. I learned this accomplishment during my second transcontinental hobo trip, in the winter of 1904, from New York to Oregon.

It was a very hard trip. When I reached Denver, after two weeks on the road, I was worn out from zero weather and hard riding. I had just a dollar and a half in my pocket, and I still had thirteen hundred miles to go. Colorado at the time was in turmoil from the great Cripple Creek strike of the Western Federation of Miners, and the police in Denver were making it hot for floating workers. However, I stayed in town a day to rest, using up fifty cents of my dwindling "pile." The division between Denver and Cheyenne, Wyoming, reputed to be the hardest in the whole country to ride, I made without difficulty. I ate and slept in Cheyenne for four bits, and from there on to Granger I rode the "tops" of the Overland Limited in below-zero weather. I had been robbed of my warm sheepskin coat in a Cheyenne "bird-cage" lodging house, and spent my last fifty cents to buy a rag of a second-hand coat. So I ate nothing in Granger.

From Granger, with an empty stomach, I turned northwest on the Oregon Short Line. The only riding I could get was on a snow-covered open coal car, exposed to the rigors of the weather. It was terribly cold and at times I feared I would freeze to death. But I held her down for two divisions, arriving in Pocatello after a grueling ride of twenty-six hours. As I walked up the main street a blizzard was blowing, and I had to turn my shoulder to the arctic-like storm. A thermometer hanging outside a drug-store registered twenty-one below zero.

Where to get food, warmth and rest in inhospitable Pocatello? I was famished, chilled to the bone and weak from riding. I did not have a red cent on me nor anything I could "peddle." The situation looked blue enough. Like hoboes generally, I scorned to go to the Salvation Army or a mission, and it was before the days of the I.W.W. which, in later years, in its union halls often furnished food and rest to hoboes in towns throughout the West. So, I hied myself to the usual hangout of the western floating worker, the saloon.

It was a honkey-tonk, like hundreds of others throughout the West, and had changed but little since frontier days. There was a dance floor, and a tin-pan orchestra banged away. Along the sides of the place were big bars. In one corner was a stage where burlesque was put on, its humor as broad as the Pacific Ocean. The hall was lined on three walls by a balcony where customers were entertained by the girls, beer selling at a dollar a bottle and girls at two dollars. Upstairs was an elaborate gambling layout, to which entry was as free as air. There were also several pool and billiard tables.

The honkey-tonk was open twenty-four hours a day, seven days a week. Already at noon the place was filling up with its usual crowd of town sports, pimps, gamblers, prostitutes, ranchers, miners and hoboes. In such places 'boes, newly arrived in town, were usually allowed to hang around for a day or two, because the busted hobo of today very often turned out to be the worker with a "stake" tomorrow. So no objection was raised to my dropping anchor there temporarily.

It was already two days since my last meal and I was ravenously hungry. I was a worker and had always earned my living, and the idea of begging revolted me. With hundreds of idle men about (the usual thing in winter), it was quite impossible to get work. So I starved along, with my stomach, as the saying goes, rubbing my back-bone. That night I spent in the honkey-tonk, sitting on a chair. Sleep was out of the question, for a wild racket continued the whole night through. A live one, a sheepherder, fresh from the hills and crazy with drink and sex, was just finishing a three days' jamboree in which he blew in eleven hundred dollars, his two years' wages.

Next morning I was in tough shape. I had had no sleep and nothing to eat for sixty hours. I was sick and faint from hunger, sleeplessness and the exhaustion of my long trip. Finally, putting my pride in my pocket, I decided that I was going to eat somehow, somewhere; I would beg a meal.

I left the honkey-tonk—I could not make up my mind to "brace" anyone there—and I went out into the bleak, wintery streets. Should I "bang" someone on the "main stem" for a dime or "hit" a back door for a "lump"? I could not make up my mind to do either. But I was not long in vacillation. My hungry stomach was an urgent master. I automatically stopped at a bakery shop, the windows of which were loaded with bread and cakes. The sight of this food made up my mind instantly. Seemingly without any conscious thought on my part, I went into the store, and without hesitation or shame—I was surprised at my directness—I told the proprietor "my tale of woe" and asked for food. But he displayed precisely no concern over my plight. "I am sorry," said he in a matter-of-fact way, "I can't give you anything; the town is full of idle men and I can't feed them all."

I was not in the least abashed by this rebuff. All I felt was my gnawing hunger, and here was food. I simply had to get it. So I repeated my request, almost like a demand. Had the baker refused me again I believe I would have seized some of the sweet buns, regardless of what might happen. I was truly a hungry man and not to be denied food. Whether the proprietor caught this fighting note in my voice and feared trouble, or whether something else motivated him, I don't know, but in any event he grumblingly handed me out half a dozen stale rolls. These I wolfed on my way to my base at the honkey-tonk.

Thus I broke the ice at panhandling. When I got hungry enough, begging turned out to be quite an easy matter. On the rest of the trip to Oregon, as well as during several other hobo tours in later years, I never allowed myself to go hungry if a bit of panhandling could prevent it. Nor did I ever again have any qualms about it. I was a worker and had a right to live. If no job was to be got, then someone who had food must give me what I needed.

A GAMBLE

I have never been a gambler, especially not a patron of mechanical gambling devices. It has always seemed to me one has to be an awful sucker to put his money into such a contrivance when it is plain the odds are heavily against him. But once, at least, I took a flyer against a gambling contraption, and with not too bad results.

I was hoboing my way west over the Southern Pacific in 1901, when I pulled into Yuma, Arizona, early one bright morning, tired, hungry and flat broke, after a long ride from Galveston, Texas. As I sauntered up the main stem of this desert railroad town I wondered where and how I was going to eat and sleep. Not even the sight of a dozen picturesque Yuma Indians lolling about in their multi-colored blankets could lure my attention away from the urgent pressure of my natural wants. A sandwich-man passed me, bearing the cryptic invitation, "Scoff at the Sunset House, ten cents, flop two bits."

As I wandered along the street my heart gave a sudden start; for there, right in the gutter, lay a small purse. I could hardly believe my eyes. No one appeared to see it or to be looking at me, so I picked it up as matter-of-factly as I could and put it in my pocket. A little way down the street I opened it and was overjoyed to find in it seventy-five cents and a thin gold ring set with a small pearl.

Now after all the sandwich-man's sign did have meaning, and I duly "scoffed" and "flopped" at the Sunset House. Breakfast, a sleep through the day and supper finished my cash. I was broke again, but I had the ring. Maybe I could realize something on that? Finally I peddled it to a jeweler for a dollar, giving him a "song-and-dance" sales talk.

I was now all set to hit the road west again, but as there was no train pulling out for several hours I went into a dance hall to while away the time. It was a huge lay-out, jammed with cow-men, railroaders and other types of the usual honkey-tonk crowd of the great Southwest. There were a dozen poker tables crowded with players; in the keno room fully four hundred men were playing this erstwhile innocent parlor game; there were also many faro, roulette, chuck-a-luck, blackjack, crap tables, etc. And above it all was the banging of the piano, the tooting of horns and the shouting of men and women in the big dance hall.

For a time I watched the gambling. As always, I was especially fascinated by the psychological struggle of the poker players. Then I began to cogitate about the big silver dollar I was fingering in my pocket. After all, thought I, what's the use of a lonesome dollar when I still have fifteen hundred miles of road before me? A couple of meals and a bed or two and my dollar will be gone and I'll be as bad off as ever. Why not take a chance with it? What had I to lose? After all, it only meant bumming a few more meals if I lost. I had been lucky so far in Yuma and maybe my luck would hold.

I surveyed the different gambling tables to pick a place to invest my "pile." Finally, I settled on the "wheel-of-fortune." I stood at the wheel watching the play, as the slick dealer monotonously called off the winning numbers. Several times I played "in my mind's eye," and in each case I lost. I was about to pass it up as a bad job and save my "iron-man" and the meals and bed that it represented, but all of a sudden I made up my mind and slapped the dollar on the "Star," which paid twenty to one. I would either leave town hungry and broke, or with enough to eat on all the way to Oregon.

The sophisticated dealer gave the wheel a spin and the paddle smacked briskly upon the passing metal number posts. Then the wheel slowed down and lo, to my amazement, the paddle teetered and finally stuck at "Star." In his routine manner the dealer piled twenty silver dollars beside my one. I was tickled. I gathered my iron-men, got bills for them at the bar, and left the place. Later I sewed the money in my shirt and caught a freight west. Need I say that I "scoffed" and "flopped" the rest of my trip to Portland? The sum and substance of my betting was that it left me twenty dollars ahead of the gambling game; for never since have I risked a dime on gambling devices.

THE FOUR TILLICUMS

Western hoboes usually traveled in pairs for protection and companionship. However, I used to go it alone, greater freedom of movement being more important to me than any other consideration. On only two of my transcontinental trips did I have a "pardner"; once Earl C. Ford, co-author with me of *Syndicalism,* and the other time, my son-in-law, Joe Manley. On another occasion also I picked up not one, but three pals.

It was early in 1907 and I was beating my way over the nearly eight hundred miles from San Francisco to Portland. I had reached Sacramento, the first division point out of Frisco, and in a local jungle I met three hoboes seated around a fire. They had a pot of "mulligan" cooking and invited me to join them, and I did. They had found a sheep killed by a train and were boiling a leg of it.

We had a good meal and got a bit acquainted. All four were typical Western floaters. They were Bob Broome, a metal miner and Klondiker; "Hank" Carter, a Kentucky mountaineer and now a logger; Ole Larson, veteran of the Philippine war and a salmon fisherman by occupation; and myself, a railroad worker, logger and farmhand. All were in our twenties.

As we were all headed for Portland we decided to travel together. We agreed that if we got separated we would meet three days later at eleven A.M. at a certain pool table in Blazier's big saloon in Portland.

Hoboing it was tough along the Southern Pacific in those days, for the shacks and bulls were hostile. Consequently I soon lost sight of Carter and Larson. Broome was a fast hobo, and he and I managed to stick together until Eugene, Oregon, where I got ditched. I made the rest of the way alone into Portland. Sure enough, next morning when I showed up in Blazier's at eleven A.M., there were Larson, Broome and Carter, all playing pool on the appointed table.

Blazier's on Burnside Street was a typical Western honkey-tonk, or "hurdy-gurdy." It was enormous and had "everything for the comfort and pleasure" of homeless workers who patronized it: girls, drinks, eats, dancing, gambling, pool, bowling, vaudeville, moving pictures. The place was open day and night and there were no locks on the doors. Right beside it was another big honkey-tonk, Erickson's, and across the street still another, Fritz's, which claimed to be the largest saloon in the world.

These "joints" were jammed with throngs of loggers, saw-mill men, fishermen, deep-sea sailors, railroad construction workers, harvesthands and the various other types of workers that make up the great armies of floating Western workers. There were also some "home-guard" (local) elements in the mass patronage. The honkey-tonk crowds were preyed upon not only by the saloon keepers, but by dozens of gamblers, pimps, prostitutes, sexual perverts, over-slick waiters, short-change bartenders, pickpockets and strong-arm men. On a railroad water-tank at The Dalles, Oregon, I once read the following realistic poetic outburst of an east-bound hobo returning from the Pacific coast:

> I came out West for change and rest;
> But the whores got my change,
> And Blazier got the rest.

A hundred yards or so from Blazier's began the huge Portland red-light district. Here the chief attraction was the block-long Paris Hotel, which housed a large number of girls. There were many such big houses of prostitution in the West, sometimes containing several hundred women each, to take care of the mass of homeless floating workers. Usually great barn-like structures, they were built so that crowds of men could saunter through the broad aisles, picking and choosing (or if they were broke, merely "taking gapings" at) the semi-nude girls in the crib-like rooms that lined the hallways. These places, entirely uncontrolled medically by the local authorities, were cesspools of venereal disease.

Blazier's was the stamping ground of the four of us—Broome, Carter, Larson and myself. Times were good—it was the hectic boom period just before the industrial crisis of 1907—and we all went to work "shoveling" railroad ties on the Portland lumber docks. The was indeed "a hard way to serve the Lord." After an eight-hour day at juggling heavy green railroad ties a man sure knew he had been working. For this laborious toil we got five dollars per day, and we all became members of the local Longshoremen's Union.

We worked steadily and we became good "tillicums" (Siwash Indian for close friends). We developed a sort of co-operative pay-as-you-go existence, spending our wages more or less in common. Each day we drew our five dollars pay and each night we spent it. With our meager living expenses deducted, we had left a total of fifteen dollars to "blow in" every night at Blazier's.

Each spent freely as long as any of us had anything left. Broome was a poker player with a perpetual streak of bad luck; Carter was also a gambler, a crap shooter, who likewise never seemed to win; Larsen got his enjoyment at the bar drinking unbelievable quantities of whiskey; and as for myself, my principal diversion was playing pool. At any rate, we managed each night to get rid of our fifteen dollars, and many times as we parted about midnight, we had trouble scaring up four bits apiece to cover our night's lodging and next day's breakfast.

So we lived for several months. But one day Broome and Carter announced they were going to the Nevada goldfields. Shortly afterward, Larson went back to his regular job, fishing for the billions of salmon that yearly crowd into the rivers of the Pacific Northwest, Canada and Alaska. And I found a job firing locomotive on the O.R.&N. railroad and became a "home-guard." Never again did I meet up with any of these three worker-hobo friends.

KAMLOOPS

A hobo on the road, beset by hardships and dangers, usually does not enjoy the scenic wonders he may pass. But on my first trip through the Canadian Rockies I found the huge, rugged mountains, bold, precipitous and wild, glorious beyond description. In the midst of these giants, with many beautiful lakes at their feet, I felt pretty small and insignificant. But the Canadian police helped to spoil their beauty for me.

It was in 1912 and I was on one of my several national hobo agitation tours, laying the basis for the Syndicalist League of North America. I had stopped at Nelson, B. C., where Jack Johnstone established the first local unit of the S.L.N.A. out of some former I.W.W. unions. From Nelson I bore north to Revelstoke, near Banff, and started west on the Canadian Pacific railway, towards Vancouver, B. C.

At the time the I.W.W. was carrying on a strike of five thousand railroad construction workers, centering at Lytton, B. C. The strike was being fought militantly by the union and the whole country was terrorized by the company. Many I.W.W.'s had been slugged and three hundred arrested.

At Kamloops two policemen grabbed me in a lunch room. They put a sudden stop to my hobo sight-seeing. Leading me off, they made slighting remarks about my origin and threats regarding my future welfare. The police station was like an arsenal, full of armed men and with several racks of rifles. Putting me into a cell, the two cops, whom I judged to be Northwest Mounted Police on strike-breaking duty, pointed out the stores of arms, and one said, "This is what we've got waiting for those goddamned I.W.W.'s."

The captain of the police was away, and the others sat in the next room, talking loudly about the strike. Said one: "By Jesus, these American I.W.W.'s certainly have gall. What do you suppose they did today at Camp Six? Why, they took the Canadian non-union cook out to the precipice at the river's edge and said, 'Now if you don't join the union we're going to dump you in.' Think of it," said the cop, "these bastards were actually going to throw a Canadian citizen into our Frazer River." The others cursed in sympathetic indignation, and made suggestive remarks about myself, the only prisoner in the jail.

Finally the captain returned, and he questioned me for an hour. I stuck to my story that I was just a floating worker on my way to the Pacific coast. The captain and his aide had a long confab. There was a question of whether or not I was guilty of vagrancy. To my amazement they actually turned me loose. Which made me smile when I thought of how unceremoniously American police would have swept aside my frail proofs of respectability and given me a stiff term in jail.

But I had no illusions. I knew these police would be only too glad to jail me if they got a chance. So that night, leaving town, I took all precautions. When the westbound passenger pulled in, being a skilled railroad car worker, I recognized a certain build of trucks on the next to last car and crawled into the complexity of wheels, axles, springs, brake-beams, etc.

In a few minutes the train pulled out and I breathed easier. But my satisfaction was short-lived. The train suddenly stopped and several police began to "frisk" her. They worked from both front and rear; some on top and others on each side. They searched everywhere; rods, trucks, side-boxes, tops, blinds and all. I had no chance to get away. So I sat tight, hoping they might not find me.

When the searching party reached my car I held my breath and crouched deeper into my nook. I could see six months in jail staring me straight in the face. The police looked around the car and shouted to each other. One flashed his lamp squarely into the trucks where I was hidden but actually missed me. I guess he did not think it possible for a human being to ride in the midst of such a tight tangle of machinery. At last our train pulled out, and was I relieved!

I held down those trucks all the way to Vancouver, some two hundred and fifty miles, and this time there was no sight-seeing of glorious mountains along the way. Twice more during the journey the train was searched, but again the police missed me. Whether such intensive hunting was just part of the strike situation or not, I was sure it would not be healthy for me to be picked up. When the train finally reached the station in Vancouver, with me half dead from the cramped riding and the cold, I did not venture to crawl out of the trucks, but waited until the car was switched back into the yards. It was weeks before the soreness wore out of my muscles from that long, hard ride.

CHAPTER IV. . . . . STRIKES

Since 1894, when I began active participation in the class struggle, I have been in numerous battles of the workers against their capitalist oppressors, including scores of strikes in many industries—by the American Federation of Labor, the Industrial Workers of the World, the Railroad Brotherhoods, the Trade Union Unity League, the Committee for Industrial Organization and various independent unions. I have also participated in many free speech fights, unemployment movements, election campaigns and political demonstrations. The more important of these struggles I have written up in my books, The Great Steel Strike and Its Lessons, Misleaders of Labor, Towards Soviet America, From Bryan to Stalin, and in a score of pamphlets. The incidents in the present chapter are selected from this general labor experience as illustrating interesting, amusing or instructive angles of the class struggle.

MY FIRST STRIKE

When, about 1890, it was proposed to establish Philadelphia's first electric trolley lines (on Bainbridge and Catherine Streets) a big howl was raised. This agitation, organized I suppose by the horse-car companies, protested against placing the new "murder machines" on the streets of the City of Brotherly Love. The trolleys came, nevertheless. Although they were hailed as a convenience, the car company was hated for its money-grasping policies, both with regard to its workers and the public.

Things came to a clash in 1895, when the motormen and conductors walked out all over the city for the right to organize, for better wages and improved working conditions. The strike, although short, was very bitterly fought. The company employed professional scabs; the police acted as a strike-breaking agency; the strikers were very militant, and the public was generally on their side. Violent collisions took place in various parts of the city.

At the time of the strike I was fourteen years old and already a worker for four years. I had begun to take notice of the many strikes in the nearby anthracite districts, the Homestead steel strike and the American Railway Union strike. So, when this fierce local street-car strike broke out, I was all seas over with interest for it and lost no occasion to attend strike meetings and demonstrations. In doing this I got my baptism in strike violence.

The striking street-car men, all uniformed, were holding a demonstration on Market Street, which I, not working that day, joined. A thousand or two strong, the parade was going west on Market, each man carrying a new broom. Its head had just got past 15th Street, when suddenly, out of the courtyard of the City Hall, a big body of mounted police came galloping and tore into the strikers' ranks, laying about them on all sides with their long night sticks.

In a jiffy the parade was in confusion from this totally unexpected assault. The strikers fled precipitately. I found myself jammed in a hall doorway together with a uniformed motorman. An unmounted policeman made a swing with his club at the striker and knocked him down, while another gave me a belt in the jaw with his fist that left me dizzy. Suddenly the hall door behind me opened, a friendly hand dragged me in, and that was the last I saw of the affair.

The attack on the peaceful parade caused widespread indignation against the police and the car company. In many parts of town the inflamed workers openly attacked the scab-operated cars, each of which was heavily guarded by armed police. The police were unable to cope with this violence, and for a couple of days the city was in confusion.

I lived in a proletarian neighborhood at 17th and South Streets, and our crowd set out to stop the scattering service on 16th Street, where cars were running at intervals of about one hour. At 16th and Kater Streets we built a sort of barricade on the car tracks out of lumber, boxes, ashes and especially heaps of waste stone from a stonecutter's yard.

Soon a trolley car came along. On the front and rear platforms, to guard the scab motorman and conductor, stood four policemen, revolvers in hand. Before the menace of the guns, the big crowd backed up Kater Street. The scab motorman, spotting the barricade from afar, decided to rush it at top-speed. But the car was derailed by the obstruction and stopped dead. The two scabs and the four policemen fled into a nearby building and stayed there until rescued. The crowd closed in on the car with a shower of chunks of marble, and in a few minutes it was a wreck. Several people were hurt by pieces of stone which, thrown from one side of the car, passed through both windows and hit those on the opposite side. That ended the car service on 16th Street, and we youngsters were jubilant at our victory.

The strike lasted only about a week, and it ended with a compromise, the terms of which I no longer remember. It all made a never-to-be-erased impression on me. It was the first in a long series of first-hand practical lessons I was later to get regarding the harsh realities of the labor movement. I count it as my introduction to the class struggle.

THE SPOKANE FREE SPEECH FIGHT

When city authorities suppress the right of free speech and assembly, militant labor unions and revolutionary political parties in the United States have long followed the policy of speaking in spite of these official bans. And almost invariably sufficient masses rally to break down the attempt to stifle the people's rights.

I have been in many such free speech fights and was arrested therefor in Kansas City, Missoula, Newark, Chicago, Denver and New York. Also during the steel campaign of 1919, when we were denied meeting rights all through Pennsylvania, I was arrested in Rankin, Braddock, McKeesport, Homestead, Clairton, Duquesne, McKees Rocks and Pittsburgh. And in the election campaign of 1932, as Presidential candidate of the Communist Party, I was arrested three times when the police tried to prohibit our meetings in Scranton, Lawrence and Los Angeles. Many of these free speech fights, closely based on the workers' economic demands, were serious struggles, but the most severe was that in Spokane, Washington, in 1909, led by the Industrial Workers of the World.

The I.W.W., now a reactionary sect, was then full of fighting spirit. It was concentrating upon the floating workers, the ranch-hands, lumbermen, construction workers and miners, who drifted from job to job as the changing seasons or the opening up of new work demanded.

Spokane was one of the largest centers for these homeless, itinerant workers. Many thousands poured in there every winter. It was also an I.W.W. stronghold and had the biggest local union in the whole organization. The I.W.W. activities, based upon a militant strike and sabotage program, were highly unpalatable to the local lumber, mining and railroad interests, and they decided to crush the I.W.W. by suppressing its right of free speech on the streets.

In November, when Spokane was full of floating workers and the I.W.W. campaign was going full blast, the city council adopted an ordinance prohibiting street meetings. This was aimed solely at the I.W.W., as religious and other organizations using the streets for meetings were exempted. The I.W.W. replied by holding meetings in spite of the ordinance. The police arrested the speakers as fast as they took the speaker's stand. The local I.W.W. therefore issued the slogan, "Fill the jails," and the national leaders sent out a call for volunteers. Soon rugged I.W.W. fighters began to drift into Spokane from all over the West. The A.F. of L. stood aloof, and the Socialist Party did pretty much the same.

Scores of I.W.W. were arrested daily. They were clubbed and packed into cells so closely they could not sit down. When they protested, the hose was turned on them, drenching them with icy water. Many were thrown into the suffocating "hot box" and then returned to freezingly cold cells. In spite of all this terrorism, however, the I.W.W. heroically continued to hold street meetings. Finally about six hundred had been arrested. The city jail was packed, and the dilapidated Franklin school was used to confine large numbers of men. This old schoolhouse became a sort of local Libby prison.

The prisoners were usually given sentences of thirty-four days, and as they refused to work on the rockpile they were put on bread and water. The ration was only two ounces of white bread morning and evening. The result was actual starvation. The school was also purposely left without heat. Many fell sick. Several eventually died from pneumonia, intestinal troubles and other diseases provoked by exposure and starvation. Scores had their health seriously undermined. The police suffered one major fatality, Chief of Police Sullivan being shot and killed.

When the fight began, I was a member of the Wage Workers Party in Seattle, a split-off from the Socialist Party, and I went to Spokane as correspondent of our journal, the *Workingmen's Paper*. I was soon arrested. I served two months in jail, and while imprisoned I joined the I.W.W. When released I became a member of the committee directing the fight. The bitter struggle dragged on all winter, with our available recruits to fill the jails growing fewer and fewer. We decided to make a strong rally for the early spring. But very few volunteers responded, our reserves having been exhausted by the hard fight. As the day approached that was advertised to begin a big re-opening of street speaking in Spokane, we were in danger of a fatal exposure of our weakness. Fortunately the police did not know our actual condition, as the town was full of floaters, and they could not tell which were I.W.W. fighters and which not.

In this crisis, with sure defeat facing us, we thought it might be well to sound out the city officials about what they thought of discontinuing the fight. We were agreeably surprised to learn that the Mayor was quite sick of the whole business and would meet our committee to settle it. He would not consent to formally rescind the anti-free speech ordinance, but did agree not to enforce it against the I.W. W. This was a victory for us, and we called off the fight. Thereafter the I.W.W. held its street meetings unmolested in Spokane.

The Spokane free speech fight was followed during the next few years by similar struggles in various cities all over the West, and also in some eastern centers. In these bitter clashes in the West the floating workers bravely faced policemen's clubs, jails and vigilante mobs armed with pick-handles. The I.W.W. successfully defended its right to speak on the streets. These free speech struggles constituted an heroic episode in the history of American labor.

ON THE I.C.-HARRIMAN LINES

One of the most important strikes I ever participated in was that of the railroad shopmen on the Illinois Central and Harriman Lines. It extended from Chicago to the Gulf and to the Pacific coast, and included thirty-five thousand workers in nine unions. The struggle was extremely long and hard-fought; it began on September 30, 1911, and lasted until June 28, 1915, when it was called off unconditionally. The companies used scabs, gunmen, injunctions and every known device to break the strike.

The issue at stake in this great strike was the right of the railroad shop unions to federate and to secure a joint contract. Many railroad craft union strikes had been lost in the previous ten years, and a strong movement had developed for common action by the shop crafts. Although twelve system federations had already been organized and had secured contracts, Julius Kruschnitt and C. H. Markham, heads of the Harriman and I.C. Lines, refused to deal with their workers' new federation, and the strike was declared.

The leaders of the railroad craft unions also had no love for federated action, which they looked upon as a long step towards industrial unionism. So they sabotaged the strike from the outset. Worse yet, the officials of the engine, train and yard service unions kept their men at work. The strike finally resolved itself pretty much into a rank-and-file-led struggle against both the railroad companies and the craft union top officialdom.

The outstanding leaders of the rank and file were Carl E. Person and L. M. Hawver, left-wing Socialist. They raised funds, organized picket lines and united the strikers despite the unfaithful top leadership. Their great weapon was the *Strike Bulletin*.

Under pressure of the left-led strikers, a general convention of western railroad shopmen was held in Kansas City in April, 1912, and the Federation of Federations (later the Railway Employees Department of the A.F. of L.) was formed. This body put out a general strike vote for the nine shop crafts on all western railroads, but it was defeated by the leaders.

During the strike Person shot and killed a company thug in self-defense. The companies tried to send him to the gallows, but after a nation-wide defense campaign he was finally acquitted. The Syndicalist League of North America, of which I was national secretary, took an active part in Person's defense, as it did in the whole strike.

Several times the top union leaders tried to call off the strike, but on each occasion the rank and file, led by Person, defeated them. Finally, however, after almost four years, they declared it ended. But pickets still surrounded many big shops, and the rank and filers made such a militant protest against calling off the strike that the Railway Employees Department was torn with bitter factional struggle for two years afterward. Person was expelled, without trial, from the Machinists' Union by its "Socialist" leader, W. H. Johnston.

Although the strike was broken, and the men forced back to work, with their unions completely wrecked, the strike nevertheless succeeded in its general objective. The railroad companies, taught a lesson by this fierce struggle, never forced another important strike over the right of federated action by the railroad unions. Indeed, even while the I.C. strike was in progress, several federated agreements were signed on big railroad systems. Nor did the notoriously open-shop I.C. escape. In the war period I was a member of the committee that opened successful federated union negotiations with this road's officials in Chicago. The heroic I.C.-Harriman Lines strike was not "lost."

In this bitter labor war Carl E. Person showed remarkable leadership. He was able, determined, tenacious and incorruptible. But after it was over he gradually faded out of the labor picture. The sabotage policies of the officialdom seemed too much for him. We tried to draw him into the left-wing trade union movement in Chicago, but without avail. He wrote his strike history, *The Lizard's Trial,* and eventually became a local lawyer. Hawver, also a very able leader, worked with us left-wingers in the Chicago Federation of Labor. He became the leader of the national "outlaw" strike of two hundred and fifty thousand railroad shopmen in 1919, and was also somewhat active in later years in the Trade Union Educational League. But finally he, too, dropped out. Person and Hawver took too seriously their "defeat" in the I.C. strike. They did not realize that it was only one battle in the long war of the class struggle.

J. B. McNAMARA

The workers of the world are well acquainted with Tom Mooney and Warren K. Billings, and the heroic struggle Mooney has led for twenty-two years to free himself and his partner, victims of one of the most notorious labor frameups in history. But workers, especially the younger ones, do not know as well two other heroes of labor, J. B. McNamara and Matt Schmidt, who have languished even longer than Mooney and Billings in California jails, twenty-five and twenty-eight years, respectively. It has been my privilege to meet with all these brave fighters many times in San Quentin and Folsom.

J. B. McNamara's imprisonment has been an especially bitter martyrdom. It will be remembered that he and his brother, J. J. McNamara, national secretary of the Structural Iron Workers Union, were arrested in connection with the dynamiting of the Los Angeles *Times* building in 1910, during a local general strike of metal workers. The bomb, intended only to make a demonstration, accidentally set off a leaky gas main, which resulted in a terrific explosion that snuffed out a score of lives. The ruthless open-shop Los Angeles employers thereupon developed a lynch spirit against the McNamaras and launched a fierce attack upon the trade unions. The workers replied by a strong, nation-wide McNamara defense campaign, officially led by the A.F. of L.

The evidence against the McNamaras was very damaging, but they determined to fight it out in court. All others connected with the case were for giving up: Clarence Darrow, the top A.F. of L. representatives, Lincoln Steffens, friends, relatives—all begged the McNamaras to plead guilty. It was the only way, they all argued, to save the threatened labor movement and to protect many other union leaders and militants from jail. And so, after a long resistance and with the understanding that no other unionists would be prosecuted, the McNamaras finally yielded, against their better judgment, and pleaded guilty. J.J. was sentenced to fifteen years and J.B. to life imprisonment.

Although the plea of guilty was not their proposal, the McNamaras were widely condemned for making it, even by those who had most militantly urged it. They were made to appear as if attempting to shield themselves at the expense of the labor movement. Friends turned against them, A.F. of L. officials excoriated them, the workers were given to understand they had betrayed the trade unions, and even the revolutionary movement itself for many years misunderstood and grievously neglected them. And the employers, ignoring their agreement with the McNamaras' lawyers, redoubled their attacks on the unions, and later on arrested Matt Schmidt and Dave Kaplan, and sent the former to prison for life and the latter for ten years.

Charges of surrender were especially unjust when directed against the McNamaras, as their unflinching courage had already been amply demonstrated in the class struggle. For years, in their heroic fight against the National Erectors' Association, they had faced great danger. Their plea of guilty, although a mistake, was in keeping with their previous courageous record: it was a brave attempt to save others by sacrificing themselves. The McNamara boys would have faced the gallows without flinching.

Eventually J. J. McNamara and Dave Kaplan served out their sentences and were released. But the California exploiters still retain their clutches upon J. B. McNamara and Matt Schmidt. Their long imprisonment has been hard, especially for McNamara. There he has been, deserted and slandered by the very ones for whom he sacrificed his liberty and freely risked his life. Denied the sustaining realization, dear to the heart of a labor prisoner, that the workers appreciate and defend him, with only the faintest hope of eventual release, and with but a few loyal friends to say a word of understanding and to bid him be of good cheer, he has had to make his lonesome fight all these long years.

It has been a situation that would break the heart of an ordinary man. But not J. B. McNamara's (no more than the brave Matt Schmidt's). J. B. has stood the storm of it all like the solid oak that he is. Never a whimper has come from him in all these bitter years of neglect and misunderstanding. He has not desponded or faltered in the harsh struggle. Not a cry for help has he uttered. Never has he asked any mercy from or made any concession to the capitalist enemy. He has not even applied for a parole, although he was entitled to do so many years ago. In his prison life, McNamara has maintained an upright attitude that not even the harshest regime could break. His prison letters, reflecting his unconquerable proletarian spirit and composed with rare literary merit, are a real inspiration. His friends love him with almost limitless devotion and admiration.

Through all these desperately hard years J. B. McNamara has retained a sublime faith in the working class that had so largely misunderstood him and, indeed, almost forgotten him. He has done that and much more. Like many another proletarian, the prison has been his university. In the long, lonesome years he has read and developed a broader understanding of the class struggle. He now realizes that the workers cannot solve their problem by a few heroic trade union battlers, such as he and his co-workers were, carrying on terroristic work, but that the workers must unite as a class, put an end to the capitalist system and erect a new, free socialist society.

McNamara is a splendid example of the invincible working-class spirit. He has in him the sheer courage and loyalty that goes to make a Dimitroff. His name deserves to stand high indeed on the roster of the heroes of the labor movement. He is the oldest political prisoner in the world in point of term served. He and his brave comrade, the bold fighter, Schmidt, are kept in a California prison year after year, while common murderers are released in droves. When will the workers of America put an end to this burning outrage and return these unconquerable sons of the working class to freedom?

A PROLETARIAN INTRODUCTION

In the winter of 1915 I was business agent of the Chicago District Council of the Brotherhood Railway Carmen of America, and we were organizing the car repairers of the Wood Street yards of the C.N.W. railroad. We had a couple of hundred of them, mostly foreign-born workers, assembled in a meeting, and there were three speakers, including Frank Paquin, first Vice-President of the B.R.C. of A.

The meeting went on in due form, the other organizer and myself being the first to speak. Then it came the turn of Paquin. He was a well-dressed, stiff-necked bureaucrat and pretty much out of place in a gathering of Polish, Lithuanian and Russian workers. The chairman, himself foreign-born and only feebly in command of the English language, spread himself out a bit in introducing the distinguished speaker of the evening. He went on:

"Now, brothers, we come to the main speaker, Vice-President Paquin. He is a fine man; he is a smart man; he is a great man—"

By this time the chairman had exhausted his meager supply of compliments in English, but felt he had not yet done justice to his subject. He belabored his mind to find further words of praise for Paquin and then, with a broad grin of friendliness, burst forth with the following:

"Brother Paquin is a good man, a very good man. I can't hardly tell you how good he is. He is just as good as a big hunk of apple pie."

The crowd of immigrant workers, accepting this as a very graceful compliment, applauded vigorously; the organizer and I laughed, the chairman sat down in triumph, and the dignified Paquin was so flustered that he could hardly speak.

THE SPIRIT OF THE OPEN SHOP

For many years the meat-packing industry was notorious as one of the very worst in the country. Extremely low wages, excessively long hours, and wretched, dangerous and unhealthy working conditions were regular things in the great packinghouse slave-pens. The dwelling places of the packinghouse workers were unspeakable slums.

It was an open shop industry, the oppressed workers having nothing whatever to say about the conditions under which they had to work and live. The will of the multi-millionaire owners was supreme and they enforced it by the gunman, the labor spy and the blacklist. I had an extensive experience as a worker and organizer in this slave industry. But one simple incident seemed to me to symbolize the ruthless autocracy of the packinghouse bosses.

It happened just before the World War, and the workers concerned were a small group of steamfitters in the Chicago plant of Armour and Company. They suffered from a special grievance that was particularly onerous. It was so unbearable that they went to the great lengths (in this totally unorganized industry) of asking a local trade union official to go with them to Armour's office to try to settle it.

To the surprise of the committee they were ushered into the palatial office of a Vice-President of Armour and Company. The union spokesman outlined their trouble, pointing out how hard the condition was on the men and how little it would cost the firm to correct it. The company official listened to all this and then casually remarked, "It's nice weather lately, don't you think?"

The workers were astonished. Their spokesman, thinking perhaps the Vice-President was absent-minded and not paying attention, went briefly over the matter again. But the boss, turning towards his broad window, said nonchalantly, "They tell me they have been having some big storms in the South recently."

By this time the workers realized what was happening; this autocrat was deliberately insulting them. Boiling with indignation, their leader said to him, "So that's the answer of Armour and Company to its workers when they present a grievance; you sneer at us by talking about the weather."

At this the Vice-President, rising from his chair and advancing belligerently towards the workers, shouted, "Yes, that's Armour's answer. Go back to your trade union friends and tell them Organized Labor will never get anything from this company that it hasn't the power to take."

I never forgot those cold, cynical words, nor did I fail to draw the full class-struggle logic from them. And I daresay this same Vice-President also recalled them when, a few years later, he faced our union committee representing two hundred thousand organized packinghouse workers. Let it be known that this time he found something more vital to talk about than the weather.

PACKINGHOUSE WORKERS

In 1917-18, the organizing movement of packinghouse workers, conducted by a federation of a dozen A.F. of L. unions, resulted in the complete national organization of the industry, two hundred thousand workers. It was the first mass production industry of the United States to be unionized. Jack Johnstone and myself, leading the movement, aimed at a countrywide war-time strike if need be, because we knew that such a strike would be short, sharp and victorious. But the government, packers and A.F. of L. leaders switched the developing struggle into arbitration and maneuvered the control of the industry under an Administrator, Federal Judge Alschuler. The arbitration hearings were held in Chicago early in 1918.

At this three-weeks-long arbitration we thoroughly exposed the frightful conditions prevailing in this rich industry. Our attorney was Frank P. Walsh. The workers had not had a wage increase in thirteen years, despite the enormous rise in the cost of living. Wages were as low as twelve and one-half cents an hour for the unskilled. One worker after another testified to the horrible conditions in the industry. For days they told of children going unfed and insufficiently clad in the bitter Chicago winters; of fathers, overworked and sick, without medical care; of widowed mothers locking up their broods of small children in foodless, fuelless shacks, while they went to earn a few dollars in the packinghouses; of health-destroying work, brutal treatment and horrifying accidents in the great plants of the beef trust.

Most of the workers who testified were immigrants and a number were Negroes. Many said they had never been to a theater or moving picture house in the United States, nor to the nearby Chicago lake beaches and parks. These workers' stories were an epic of proletarian poverty, misery and exploitation; a long recital of starvation, exhausting labor, sickness, mutilation, ignorance, drunkenness, insanity, despair and death.

As against this picture the unions showed the gigantic profits made by the parasitic profiteering owners of the industry. Armour and Company, for example, had cleared forty million dollars in 1917, half of which went to the already fabulously rich Armour family. Several multi-millionaire beef-trust magnates testified. They were cold and cynical at their victim's stories of poverty and hardships, and they stubbornly resisted the workers' demands for improved conditions.

We had made up a budget of a worker's necessary living expenses, and the many-times millionaire Morris was not ashamed, on the witness stand, to check over this modest list item by item and to point out what he considered to be extravagant. He had the brass to declare, for example, that our allowance of two pairs of shoes yearly for a child was too much; he was sure one pair should do. He also said that five dollars a year was a too liberal provision for a worker's family's visits to theaters, movies and parks.

I especially remember a Polish woman worker witness, who told the usual harrowing story. She wore no hat, her head being covered with a kerchief, old-country peasant fashion. Walsh, noticing this, asked her:

"Where is your hat?"

"I haven't any," she answered.

"Did you ever have a hat?" persisted Walsh.

"Yes," said she, "once, in Poland, but since I came to America it got worn out and I've never been able to buy another."

This poverty-stricken worker was a symbol of the blasted hopes of millions of immigrants who had streamed to America, land of promise, only to have their lives burned out in ruthless profit-making industries.

Then there was Grump, the coal shoveler, a witness for the companies, brought to tell how good conditions were in the packing industry. He was a native-born American. For years the charge had been made justly against the packers that they had flooded their plants with immigrant workers, non-English speaking, inexperienced in American conditions and helpless to defend themselves. Here at last, the packers thought, was a good chance to publicly refute these charges. Through Grump they would show they employed Americans.

But the clever packers' lawyers were too clever; they slipped up a bit on Grump. They made the mistake of taking some foreman's word about him instead of examining him themselves beforehand. Grump's entry into the packed arbitration room caused a sensation. He was like "The Man With The Hoe" come to life. Worn and twisted and bent from excessive drudgery, he said that for many years he had worked from twelve to seventeen hours daily, Sundays included, unloading coal from railroad cars. His age was unguessable, he was so warped and deformed from years of grueling labor. His arms hung down loosely and his hands were hooked from grasping the shovel. Muscle-bound and clumsy, he awkwardly struggled to take off his outer coat, while the whole court room watched him fascinatedly. He had so much trouble with his coat that the superintendent of Swift's pressed forward to help him.

A gasp went through the crowded courtroom as this pitiful example of exploited humanity took the stand. Grump cut a sorry figure as a witness. Feebly he tried to tell how good his job and the bosses were. Illiterate, he did not even know the meaning of the word "average" when Walsh asked him what was his average weekly wage. So this crushed native-born worker was the type of American being produced by the ultra-patriotic packers. Double-distilled anti-climax!

With tact and gentleness, Walsh questioned Grump. His mere appearance was a powerful argument for us. He was a living example of how the packinghouse exploiters were sucking the life out of their worker victims. As Grump left the stand and shambled towards the door we could hear the packers' attorneys angrily quarreling among themselves over the responsibility for fishing up this shocking specimen from the depths of the packinghouse jungle.

Finally, the ghastly parade of workers' miseries ended and the arbitrator, Judge Alschuler, handed down his decision; it was a victory for the workers. Through Alschuler the packers had to make concessions or face a great national war-time strike which they could not defeat. The decision provided for the eight-hour day with ten hours' pay, substantial wage increases, improved working conditions and partial recognition of the unions. I, as one who had worked under miserable conditions in the Chicago packinghouses, was especially pleased at the outcome. This victory was the first ray of hope that had penetrated into the benighted packing industry since the unions were destroyed in the great strike of thirteen years before.

A CHICAGO STOCKYARDS STRIKE

The Alschuler arbitration proceedings in the packinghouse movement early in 1918, covered at first only the five biggest national packers. Therefore, it became necessary for us to bring also under their scope the hundreds of smaller packinghouses, by-product plants, etc., all over the country, including the Union Stockyards and Transit Company of Chicago.

The U.S.T. Co., controlled by the great packers in defiance of the anti-trust laws, served as a depot and sales market for the tens of thousand of livestock arriving daily in Chicago. Its three thousand workers unloaded, fed, graded, segregated and drove the cattle, sheep and hogs to the killing beds of the packinghouses. It was a highly strategic section of the packing industry.

As national secretary of the movement, I headed the union com-

mittee which demanded that this company accept the eventual arbitration decision. Mr. Leonard, the manager, met us coldly and told us
that his men were not members of our union, that they were satisfied
with present conditions and that he would not sign his company into
the pending arbitration proceedings. Unfortunately, there was truth in
his remarks about his workers being unorganized. They were mostly
Irish and Americans who had worked there for long periods, and
they were hanging back, waiting to see what the foreign-born and
Negroes, who had taken the lead in the organizing campaign, were
going to gain from the new organizations. Therefore, it was impossible
to strike them, and we had to go to arbitration without Leonard's
signature.

When the arbitration award was handed down the workers considered it a real victory, and those who were still unorganized piled
into the federated craft unions by thousands in every packing center
in the country. Nearly the entire industry became solidly organized,
including the workers of the Union Stockyards and Transit Company.
So, again I headed a committee to insist that this company accept the
Alschuler award for its workers.

This time Leonard sang a different song. He knew his workers were
unionized and he started out by "jollying" us. "Well," he said, "you
boys have done a wonderful job in organizing the national packing
industry after the A.F. of L. failed completely for thirteen years. Not
a single packer believed it could be done, yet you've done it. But why
come to the U.S.T.? We aren't part of the packing industry; we're
just a sort of hotel for animals. Besides, our men are well-paid and
contented."

We told Leonard his men demanded the terms of the Alschuler
award, and that if he did not sign they would strike. This got under
his hide and he shouted at us: "You can't bluff me! You can't strike
my men! Here we have son, father and grandfather working together.
We are all one big family. I know every one of my workers personally
and they respect me as a friend. You are total strangers and they
won't follow you and your 'hunkies' into a strike. They are patriotic

American citizens and will never tie up the 'yards' in these war times."
A main government slogan was, "Food will win the war," and Leonard
did not think we would dare strike the great packing industry.

That night we held a big mass meeting of the U.S.T. Co.'s
workers, and I reported Leonard's refusal to sign. No sooner had I
finished then a dozen men leaped to their feet and moved for an
immediate strike. With a shout the motion was adopted and the strike
was on. The workers streamed out of the hall to mass picket, for the
night shift was due to go to work.

An hour later the whole stockyards district flared crimson from a
great fire. The huge hay barn of the U.S.T. Co., largest in the
world and containing many hundreds of carloads of hay, went up in
smoke. The fire was caused by an accident, seen by several people, so
the company, although casting hints, never ventured publicly to
blame us.

Powerful effects of the stockhandlers' strike were felt immediately.
Frantically the U.S.T. Co. wired all over the West to stop ship-
ments of stock and to turn back those already en route. But the stockyards trackage quickly clogged with stock trains; for the packing
industry had been working at record speed to meet the insatiable war
demands of the United States and its allies. With difficulty the boss
stockhandlers and office help watered and fed the stock already in the
yards and unloaded a few cars.

Meanwhile, the huge Chicago packing industry, employing seventy-
two thousand workers, began to slow down. The union killing gangs
refused to kill scab-delivered stock and already on the first day of the
strike department after department of the great packing plants ceased
operations for want of slaughtered animals.

The packers were obviously afraid of the national packinghouse
strike which was looming. There was a great buzzing about by government people, packers and top A.F. of L. officials, trying to slough
off the strike. Jack Johnstone, myself and other packinghouse union
leaders were hauled to the Department of Justice office and menaced
with prison as sabotagers of the government's war program. The
press denounced us as reds who had called the strike for anti-war

purposes. The strikers were deluged with an ocean of patriotic propaganda in an effort to stampede them back to work. But they stood their ground and daily the strike became more effective.

On the fourth day the packers, real owners of the U.S.T. Co., gave in. These great open shop overlords of industry had been checkmated by the solidarity and militancy of their workers. So, again, I headed a union committee to meet with Mr. Leonard. This third time we found him more tractable, an industrial autocrat brought to book. It was one of the pleasantest experiences of my life to watch him put his "John Henry" to the Alschuler award. With a pretty wry face, after signing, he turned to me and said, "Well, Foster, I must admit you fellows have taught me a few things about my workers that I never knew before."

GOLD DUST TWINS

Seldom have I got more satisfaction out of winning a strike than from one in the Chicago plant of the Fairbanks Company, makers of the well-known "Gold Dust Twins" washing compound. Only about fifteen hundred workers were involved, but the strike had a special interest in the decisive way the unity of the workers triumphed over the bag of tricks of a strike-breaking efficiency engineer-manager.

The Fairbanks Company, a Rockefeller concern, was working on war orders, and we undertook to organize its workers in connection with our big packinghouse drive. The manager was a slick open-shop efficiency engineer who thought he knew just how to defeat trade unionism. So when we began he tried to terrorize the workers by firing a few of the most active ones. This, however, only incensed the mass, and the union went right ahead. The smart engineer then tried his next stunt by launching a company union. This was dangerous, because at that time company unions were something new, and the workers were not yet awake to their hypocrisies. But we continued on with such success that the engineer-manager was soon forced to make some more "concessions" if he were to prevent the unionization of his plant. Hence he hurriedly announced an elaborate plan of "welfare work," including pensions, sports, improved sanitary conditions, etc. He also increased wages a bit. And all the while he carried on a big patriotic campaign for the necessity of producing war munitions and against the menace of the reds who were trying to strike the plant and ruin the war.

This combination of terrorism, trickery, patriotic demagogy and economic concessions made it plenty tough for us. But our Stockyards Labor Council, having just led the victorious national movement against the big packing trust, could not afford to be defeated in its effort to organize the Gold Dust workers. Jack Johnstone and I took the work personally in hand. Finally, after hard slogging, we got about half the workers organized. A settlement or a strike was our only chance to win over the rest. So the workers elected a negotiating committee of which I, as head of the Stockyards Labor Council, was chairman.

The committee proceeded to the office with the workers' demands and were met by an assistant superintendent. "Too bad," he said, "the manager has just left for the downtown office." So down to the Loop office of the company we went. Here we were also informed that, regrettable as it was, the manager had just gone back to the plant. Several times the manager kept us trotting back and forth from the plant to the downtown office. It was one more of his union-smashing tricks.

We stood this runaround until the fourth day, when we gave the assistant an ultimatum. Our committee would again come to the plant two days later, on Friday, and if the manager did not meet us we would strike the works, even if it were on war munitions. But it was the same old story. When we called, an underling blandly informed us that the manager had left for St. Louis the night before. Then I exploded: "Well, he'll leave St. Louis for Chicago tonight, because we're going to tie up your plant as tight as a drum tomorrow morning."

I was doubtful whether, with our weak union, we could pull the plant, but events put these fears to rout. We had a rousing meeting, the workers adopted as the strike slogan the company's widely advertized motto, "Let the Gold Dust Twins Do the Work," and next morning our picket lines stopped the works completely; there was not enough workers left in it "to blow the whistle." The company officials were amazed and we were overjoyed.

The company unionism, welfare work, patriotic blather and wage increases of the strike-breaking efficiency engineer-manager had failed. The workers, realizing that their only protection was in a trade union, were on the street a hundred per cent and bubbling over with fighting spirit. I felt certain that with the powerful support of the Stockyards Labor Council we could give the Fairbanks Company a battle it wouldn't soon forget.

Next morning, as I was about to leave my home for the strike headquarters, the telephone bell rang. An unknown man inquired if I were Foster. He then informed me that he was the engineer-manager of the Fairbanks Company. When I had caught my breath I said: "Well, and I've located you at last; I was sure we would get around to it finally. So you did take the train from St. Louis last night after all, as we said you would?"

He laughed and was all affability. "Don't be sore at the maneuvers we made against the union," he said. "I just wanted to see your credentials. Well, now I've seen them and they seem to be O.K. I didn't think it was humanly possible to strike our plant. Can't we get together today and settle the thing?"

I replied that we never worked on Sunday and that he would have to wait until next day. The company, loaded up with war orders, was in no position to fight and the manager had to agree with the union. But it was my bad luck that other business prevented my sitting into the settlement conference, which was handled by Jack Johnstone. So I never got to see this slippery manager at all, my only contact with him being that one telephone talk. It would have been a real pleasure to see him signing on the dotted line.

A STEEL ORGANIZER'S DAY

Violence by the steel trust to prevent the organization of its workers is an old story. Organizers especially are subjected to it. Years ago I knew of an organizer who, one cold winter night, was taken to the bank of the Allegheny River by steel trust gunmen and forced to swim across, while they pot-shotted at him with their revolvers. And there was another, awakened at night by a tapping at his hotel room door, to find a little girl there with her clothes unbuttoned; but fortunately a fellow organizer was in the room, a fact which saved the former from a frameup and a long prison term.

In the 1919 steel organizing drive we met plenty of such violence. One of our organizers, Fannie Sellins of the U.M.W.A., was brutally murdered by steel trust gunmen at West Natrona, Pa., on August 26, 1919.* In the company towns, where the steel corporations owned everything but the post offices, the organizers walked in the peril of their lives.

During our big strike the bosses' terrorism reached extreme lengths. Wholesale shootings, sluggings and arrests of strikers and organizers were the order of the day. Troops were used in various places, and a sheriff in a Pennsylvania steel district testified that he had more armed deputies in his county than there were actual strikers. Throughout the great Pennsylvania steel areas free speech was suppressed, the A.F. of L. steel unions not being permitted to hold a single open meeting during the three and one-half months of the strike. The following typical incidents occurred in Wheeling, W. Va., and Steubenville, Ohio, districts where conditions were about the least terroristic of any place in our entire lineup.

In these two contiguous areas we had twenty-seven thousand men

* In my book, *The Great Steel Strike,* I gave an account of this savage murder. Unfortunately, however, a typographical error slipped past the proofreader. The original text read: "Rightly and strongly, the steel workers, almost to a man, felt that this devoted woman was a martyr to their cause." But the printer made it read: "Rightly or wrongly," etc. Some wiseacre book reviewers sharply criticized me for this, ignoring the fact that the whole text of my account pictured Fannie Sellins as a noble martyr to labor's cause.

on strike, of our national total of three hundred and sixty-five thousand. The strike had been on for two months and was still airtight. The steel companies were trying desperately to break the workers' solidarity, but as the whole country roundabout was strong union territory (miners especially), they had been unable to prohibit our meetings.

One Sunday I was billed to speak in both towns. Just before I arrived at Wheeling I was informed that the Chamber of Commerce had publicly announced it would prevent my speaking by force, and the officer-leaders of the American Legion had also stated in the newspapers they would throw me into the Ohio River, which flows conveniently by. The city officials hemmed and hawed, but refused to either suppress or protect our meeting.

The steel workers organized themselves to defend the large meeting. When I alighted from the train I was surrounded by an armed guard of a dozen workers. In the meeting hall the platform was banked with some two hundred determined workers, sentinels were placed at the doors and huskies stood about at strategic points.

But nothing happened. The meeting, a big success, passed off peacefully. The vigilante elements gathered their forces, but dared not go through with their planned violence. The fine gentlemen of the Chamber of Commerce thought better of attacking the armed steel workers, and so did the American Legion. Indeed, most of the latter organization's membership was made up of striking steel workers who could not be mobilized to break up their own meeting, and naturally the officer-leaders of the Legion were not risking their own precious necks in such a hazardous venture. After the meeting I was escorted to the train, heavily surrounded by workers.

That was Wheeling; next came Steubenville, an hour or so's railroad journey away, where I was to speak that evening. I was accompanied on the train by an organizer of the Mine, Mill and Smeltermen's Union, and just as we were leaving Wheeling we were told that the Steubenville American Legion leaders were boasting they would "get" me. So reverting back to my hobo technique, as we were pulling into town I worked my way to the head of the train and dropped off in the railroad yards while she was still moving fast. I had previously agreed with my companion upon a certain restaurant where I could be found. The workers came to get me, thirty strong and all armed, and we went to the meeting.

The situation in Steubenville was very tense. The newspapers were carrying on fierce red-baiting; the town was full of steel trust gunmen and the companies were making violent efforts to stampede the men back to work next morning. The meeting hall, the biggest theater in town, was literally packed to the rafters with steel workers. Just as the meeting was about to begin a messenger came from the American Legion leaders to inform me that if I dared to speak they would take me from the platform. The workers' committee replied that if they interfered with the meeting they could prepare to drape their charter, for many of them would be carried feet first out of the hall. The crowd greeted this answer with frantic applause.

As in Wheeling, with the workers prepared to defend their rights, the meeting went off peacefully. Again the Legion leaders thought better of their projected attack, and probably for the same reason—that most of their members were union miners and steel workers. The meeting closed with great enthusiasm. I was escorted to the Pittsburgh train by a large body of workers, some of whom accompanied me part way to Pittsburgh to make sure I would not be waylaid. Thus one more day of the great steel strike came to an end.

A BLUFF THAT WORKED

In the class struggle to bluff is dangerous but sometimes, as in poker, it succeeds. Once a bluff saved me from disaster.

It was in the early phases of the big 1919 steel organizing campaign. The situation was a tough one. The local governments had abolished our right to hold meetings all over the Pennsylvania steel districts; the companies were discharging thousands of workers for union activities, and to kill the workers' militancy they also gave wage increases and the basic eight-hour day; gunmen were terrorizing the steel towns;

and the A.F. of L. top leaders were sabotaging our work. Union recruitment, in face of these difficulties, proceeded but slowly.

Just at this critical juncture the Pittsburgh *Labor World,* a corrupt sheet financed by employers, began a virulent attack upon me. Its editors declared I was an I.W.W. at heart and only awaiting a favorable opportunity to swing the new steel unions into the I.W.W. They got out special editions, filled with my former writings in the I.W.W. press and from my pamphlet, *Syndicalism,* and at the steel companies' expense they distributed scores of thousands of copies free in many steel centers. Besides, the *Labor World* held a "trial" of me, inviting newspapermen and fake delegations of steel workers. I was found "guilty" and my removal as head of the steel campaign was demanded. These Steel Trust tools thought that if I were ousted from leadership, some local A.F. of L. faker would get my job and the steel compaign would be ruined. This being the time of the Palmer "red raids," their campaign against me caused much excitement throughout the steel industry.

Following up their "trial" verdict, the *Labor World's* editors sought to have labor councils in steel centers demand that the A.F. of L. withdraw me from leadership. They figured that an easy and most important place to have such a resolution adopted against me was in the Pittsburgh Federation of Labor, then one of the most corrupt labor bodies in the United States. And they hoped to accomplish it through the so-called Committee of Ten, which had been selected by the P.F. of L. to "co-operate" with our national steel committee. The reactionaries, including some later exposed as stool pigeons, constituted a majority of the committee. A few honest trade unionists were also members to give it a flavor of respectability.

One day I got word that the crooked Committee of Ten leaders, who were in cahoots with the *Labor World,* would meet that afternoon, adopt a resolution against me and jam it through the P.F. of L. the same night. Had they succeeded it would have been fatal to me, for the reactionary and hostile top A.F. of L. leaders in Washington would have been only too glad for such an excuse to get rid of me and the whole steel business. I was in a tight corner.

That afternoon I attended the Committee of Ten meeting "with blood in my eye." My only hope of defeating the reactionaries lay in a bold course. I had to forestall even the presentation of the censure resolution in the Committee of Ten. So, immediately the meeting was opened I got the floor and made my grand bluff, speaking substantially as follows:

"Before coming to Pittsburgh as head of the steel committee I heard much about the notorious corruption of the Pittsburgh Federation of Labor. And since arriving here I have heard much more, especially from men now in this room. Indeed, many of you have named each other to me as leaders in this crooked work.

"Now, you have all been very friendly to me. On my arrival, one of you, speaking for several others, offered me a big limousine for my personal use, which I declined. But despite this show of cordiality I realized that the corruptionists in the P.F. of L. would be alert to sell out the steel campaign if they saw the chance. Now these crooked elements think they have their opportunity. I have positive information that their plan is to try to put through the Committee of Ten this afternoon and the P.F. of L. this evening a resolution condemning me along the lines of the *Labor World* campaign.

"But I challenge them to try it. This steel campaign is very important. The A.F. of L. is pouring into it lots of organizers and hundreds of thousands of dollars. If it succeeds it will mark a turning point in American labor history, as many other industries will also be organized. The A.F. of L. is not going to permit such a vital campaign to be injured or destroyed by a few local corruptionists. If these crooked rats dare to stick their heads out of their holes, the A.F. of L. will snap them off. Every man who has anything to do with such a resolution will be driven out of the trade union movement."

After this I sat down. Then Gunther and J. G. Brown, steel organizers, gave them another blast on the same lines.

The labor leaders on the Committee of Ten were astonished and confounded by our sharp attack. Second-line union officials as they were, they did not know precisely what the top A.F. of L. policy was. All they saw were numerous organizers on the job and much activity.

Maybe I was right. They did not know that the A.F. of L. was shamelessly sabotaging the campaign and that Gompers would have been glad to get rid of it. They did not realize that my threats were therefore nothing but bluff. So they feared for their own skins if they went ahead.

The reactionaries looked from one to another, not knowing what to say or do. Finally, the shrewd Kelly, business agent of the Carpenters, and a leader of the conservatives in the P.F. of L., whispered something to his close crony, Norrington of the Bill Posters. Whereupon the latter, a slick article, made a clever proposal. In a genial tone he said: "Bill, you are wrong. We are all your friends and we want to see the steel campaign succeed. I, therefore, move that the Committee of Ten prepare a resolution for the P.F. of L. in which we endorse the A.F. of L. organizing crew in the Pittsburgh district."

I took the floor again. "No," I said, "such a resolution won't do. It's not the A.F. of L. organizing crew that's under fire, but me, personally. I propose a resolution specifically endorsing William Z. Foster. If you adopt Norrington's motion it'll be just what the *Labor World* wants and you will have the responsibility. Before nightfall they'll have an edition on the streets claiming that the P.F. of L. has condemned Foster by rejecting a specific request to endorse him."

More confusion and silence in the committee. Then Kelly, seeing their plan was upset, made a motion endorsing me by name. Now that their cause was lost, typically enough, they all wanted to get on the bandwagon, and they poured out assurances of goodwill to me. The meeting of the P.F. of L. that night passed the endorsement resolution unanimously, and the *Labor World* campaign was killed. My bluff had succeeded completely.

JACK BEAGHEN

Despite our victory in the Committee of Ten, the Pittsburgh labor reactionaries were soon threatening to protest to the A.F. of L. that I was appointing only "reds" as steel organizers. They wanted me to let them name an organizer to go on our payroll. This looked like blackmail, but I had to agree.

Clearly the new organizer would be an encumbrance, and probably also a talebearer for the Pittsburgh labor fakers. My bad opinion was confirmed when I learned that the new man, Jack Beaghen, was a former president of the local Bricklayers Union. Of all people, a building-trades official! How could he, saturated with craft ideas and tied up with the local Gompersites, be of any value in our broad industrial, fighting movement of steel workers? Beaghen, a man in his middle forties, had the typical cocky, hard-boiled air of building-trades business agents, and I at once took a strong dislike to him.

Beaghen soon got his test. The steel companies were viciously resisting our campaign and, among other violent measures, they had suppressed free speech in Pennsylvania so we could not hold hall meetings anywhere. We had to break this embargo at all costs, and the only way to do so was by holding meetings on the streets in spite of prohibitions by the local authorities.

Our first free speech battle was at Monesson, which we won hands down with the help of ten thousand union miners who flooded the town. Then we called a street meeting in McKeesport, a big steel center. Here the situation grew very tense; the steel workers were deeply stirred; the police declared they would smash the meeting, and the National Tube Company's gunmen openly boasted they would shoot down the first man who dared speak at the meeting.

As the chief steel organizer, I was scheduled to open the McKeesport meeting. The question was, who were to be the succeeding speakers, if any. Here I saw a good chance to put the Pittsburgh labor fakers "on the spot." So I asked several if they would speak and thus lend "prestige" to our meeting—this was only a short while before the meeting was to begin and we were gathered in the tiny headquarters of the McKeesport Labor Council. As I expected, they all declined. One said, "I can't make street speeches, my voice don't hold out"; another replied, "Oh, you've got lots of speakers, I'm a poor talker"; a third had to leave shortly, and so on.

Then I came to Beaghen. Perfunctorily, I asked him if he would speak. He cocked an eye at me and said, "Of course I will, what the hell do you think I came out here for, to be a decoration? I'll open the meeting if you say the word!"

I was flabbergasted. My hostility to him evaporated instantly. I realized I was dealing with a man and a fighter. So I listed him as one of the speakers. The meeting went off without a hitch, a splendid success. Neither the police nor the company gunmen dared to break it up, being obviously overawed by the thousands of assembled steel workers.

After this meeting Beaghen plunged wholeheartedly into the organizing campaign, needless to say with my fullest co-operation. He became a splendid organizer and volunteered for the most dangerous post in the whole organizing crew, the head of our "flying squadron."

The flying squadron was composed of a small body of picked organizers, Manley, Gunther, Brown, myself and others, and its job was to lead in violating openly the anti-free speech ordinances. This crew held street meetings in such hard-boiled towns as Homestead, where there had been no labor meeting since the famous strike twenty-six years before; in Duquesne, where the mayor declared that not even Jesus Christ could speak under the auspices of the A.F. of L., and in many other gunman-controlled steel towns. The crew members were thrown into nearly every jail in the Pittsburgh district. Their bold course so roused the masses of steel workers that, up till the strike at least, they established free assembly everywhere and they drew thousands of steel workers into the unions' ranks.

Jack Beaghen, so unpromising at the start, stood at the head of this dangerous work. And throughout the eventual bitterly-fought strike he was one of the most intelligent, courageous and trustworthy organizers in our whole crew. All of which goes to show that as you cannot judge a book by its cover, you can never know where you may unearth the rich gold of the working class.

THE DOUBLE-CROSS

In their internal struggle for positions, A.F. of L. bureaucrats make free use of the double-cross. During the 1919 steel campaign this was made very clear to me by William Hannon, vice-president of the International Association of Machinists.

Hannon represented the I.A. of M. (which had about three hundred and fifty thousand members) on our national committee. Constantly expressing himself in favor of the organization of the steel workers and endorsing our general methods of accomplishing it, it was not long until he became one of the key figures in our organization. Seldom was there an important policy adopted by the national committee that John Fitzpatrick (our chairman) and I did not first talk over with Hannon. He, with Fitzpatrick and myself, became the very center of this committee.

But W. H. Johnston, president of the I.A. of M., whom Hannon represented on our committee, was very much against our whole program. Following the typical Gompers policy of sabotaging the steel campaign, he starved it for funds and organizers and flatly opposed every decisive step in policy that we took.

This situation—with Hannon endorsing the campaign, and his chief, Johnston, opposing it—led Hannon to develop a double policy. Thus, in private talks with us he condemned Johnston as a reactionary and supported our policies energetically, but when it came to the committee meetings and he had to go officially on record, he voted in accordance with Johnston's policy. Hannon had long been in opposition to Johnston in the I.A. of M., and we knew the latter was watching for an opportunity to "get" him. His negative official votes, he said, were therefore only in self-protection, as his heart was in the campaign.

Thus, Hannon in the committee discussions favored putting out the decisive national strike vote, but voted against it; likewise, also, he spoke for launching the strike, but registered his committee vote negatively; and similarly, when the strike was eventually lost, he helped us formulate the resolution calling it off, and then voted against it; and so on in other decisive instances.

This two-faced action did not sit well with me, but Hannon always expressed himself so militantly for the policies of our movement and for the necessity of his making an official record in accordance with Johnston's wishes, that I could do nothing about it. He repeatedly deplored the duplicity that Johnston's reactionary attitude forced him into.

Hannon thus found himself in a strategic position. He stood to gain no matter how things turned out. If the great strike were won he could take credit to himself for his personal stand, and if the strike were lost he could rely upon his official votes and say, "I told you so." It was a sort of "heads I win, tails you lose" proposition.

Indeed, hardly had the strike been called off as lost, then Hannon played his hand, based on his official votes. He wrote an article in the official journal of the I.A. of M., condemning the steel strike leadership and policies, much as the Gompers clique were doing. Especially was he violent against me, with whom he had been so friendly and worked so closely. He denounced me as a dictator and an incompetent. According to him, I had at my disposal the biggest corps of organizers in labor history, yet accomplished nothing. The members of the national committee, he said, had little or nothing to say in the campaign, being constantly confronted with ready-made plans and *faits accompli* by me. As for himself, he had deemed the whole strike movement inadvisable, and he paraded his various negative votes to prove it. It was the double-cross *par excellence,* and it virtually freed Hannon of responsibility for the loss of the great struggle.

MIKE CASTS HIS VOTE

Shortly before the big steel strike of 1919, a strike ballot was taken in all the important steel centers to determine the attitude of the workers. The affirmative vote was almost unanimous. But in the Youngstown, Ohio, district, where eventually fifty thousand workers struck, there was one rather celebrated negative vote registered. It was cast by "Mike," a Croatian laborer in the big plant of the Youngstown Sheet and Tube Company.

Our strike ballot was formulated in such a way that a worker who favored striking in support of the miners' demands signified so by marking a cross in the "Yes" column. But Mike developed a method all his own. After depositing his ballot he shouted:

"I vote NO! I no like twelve-hour day; I no like company union; I no like seven-day week; I no like low wages; I no like scabbing; I vote No! No!! No!!!"

A HORSE APIECE

In the spring of 1922 the Chicago Federation of Labor, upon the initiative of members of the Trade Union Educational League, adopted a resolution calling for the amalgamation of all A.F. of L. crafts into industrial unions. This started a sweeping movement all over the country for industrial unionism and gave a sharp shock to the reactionary trade union bureaucracy. Samuel Gompers, president of the A.F. of L., hastened to Chicago to stem the rapidly rising tide of industrial unionism. He called a hand-picked conference of some fifteen hundred local trade union officials in the Hotel Morrison and exhorted them to "rescue the C.F. of L. from the reds."

At this meeting Emmett Flood, ultra-reactionary A.F. of L. organizer in Chicago, made a bitter attack upon me and charged that the Trade Union Educational League, of which I was secretary, was financed with Moscow gold. I denied this allegation and demanded that the conference appoint a committee of three to go over our books to ascertain the sources of the T.U.E.L.'s income.

Gompers spoke, and he paid special attention to my demand for an investigation committee. Addressing me directly, he said, "Brother Foster, let me tell you a story," and he related substantially the following:

"Once a newly-appointed union organizer submitted his first month's expense account and the secretary made some objection. 'What's this,' said he, 'one pair of shoes, six dollars; one suit of clothes, forty dollars? Now you can't put in such expenses; you must confine yourself to outlays directly incurred in your work!' and he crossed out the objectionable items.

"Next month," went on Gompers, "the organizer again put in his expense account. This time, however, the secretary, running his eye over it, said approvingly: 'Now you're railroading: I don't see any such items as shoes and clothes.' 'No,' said the organizer, with a knowing look, 'you can't see them, but they're there just the same.'

"And," said Gompers, "that's how it is with your T.U.E.L. books. I haven't the slightest doubt that they are in perfect order, but the Moscow gold is there just the same."

Everybody laughed, myself included. Although few believed Flood's charges, all could appreciate a pat story. I got no investigating committee, and I counted the incident one up for Gompers.

But the "old man," in going ahead with his speech, "put his foot in it." He said: "Brother Foster, I propose we settle this industrial union controversy in an intelligent way. Let's have a public debate on the question, you and I. We'll hire a big hall, you pick one judge, I'll choose another, and these two can select the third. Then we will each present our point of view and let the crowd and judges decide."

I was amazed at this proposal and promply accepted it. I was confident that despite Gompers' speaking ability and prestige I could hold my own on the matter of industrial unionism. Such a debate would surely give favorable publicity to the T.U.E.L. amalgamation campaign.

Gompers' friends were appalled by his proposition. The last thing they wanted was a public discussion of amalgamation versus craft unionism. Their way of fighting industrial unionism was by strong-arming it in the unions. So Gompers welched on the whole business. As weeks rolled on and we heard nothing further from him, I challenged and rechallenged him to debate. I wrote him letters reiterating my formal acceptance of his proposal; I gave out stories to the daily press; I sent him messengers with challenges and I printed defies in the T.U.E.L. paper, the *Labor Herald*.

We did not let Gompers rest for months. But he would have none of the debate. Meanwhile, trade union officialdom was snickering at him for his embarrassing position of having proposed the debate and then refusing to go through with it.

So, all said and done, the Chicago anti-amalgamation meeting's clash was not so one-sided. Gompers got the best of me on the investigating committee, but I surely won out on the debate. It was a horse apiece.

GOMPERS

Samuel Gompers, who for forty years stood at the head of the A.F. of L., was a capitalistic-minded trade union bureaucrat. When fighting for his own personal interests, within the labor movement Gompers was very militant. He was a hard-fighting, hard-drinking, hail-fellow-well-met leader, who intellectually stood head and shoulders above any of his associate officials. Proof of his high ability is the fact that for four decades he, a Jew, was able to dominate a clique of trade union bureaucrats mostly Irish Catholic and often saturated with anti-Semitism. In his many struggles against opposing leaders he was bold, relentless, unforgiving, successful. And he was worse than vicious against revolutionary minorities in the A.F. of L.

But when it came to fighting the capitalist class Gompers had not even a spark of proletarian revolt in him. In practice he acted as though the capitalist system was God-given and the working class the natural servants of the capitalists. With all his vigor and ability he resisted every policy that would make the trade union movement a real weapon against capitalism. He fought against the development of class consciousness, against militant strike policies, against trade union democracy, against industrial unionism, against the organization of the unorganized millions in the basic industries, against every attempt to form the workers into a party of their own. He supported corrupting alliances with capitalist organizations—economic, political and social. He tried to keep the working class tied to the chariot of capitalism, although he knew well enough, when the situation demanded it, how to cloak his subservience with radical phrases.

Let a couple of simple incidents illustrate Gompers two-sidedness—his subservient holding towards the ruling class and his dictatorial attitude within the A.F. of L.

The first was in 1919. We were on the verge of the great steel strike. Thirty thousand men had been discharged for union activities; the companies had refused our overtures for a conference and had turned the steel districts into armed camps; the workers were all set for the struggle. In this crisis we elected a committee to urge President Wilson to arrange a meeting with the steel barons. It consisted of Gompers, John Fitzpatrick, myself and two or three others. At the White House we met with Wilson, and Gompers started the presentation of our case. I was astonished at the way he did it.

Gompers was obviously deeply overawed by Wilson. His face took on a submissive look, his voice was obsequious and his manner servile. He began by recalling to Wilson a few trivial incidents of their activities in Versailles at the end of the World War. Then, in an almost apologetic manner, he presented our case, ending by most respectfully requesting Wilson to try to arrange a steel conference. I was amazed to see the mighty Gompers, such a haughty autocrat in his own circles, acting thus humbly before the President.

Then came Fitzpatrick's turn to speak. In those days he still retained something of a fighting spirit, and he stated our case aggressively, speaking in a firm voice, banging the table and warning Wilson of a serious struggle if the steel magnates refused to come to terms.

Gompers was manifestly shocked and visibly in pain. His whole demeanor was a protest against Fitzpatrick's militant speech in the Great Presence. Wilson himself took Fitzpatrick's speech good-naturedly, and generally acted quite informally. Once, during our conference, he excused himself from the room with the remark that he had "to go and pump ship." We laughed outright at this—which further pained the obsequious Gompers. Now all this was a very simple incident, but in it Gompers revealed his true character. All his life he was a servitor of capitalism, and as we spoke to Wilson, the leader of the employers' government, this fact was curiously and emphatically dramatized.

Gompers, however, was plenty dictatorial in his own bailiwick. Although he was considerate enough of the powerful heads of the strong trade unions, leaving them quite without interference in their regime of craft autonomy, strike-sellouts, racketeering, fat salaries, gangsterism and general corruption, so long as they did not conspire together to take away his job and elect one of themselves—but when it came to Gompers' handling of the weaker elements in the Federation it was quite a different story. Then he ruled with an iron hand as an intolerant bureaucratic dictator. He constantly sacrificed the interests of the smaller international unions and the weak federal unions to the ruthless leaders of the larger organizations, and he turned a deaf ear to rank and file protests and opposition movements—when he did not fight them openly. Largely through his influence, the Federation conventions were reduced to mere collections of the top union bureaucrats, with no semblance of rank and file democracy. Any worker, outraged in his union by the corrupt leadership and seeking justice, might just as well appeal to the Atlantic Ocean as to Gompers.

From my personal experience I could cite many examples of Gompers' autocratic rule, but let just one little incident suffice. I thought it well illustrated Gompers' crass bureaucracy. It happened in the 1918 convention of the A.F. of L., at which I was a delegate. Gompers was doing the job in person of accepting resolutions from the delegates. While the bulk of the convention sat idly, a crowd of delegates assembled before the broad speakers' stage, resolutions in hand. Strutting along the platform, Gompers slowly gathered up the resolutions, one by one. He would select one from the many offered, glance through it ostentatiously, cumbersomely mark it for the committee, and then leisurely wander along until the spirit moved him to take another resolution.

Back and forth he stalked. Once in a while he would stop to chat casually with some delegate or other about an extraneous matter. And meanwhile the convention of several hundred delegates sat and waited as the leader of the American labor movement went through this childish exhibitionist rigmarole.

I remember what Gompers did to one delegate, evidently a worker and a newcomer. He had no less than thirteen resolutions and tried to pass them up to Gompers all at once. But Gompers drew back indignantly, his bureaucratic soul deeply shocked at the idea of a progressive worker asking the A.F. of L. really to do something. "How long do you think this convention is going to last, with you and your thirteen resolutions?" he shouted at the delegate. The gathering, nearly all top officials, guffawed. Then Gompers took one of the thirteen resolutions, read it, assigned it to the committee and went across the platform, collecting resolutions haphazardly from other delegates. After that, every time he passed the worker delegate in his criss-crossings he would take only one resolution, meanwhile making a wise-crack, at which the convention laughed. The delegate was deeply humiliated, and I was nauseated and disgusted.

Such was Gompers: a cringer before the capitalist rulers and a tyrant to the weaker ones in his own organization.

"SAVE THE MINERS UNION"

One of the most interesting struggles I ever participated in was the "Save the Miners Union" movement in the coal industry in 1926-28. As general secretary of the Trade Union Educational League, I spent six months in the field organizing this movement. It was a tough assignment.

By the beginning of 1926 the United Mine Workers of America found itself in a dangerous position due to the crisis in the coal industry. This crisis was caused chiefly by an over-development of mines during war-time and the growth of the use of substitutes for coal. It resulted in great unemployment even during the Coolidge "good times." The position of the union was further made precarious by tendencies of the industry to move to the non-union South, by militant anti-union attacks by the operators, and also by the fact that the Lewis administration of the U.M.W.A. was following a conservative line unfit to cope with the situation.

Evidently the union was facing disaster. It had already been smashed in many important areas—West Virginia, central Pennsylvania, Missouri, Oklahoma, Kansas, etc., and the great Pittsburgh Coal Company had just repudiated the Jacksonville agreement and gone open shop. In this crisis the Communist Party, through the Trade Union Educational League, put out the slogan "Save the Miners Union," and called for the formation of a left-progressive block of miners to fight for the life of the threatened union. Pat Toohey was elected secretary of the movement.

The "Save the Miners Union" movement was one of the most important struggles ever conducted by the left-progressive forces in a trade union. Its program called for the organization of the unorganized, the establishment of more democracy in the U.M.W.A., for a progressive leadership, for a Farmer-Labor Party, for government ownership of the mines, etc. Naturally the movement came into a head-on collision with the Lewis administration.

The "Save the Union Committee" made its first big crystallization of forces in the national U.M.W.A. elections in the latter part of 1926. Heading the left-progressive united front slate against John L. Lewis was John Brophy (who by the whirligig of developments is now Lewis' right hand man in the C.I.O.). We made a vigorous campaign all through the union on the basis of our program. Finally the official figures showed Lewis had 173,323 and Brophy 60,661.

The second point of concentration of the "Save the Union" movement was the national U.M.W.A. convention in January, 1927. Here the combined left-progressive forces numbered about one-third of the total convention delegates, but Lewis was in firm control and the whole progressive program was voted down.

Then came the great strike, beginning April 1, 1927, which was our third phase of struggle. This strike, one of the most important in American labor history, was desperately fought. But with more than half the bituminous miners in the country unorganized and remaining at work, with the union anthracite miners also staying on the job, with the reactionary Coolidge administration in power, the union had hardly a chance. Nevertheless, under Lewis' official slogan of "No Backward Step" and ours of "Save the Miners Union," the miners fought on desperately month after month.

The "Save the Miners Union Committee" was a basic force in strengthening the embattled miners. Their great strike had such enormous vitality that our committee called a national conference in Pittsburgh on April 1, 1928, precisely twelve months after the strike had started. Present were over eleven hundred delegates, representing approximately one hundred thousand miners from many districts. The conference adopted a program to strengthen the strike by rebuilding the picket lines, improving the relief system, drawing the anthracite miners into the strike, and extending the strike into the various unorganized districts.

After this the strike took on new vigor for a while—we struck twenty thousand unorganized miners in the Fayette and Westmoreland coal counties, and the relief and picket systems were much improved. But the strike could not be won, and shortly afterward the national U.M.W.A. leadership instructed the districts to make the best settlements they could. The general outcome was that the U.M.W.A. was wrecked everywhere except in Illinois and the anthracite districts.

The "Save the Union" movement did not achieve the goal it set for itself of organizing the unorganized and winning the strike. Despite its efforts, the U.M.W.A. suffered a tremendous defeat and with it the whole A.F. of L. But our committee made a noble struggle, and it wrote a bright page in militant trade union history.

THE 1931 COAL STRIKE

Following the defeat of the U.M.W.A. in the great strike of 1927-28 and with the breakup of the organization in nearly all soft-coal districts, the miners in the Pittsburgh area sank into slave-like conditions. By 1931 wages had dropped from seven-fifty per day to about two dollars; hours of work had increased and working conditions degenerated;

unemployment ran as high as seventy-five per cent, and no relief was given by the coal town authorities; the district was overrun with armed company thugs. The destitution and misery of the miners were beyond description, and the broken U.M.W.A. could do nothing about it.

Into this desperate situation came the militant National Miners Union, affiliated to the Trade Union Unity League. During that period, in industries where the A.F. of L. unions were non-existent or very weak, the Communist Party supported the formation of independent unions. Hence, seeing that the U.M.W.A. had practically collapsed in many districts, the C.P. actively backed the N.M.U. The N.M.U. was thus the continuation, under new conditions, of the earlier "Save the Miners Union" movement.

It was not long before the oppressed Pennsylvania miners began to respond to the N.M.U. On May 27, 1931, a small strike against a wage cut developed near Pittsburgh. The strike fever ran swiftly. All we had to do to pull a mine was to send a delegation there. The miners marched from mine to mine halting the industry. Soon the strike spread over several counties in Western Pennsylvania, Eastern Ohio and the Panhandle of West Virginia. By the latter part of June there was a total of forty-two thousand out, and the largest strike ever conducted by a revolutionary union in the United States was under way.

As national secretary of the T.U.E.L., I went into the area at the outbreak of the strike and remained there until the finish, a total of five months. It was one of the severest strike tests I ever went through. It was a heart-breaking affair to see the starving miners being cut to pieces by the ruthless operators and to be able to do nothing about it except to work eighteen hours a day to hold the men in line. At the end of the fight I was almost finished myself.

The enemy comprised some of the biggest, most ruthless corporations in the United States, for the mines of the Pittsburgh Coal Company, Pennsylvania Railroad, U.S. Steel Corporation, General Motors, were located here. To help the miners fight these vicious exploiters, the Communist Party either already had on the ground or sent into the strike field numerous leading forces, including Bill Dunne, Jack Johnstone, Al. Wagenknecht, Frank Borich, Tom Meyerscough, Tony Minerich, Dan Slinger, Leo Thompson and others.

The mine operators viewed with amazement and alarm the sudden appearance in strength of the revolutionary N.M.U. The miners whom they had thought hopelessly beaten by the breakup of the U.M.W.A., had rallied again, this time under Communist leadership, and the employers feared the N.M.U. would spread to other districts. The strike had to be broken at all costs. To do this the coal bosses evicted at least one hundred thousand men, women and children from the company-owned houses; they cut off all credit at the company and private stores; they brought in large numbers of strike-breakers; they flooded the strike districts with gunmen and set up a reign of terror. They killed two, slugged scores and arrested hundreds. And this terror campaign had the support of the state and local authorities. The strike was pictured in the press as an attempt to overthrow the government and to establish Communism.

Besides all this, the coal operators sought to undermine the strike by coming to terms with the U.M.W.A. Agreements were signed at several mines, although the U.M.W.A. had only a few members. This led to physical clashes between the two unions. The old-time struggle between the Lewis administration and the "Save the Miners Union" movement grew into open fights on the picket line.

Meanwhile, the Hoover government became alarmed and tried to bring the coal operators and U.M.W.A. together for a general settlement. The A.F. of L. also took a hand against the militant N.M.U.

Facing all these hostile forces, the N.M.U. battled bravely. Inspired by its fighting slogans, the miners and their families poured out in the big marches and mass picket lines. It was a strike against starvation. Negroes and whites fraternized in a way never before seen in the mining districts. Broad rank and file united front committees controlled the strike at each mine and also in Pittsburgh. An elaborate relief organization was built and tent colonies were set up for evicted miners. The fighting spirit of the workers was high. Like a storm the strike raged on.

This was in the depth of the great industrial crisis, and the workers in all industries were full of discontent. Consequently, in the strike region, they became infected with the miners' burning spirit. Huge unemployed demonstrations were held in various towns; steel workers in numerous mills demanded that organizers be sent to unite them. For a time it looked as though the Pittsburgh area would develop a big local general strike movement such as various American cities— Akron, Minneapolis, San Francisco—experienced a couple of years later.

But the forces of the strikers were too weak to prevail in the face of their many powerful enemies. The N.M.U. could not spread the strike far enough. Heroism was not enough to win against such superior odds. So, on August 8th, after twelve weeks of bitter struggle, the strike was given up. The workers had to return to work unconditionally.

The employers followed up their victory by blacklisting hundreds of good fighters. The defeat also dealt the N.M.U. a fatal blow. But the strike was not entirely lost. For one thing, it threw such a scare into the coal operators that they largely put a stop to the worsening of the miners' conditions; and also when, in the great upsurge of the workers two years later in the days of the N.R.A., the miners began to stream back into the U.M.W.A., the resistance of the bosses was greatly reduced. With the memory of the N.M.U.'s great fight clearly in their mind's eye, they were not so unwilling to see the U.M.W.A., which they had fought so hard in 1927-28, re-establish itself.

KNOXVILLE

When the National Miners Union (Trade Union Unity League), as a result of its big Pittsburgh strike in 1931, took over the leadership of the Kentucky miners and struck several thousand of them in bloody Harlan and Bell Counties, the workers had been engaged for several months (under the U.M.W.A.) in a desperate losing battle against the coal operators. A reign of terror existed throughout the Kentucky and

Tennessee coal fields. Several men had been killed and scores thrown into jail for long terms.

The N.M.U. strike began on January 1, 1932. It was greeted with a wild blast of red-baiting by the company-controlled local officials and press and by an outbreak of company thug violence. The police raided the union headquarters and arrested almost all the top strike leaders. A new leadership had to be set up, and for this purpose a number of us went into the district, including Frank Borich, secretary of the N.M.U., Alfred Wagenknecht, head of the Workers International Relief and myself, head of the T.U.U.L. We could not hold our meeting in the coal areas, as they were everywhere overrun with police, gunmen and vigilantes, all of them looking for us. So we decided to convene our session in Knoxville, the nearest big center.

Knoxville was jittery over the intense strike situation, and Communist leaders, especially from the North, were most unwelcome. In order to hold our meeting without publicity, therefore, someone got the not-too-happy idea that we pose as an organization of tobacco growers. On this basis we engaged a small hall in the middle of town.

Unfortunately, however, the delegation of local miners' leaders coming from the coal fields were late in arriving, what with plugging over bad roads and dodging vigilante patrols. They did not reach our meeting place until ten-thirty P.M. This was an ungodly time to begin a meeting in a town like Knoxville and, to make matters worse, the hall-keeper had become suspicious of us. But the situation being urgent, we had to go ahead.

Things went along all right for an hour or so, when there came a knock at the door. It was the police, called by the landlord to investigate the mysterious meeting. Wagenknecht went out to confer with them, we meanwhile expecting a pinch at any moment. Soon "Wag" returned, with everything straightened out. How he succeeded in talking us out of being arrested always remained a mystery to me.

We felt quite relieved at this lucky escape, for many strike leaders were being prosecuted under the syndicalism laws. But the Kentucky miners took the whole matter with surprising nonchalance, and soon I learned why. One of them, pulling out two big 45's, informed us that there never had been a chance of our being arrested; for if need be they were going to shoot their way out. This the miners had decided among themselves. They were fresh from the semi-civil war conditions in Harlan County and such a bold course seemed natural to them. Now, indeed, after this revelation, we breathed easier. I have often speculated on the tragic consequences that might have ensued had that Knoxville police official been less responsive to Wagenknecht's persuasive tongue.

MARCH 6, 1930

March 6, 1930, was a memorable day of struggle. On that day a million and a quarter unemployed workers, led by the Communist Party, Trade Union Unity League and Unemployed Councils, demonstrated nationally for unemployment insurance and relief. In Detroit one hundred thousand turned out, in New York one hundred and ten thousand, and the demonstrations elsewhere were also huge.

The great industrial crisis had been on for several months. Millions were out of work. The national, state and local governments gave them little or no relief. The A.F. of L. did not bestir itself in their behalf, and the Socialist Party was also inactive. The Communist Party, however, had launched a militant fight. Among many other actions, it organized a great national protest and demand for relief and insurance for March 6th. The A.F. of L. denounced the proposed demonstration, Matthew Woll declaring it was being financed with two million dollars of Russian money. The local police everywhere took measures to crush the movement by force. But on the date set the workers startled the country by their gigantic turnout.

The New York demonstration, the largest of all, was held in Union Square. Our plan was to march down Broadway to the City Hall and lay our demands before Mayor Walker. But Walker prohibited the march and Police Commissioner Whalen declared that if it were attempted it would be broken up by force. He announced that eighteen thousand policemen and seven thousand firemen, the city's total force, were being mobilized to defeat the threatening "red revolution." On our side, we stated we would march, permit or no permit. The whole city became highly excited, and the tension increased hourly.

Union Square on March 6th was an unforgettable sight. The workers were massed in the Square, and all the surrounding streets were crowded. The unemployed had come together to demand the right to live. The police and firemen were in the Square in great force and thousands more were stationed in nearby buildings as reinforcements. On roofs surrounding the Square were machine guns. Commissioner Whalen had established his headquarters about a hundred feet from our main speakers' platform.

The meeting went off with great mass enthusiasm. The workers adopted demands and elected a committee consisting of Bob Minor, I. Amter, Harry Raymond, a young fellow named Lester, a Negro worker whose name was lost and myself. I was chosen spokesman. This committee was to lead the march. But before starting the parade, it decided to make another effort to secure a permit from Whalen.

Our committee pushed its way through the dense crowd to the temporary police headquarters. To reach Whalen we had to pass hundreds of "dicks," patrolmen and newspaper men. He was in a small room, surrounded by twenty police. Our committee demanded a parade permit. We pointed out that only recently the Queen of Roumania, sundry military butchers and many capitalist organizations had been allowed to parade freely, but now the class that built Broadway was being denied the right to walk along it. Whalen flatly refused to give us a permit. Whereupon we told him we would march without one. He declared he would break up our parade by force and that we would be held personally responsible for any bloodshed.

Our committee returned to the speakers' stand. As spokesman, I reported to the crowd what had taken place and put the question: "Shall we march in spite of Whalen and his police?" It was a tense moment. Then tens of thousands of workers shouted, "Let's march!" So I gave the signal to start, and the huge throng began to shape itself into a procession to move down Broadway.

But immediately, before the parade could even form, mounted police charged through the crowd, clubbing right and left; heavy forces of police on foot used their night sticks unmercifully, and hundreds of plainclothesmen, stationed at strategic points in the crowd, drew out blackjacks and attacked the workers, while fire engines played the hose upon the great throng. Under this heavy and swift assault, the unarmed workers had to give way. Within a short while the demonstrators were driven from the Square into adjoining streets.

Hundreds of workers were injured, but fortunately none fatally. The reactionary capitalist press gloated sadistically over the brutal clubbing of the unemployed, who were denounced as "reds." Several police were injured, one seriously. Only a few workers were arrested, the policy of the police being to club the workers off the Square, rather than to arrest them wholesale.

Meanwhile, our committee was having a strenuous time. The police attack was so sudden that we had no chance to squeeze through a hundred yards of dense humanity to head the parade. No sooner had we stepped from the platform than we were jammed in an immense sea of surging workers who were being attacked on all sides. The committee tried to stick together, but we were almost immediately split up and scattered by the police charges.

As for myself, I fell in with George Siskind and a knot of workers, and we made our way through the surging mass, from 17th and Broadway to 14th and University. All about us the police were riding down and slugging workers. Soon the demonstration was broken up, so I went downtown to the place, a couple of blocks from the City Hall, where the committee had agreed to meet in case it got separated. When our committee was assembled, we went in a body to the City Hall, around which many workers were milling, and we demanded to see the Mayor to place before him the demands of the unemployed. At once were were all arrested.

For several days we were held without bail, while the reactionary press carried on a wild campaign against us. Whalen declared that if the injured policeman died we would be charged with murder. Finally, we were released on bail, and a few weeks later were convicted, jury trials being denied us. Minor, Amter, Raymond and myself were given three-year indefinite sentences in the New York penitentiary.

March 6th had many important consequences. Locally, it taught the police that the workers were prepared to fight for their right to use the streets. Whalen became badly discredited and was soon removed as Police Commissioner. Since March 6th, the workers have never been refused the right to parade to or from Union Square. Besides, the city government was compelled to substantially increase its relief appropriation.

The March 6th demonstration raised the question of unemployment insurance into a live national issue. It also brought the Communist Party forward sharply as the outstanding leader of the huge masses of unemployed, to the astonishment and dismay of all shades of reactionaries. It gave a tremendous impulse nationally to the unemployed workers' struggle, and many cities were soon compelled to grant relief. March 6th was one of the historic days in the long struggle of the American proletariat.

THE FIRST NATIONAL HUNGER MARCH

The winter of 1931-32 was a desperately hard one for the approximately sixteen million unemployed. They were receiving no relief whatever from the Federal government and little from the states and cities. Wholesale starvation stalked the country. But the ultra-reactionary Hoover government handed out hundreds of millions of dollars to help the capitalist corporations.

The A.F. of L. leaders were still tailing after Hoover's hunger program and were making no fight to relieve the mass distress. The Communist Party was intensifying its efforts to unite the unemployed workers to fight for unemployment insurance and relief. It was organizing hundreds of big demonstrations, hunger marches and anti-eviction fights. In these fights it faced ferocious police attacks, a score of workers being killed and many hundreds clubbed and arrested.

One of these struggles was the first national hunger march of

December, 1931. With seventeen hundred delegates from all over the country, it arrived in Washington, December 7th, for the opening of Congress. Its central demands were for unemployment insurance and winter relief. The march was under the auspices of the National Unemployed Councils and was headed by H. Benjamin, with A. W. Mills as chief organizer. I participated in its organization and took part in the march. So successful was it that it was soon followed by Father Cox's Pittsburgh march, the national bonus march, the second hunger march and similar events.

This first national hunger march was the best organized march in the history of the American proletariat up to that time. It had an almost military structure and discipline. The delegates traveled in trucks and autos, borrowed or hired. The march was in four columns, starting from St. Louis, Chicago, Buffalo and Boston. Far Western contingents assembled at St. Louis and Chicago. Each column had its specified route. At Pittsburgh the two western columns joined forces and at Philadelphia the two from the Northeast came together. In Baltimore these two fused columns united to march into Washington. The marchers touched at almost every big industrial center east of the Mississippi and north of the Ohio, where the millions of starving unemployed were congested.

The columns traveled with machine-like precision. The night stop-overs, carefully scheduled weeks in advance, were about one hundred and fifty miles apart. Well-organized local committees arranged for food, beds and auto supplies for the marchers and they organized local mass demonstrations. The number of delegates picked up at each point was strictly limited. No stragglers were allowed to join the march.

The columns themselves were highly organized. Each truck had its captain and each column its governing committee and leader. There were also volunteer doctors, dentists, nurses and auto mechanics. Each column also had a defense corps, strategically placed while the column was traveling and camping. Column movements were regulated by whistle and horn signals. Strict discipline prevailed. The marchers had ample printed propaganda material, and the march was financed by each locality providing the funds for its own delegation by popular subscription.

This splendid march of the unemployed, with its definite program, militant leadership and thorough organization, was a big advance over its historic predecessor, the confused, straggling Coxey's Army of thirty-seven years before. The heart of the march was the Communist Party.

The 1931 march aroused national attention. Everywhere great masses turned out to meet it. At many places local police and vigilante thugs tried to break it up; but the solidarity of the local workers and the good discipline and fighting spirit of the marchers defeated them. With clock-like regularity, the four columns moved forward, making all the scheduled stops without a hitch the entire way to Washington. In various towns so great was the employed and unemployed workers' support that the local city officials had to furnish the marchers with food, lodgings and gasoline free.

Great throngs greeted the marchers in Washington, and there was a huge police mobilization. As the marchers moved along Pennsylvania Avenue they were flanked by two solid rows of policemen, probably one thousand in all. The hunger marchers were virtually under arrest. At the Capitol building it looked as though the authorities expected a revolutionary attack. Two to three thousand more police were banked there with machine guns planted openly at strategic points. There were hundreds of plainclothesmen in the crowd. Besides all this, there were also about a thousand soldiers brought in from neighboring forts and held in readiness close by. The police and soldiers outnumbered the marchers at least three to one.

The police isolated the marchers on the Capitol plaza so they could be more effectively attacked. The vast crowd had been pushed far back in a big semi-circle, in front of the great building, and as the marchers entered the plaza they were bunched together in a sort of human island and heavily surrounded by police. Hemmed in on all sides, with machine guns aimed at them from various points, the marchers could have been mowed down upon the slightest provocation. All this force was a foretaste of Hoover's later murderous military attack upon the bonus-seeking war veterans.

The hunger marchers, undeterred by these sinister threatenings, sang and shouted slogans, while their committee, headed by Bill Dunne, tried in vain to present the demands of the millions of starving unemployed upon the floor of Congress. Only a minor government official would meet them. Meanwhile, the workers staged a thrilling demonstration in front. The New York delegation had a band, a former German Red Front unit, which played revolutionary tunes. Finally, it burst into the *International*, the first time this glorious air had been played on the Capitol plaza, although certainly it will not be the last. The crowd applauded enthusiastically and the police glowered menacingly. It was one of the most inspiring moments of my life. The awakening workers were at last raising their rebellious voices in the very sanctuary of the ultra-reactionary Hoover capitalist government.

Then came the march to the White House, to lay the unemployed's demands before President Hoover. Again the procession was locked between two strong lines of moving police. At the White House there was another big crowd and a further heavy police mobilization. As the marchers came to a standstill, the accompanying police banked themselves on the street side between the marchers and the White House, their purpose being evident.

Hoover refused to meet the committee; so the marchers, leaving their demands at the White House, proceeded on to the A.F. of L. headquarters. Here the police had also placed a heavy guard, for they realized the mass resentment against the A.F. of L. top leaders who were supporting Hoover's outrageous policy of no unemployment insurance and no Federal relief program for the unemployed.

William Green met with our committee; but only to attack the demands of the unemployed for the benefit of the capitalist press present. He lectured the marchers' committee to the effect that unemployment insurance would destroy the workers' individuality and break up the trade unions.

The marchers remained two days in Washington, and held a big conference to better organize the national struggle for unemployment insurance and relief. Then came the homeward journey, with each column making its regular night stops, scheduled weeks ahead. The marchers were received by enormous crowds everywhere.

Today the necessity for unemployment insurance and Federal relief are accepted facts. The Roosevelt administration has instituted the beginnings of a system of social security. The reactionary A.F. of L. leaders have been compelled by mass pressure to give up their Hoover-like opposition to unemployment insurance. Great credit for all this must go to the Communist Party, with its long and militant struggle for the unemployed during the depth of the crisis. And of the innumerable battles led by the Party, among the best was the first national hunger march.

THE FORD MASSACRE

For many years Henry Ford has been represented as a big-hearted philanthropist, highly solicitous about the welfare of his huge army of workers. This legend, carefully cultivated by the Ford Motor Car sales department, is a valuable business asset.

But the great crisis of 1929 stripped this hypocritical mask from the sainted Ford's face and exposed all its capitalist ugliness. Ford, even more ruthlessly than other capitalists, threw his workers out of their jobs and left them to starve. And he distinguished himself among the bitterest enemies of every social security measure tending to relieve mass suffering. Ford is ripe to back an eventual American fascist movement.

Ford's anti-labor policy came to full flower on March 7, 1932, in the so-called Dearborn Massacre. This bloody affair occurred in the depths of the crisis, when half the workers in Detroit were unemployed. Masses were actually starving and the destitution defied description. At that time the Communist Party was in the midst of its great national campaign for unemployment insurance and relief, and in the course of this campaign the Auto Workers Union (T.U.U.L.) and the Unemployed Councils organized a demonstration at the big

Ford plant in Dearborn. A preliminary meeting of the unemployed, to mobilize for the demonstration, was held the night before and I, being on tour organizing the unemployed, was billed as the principal speaker.

This preliminary meeting, with several thousand workers present, went off peaceably, and I took the night train to Milwaukee, where I was scheduled to speak the next day. In Milwaukee I was horrified to read in the papers that there had been a massacre by the Dearborn police.

The plan of our demonstration was that the unemployed should march to the gates of the Ford works, present their demands for work and relief and then disperse. But the autocrat, Ford, denied his starving workers even this thin right of petition. When the procession of unemployed entered Dearborn and approached the huge plant, the city police and Henry Ford's private army of gunmen opened fire upon it with tear gas, rifles and machine guns. The peaceful demonstration was broken up, with four workers killed and fifty wounded. It was cold-blooded, premeditated murder.

Of course, the Detroit capitalist press immediately blamed the workers for the fatal "riot." The news agencies also sent out a story, printed with big headlines all over the country to the effect that I, as main speaker at the mobilization meeting, was personally responsible for the killings, and would be arrested with other Detroit Communist Party leaders for murder. This news reached me in Milwaukee, so after my meeting there I took a train for New York to prepare my defense.

Now it so happened that at this time I was on parole, as part of the three-year penitentiary sentence I had received for participating in the March 6, 1930, demonstration in New York. This required me to make personal parole reports semi-monthly, and one was due precisely on the day I got back to New York. I shall not forget the circumstances of that report. No sooner had I put my foot inside the parole office then half a dozen police surrounded and grabbed me.

"Just the guy we want to see; they only want you for murder, that's all," said one, and the rest laughed and made wisecracks about the hot seat at Sing Sing.

The parole commission was in session at that moment and my case was acted upon at once. I was prepared to go back to the penitentiary as a parole violator, and also to face a murder charge. But the Dearborn police (which means Henry Ford) had resolved that the best course was to hush up the massacre. Their brutality simply could not stand investigation. So they decided not to press charges against me and the local leaders, as this would lead to unwelcome exposures and publicity.

Still the New York police had to do something. It would never do, they said, to have a paroled man running up and down the land organizing the unemployed. Therefore, the parole commission sentenced me to serve the rest of my parole, two years, within the confines of New York City. If I should leave the city under any pretext I would be immediately returned to prison to serve the balance of my term.

Now this was a pretty kettle of fish. I have never liked New York as a place of residence, and to be compelled by the police to live there was, I thought, laying it on a bit thick. But I had to make the best of it, and for the next several months the city limits of Greater New York were the walls of my prison. And so things remained until I was nominated as Presidential candidate of the Communist Party in 1932. My nomination put the New York police in a quandary. They did not want me to travel around the country "agitating" the workers, yet they were afraid to hold me in New York for fear I might appear as something of a martyr. They finally decided to lift the city limit ban from me, but kept me under the menace of being returned to jail upon the slightest provocation.

SAN FRANCISCO GENERAL STRIKE

My contact with the great Frisco general strike in the summer of 1934 was a rather trying one. Slowly recovering from an almost fatal heart attack, which I suffered in the 1932 election campaign as Presidential candidate of the Communist Party, I had gone to California to recuperate. My nerves were badly shattered and I had to have complete quiet and rest—especially total freedom from all political excitement. So, appropriately enough, hardly had I landed in San Francisco than there began to develop one of the greatest and most exciting labor struggles in American history.

The San Francisco general strike grew out of the coastwide strike of the longshoremen, begun on May 9th and led by Harry Bridges. It being evident that the waterfront employers were trying to smash this powerful longshoremen's union, it was not long before the ten marine crafts made common cause and tied up the whole Pacific coast shipping industry, striking thirty thousand workers.

Now, indeed, the situation became tense. The employers tried every means to break the marine strike—scabs, controlled mediators, crooked labor leaders, police brutality—but the workers' ranks remained solid. The daily press screamed its hostility to the strike, while the workers in all industries rallied more and more closely around the embattled marine workers.

Frisco, by this time, was in a high state of excitement, and so was I. With my shattered nerves I was about ready to explode. To make the misery worse for me, I was unable seriously to help in the great strike, as I was so very sick that I could not even meet with our local Party leaders, except in a desultory manner. The doctor warned me that I must leave Frisco at once, on pain of another heart attack.

Daily the fighting spirit of the masses rose. They realized that a defeat of the maritime workers would be a disaster to the whole labor movement. The Communist Party, of which Sam Darcy was the California leader, put out the slogan of a general strike. General strike spirit began to run like wildfire, one local union after another endorsing the proposal of a complete tie-up, despite the efforts of conservative trade union leaders to check them.

On July 6th, the police brutally murdered two pickets, and thus touched off the already rapidly developing general strike. The workers' indignation was boundless. On July 8th, the truckmen, overriding their officials, decided to strike July 12th. They were quickly followed by other unions in San Francisco and Oakland, and by July 16th there were one hundred and fifty thousand workers out in the Bay district, and the movement was quickly spreading throughout the Pacific coast. Paralysis lay upon the whole Bay area. The entire United States was astounded at the magnificent movement.

The capitalist elements of California were amazed and frightened. They turned their every weapon to breaking the strike. In a day or two they confronted the strikers with at least thirty thousand soldiers, police, deputies and vigilantes. Their newspapers shrieked "insurrection" and yelled that the Communists were about to set up Soviets. Their government mediators and subservient labor officials set about disintegrating the unparalleled strike both from without and within, their police and vigilante gangs began terroristic raids against the Communist Party and other left-wing organizations.

By this time I was virtually in a state of collapse from excitement and my inability to give any real help. Then a new factor entered in to make my position untenable altogether. My being in San Francisco was not generally known and there was the danger that if the police or press should locate me, living privately and making no public appearances, this would play right into the hands of the red-baiters who were shouting that the Communists were trying to make a revolution. The disclosure of my presence could have been given a sinister meaning and might have had serious consequences in the strike. And to make the hazard more acute, William Green, like a faithful capitalist henchman, had condemned the general walkout and declared that "Foster is the man behind the strike." So, in the midst of the struggle, I had to be withdrawn to a less exposed position in the nearby country.

Meanwhile, the capitalist forces tore into the great strike. Their principal aides were Vandeleur and the other reactionary labor leaders in the San Francisco Labor Council. These people refused to call out the newspaper, power house and ferryboat workers; they issued indiscriminate trucking permits; they allowed many restaurants to open instead of setting up feeding stations; they failed to establish a workers' patrol in the city; they sent the Market Street carmen back to work on the first day of the strike; they did nothing to extend the strike along the coast. In short, they undermined the strike in every possible way, and their disruptive work dovetailed with the vigilante terrorism that was aimed at the heart of the strike, the Communists and other militant workers.

Finally, on July 19th, with the general strike four days old, Vandeleur and his A.F. of L. cronies deemed the time ripe to kill it. They presented a resolution in the Frisco general strike committee to call off the general strike and to appeal to the bosses to arbitrate the marine workers' demands. A bitter struggle occurred. Many rank and file delegates, full of fight, demanded that the strike be continued and extended. But the matter was rushed to a vote in the general strike committee, packed from the start with conservative officials. The vote was by a show of hands. The official count gave 191 to 174 in favor of ending the general strike. Delegates charged this was a crooked figure, insisting a majority had voted against. Demands for a roll call vote were arbitrarily refused, the resolution was declared carried, the meeting hastily adjourned, and the great San Francisco general strike was over. Next day similar action was taken in the other Bay cities. The thirty thousand marine workers were left to fight alone.

The general strike was not broken by the fierce frontal attack of the employers and the government, nor by the weakening of the workers' fighting spirit; it received its death blow from the reactionary A.F. of L. leadership. At the time the strike was called off, the movement as a whole was on an ascending curve. Greater and greater masses were either joining it or preparing for the struggle. Up to the day of the betrayal new cities in the Bay district were joining the strike. The whole Coast was rapidly becoming involved. The Portland unions had voted for a general strike and there was a strongly developing strike sentiment in Tacoma, Seattle, Los Angeles and many smaller Coast cities. Besides, the California railroad men were in a growing foment, so deep was the stir caused by this great battle generally throughout the whole Coast proletariat. If a general strike call had come from the San Francisco strike committee the workers throughout the Pacific coast would have responded. But the A.F. of L.

leaders dreaded such a struggle hardly less than the employers and they proceeded to cut it to pieces as quickly as possible.

The San Francisco general strike was politically the highest point reached by the workers in the great national strike wave of 1934, and the Communist Party played a vital role in it. Despite the formal loss of the general strike, the marine workers eventually secured a favorable settlement, and the trade unions strengthened themselves generally along the whole Pacific coast. It was all a very important chapter in the development of the American labor movement.

STEEL IN 1937

When the C.I.O., headed by John L. Lewis, began its 1936-37 campaign to organize the steel industry, not unnaturally it carried my best hopes for success. I was glad to see organized labor again taking up the cudgels in the slave-ridden steel industry. And I rejoiced when the campaign finally culminated in the U.S. Steel Corporation signing an agreement with the newly-built union.

John L. Lewis has shown real vision and ability in his work of organizing the unorganized. I have, of course, seen much of Lewis in A.F. of L. and U.M.W.A. conventions, but the only time I ever had any direct business with him was during the 1919 steel organizing campaign. As the new head of the U.M.W.A., he had delegated a dozen coal-miner organizers to help in our work, one of whom, especially capable, we had stationed at Youngstown, a particularly difficult spot. This organizer was doing good work, after long months of failure by others, when one day he got a letter from Lewis ordering him to come back to Indianapolis for another assignment. This presented us with a serious problem. It was very dangerous to withdraw our key man from Youngstown at such a critical juncture of the work. So I packed myself off to Indianapolis to try to talk Lewis out of his organizer.

But I did not succeed. Lewis said he appreciated our great difficulties in trying to organize steel without any real backing from the trade union movement, but he had definitely promised this man months ago to a western district of the U.M.W.A. and could not break his word. He offered, however, to let us have in his stead any two foreign-language-speaking organizers in the U.M.W.A. that I might name. As it turned out, despite the loss of this capable man, we managed to organize the whole Youngstown area practically solid.

My conference with Lewis lasted a considerable time. Lewis, who had been the general A.F. of L. organizer in Pittsburgh a few years before, displayed a keen interest in our campaign. He plied me with dozens of questions. Did we really have the mass of the workers organized? Were the Americans also in the unions? Would the steel workers actually strike? And as he quizzed me, getting a detailed report on our whole situation, a messenger kept coming in to tell him that his executive board was waiting very impatiently in the next room. I little dreamed at the time that Lewis would be the man to one day succeed in the great task of unionizing steel, a job at which in 1919, because of sabotage by the A.F. of L. leadership, we were doomed to fail.

The Communist Party, in harmony with its policy of backing every economic and political struggle of the masses, whether conducted by the A.F. of L., C.I.O. or other labor organization, gave active support to the 1937 C.I.O. steel campaign and was an important factor in its success. As for myself, the only help I could render personally was by writing a series of pamphlets embodying the lessons of the 1919 campaign and of industrial union experience generally. These booklets were *Industrial Unionism* (a general argument for industrial unionism); *Unionizing Steel* (organizing strategy); *Organizing Methods in the Steel Industry* (organizing tactics); *What Means a Strike in Steel* (strike strategy and strike tactics); and *A Manual of Industrial Unionism* (organizational structure and general policies of industrial unionism).

The real success of the C.I.O. steel campaign (despite its failure as yet to defeat "Little Steel") is a testimonial to the much higher level that this movement was carried on, in contrast with ours in 1919. At that time the campaign was the work of a few militants without powerful trade union backing. The big trade unions then were either indifferent or hostile and we had to begin our campaign with the totally inade-

quate sum of fourteen hundred dollars.* But when the C.I.O. undertook its campaign, it had the solid support of a million organized workers and was possessed of a fund of five hundred thousand dollars, with
millions more to draw on if necessary.

These greater resources gave the C.I.O. an enormously better chance
for success than we had in 1919. Besides, the political situation in 1936-
37 was far more favorable for the campaign. The right of organization
and collective bargaining had been written into Federal law, whereas
in 1919 the steel companies discharged their workers literally by tens
of thousands for joining the unions. In 1936-37 the steel companies
were compelled by law to meet with their workers, but in 1919 Judge
Gary haughtily refused to meet the steel unions' committee. In many
steel towns and states there were in 1936-37, as part of the New Deal
victory, authorities sympathetic to the workers; but in 1919 the entire
steel areas were completely dominated by steel trust tools who ruthlessly suppressed and terrorized the workers.

Added to its economic and political advantages, the C.I.O. movement had various others, such as the lessons of our experiences in 1919
to help guide it, a less acute language problem among the workers,
a rising industrial production (we had a slump), a forward movement
generally by the workers (in 1919 they were on the defensive), etc.

Notwithstanding our lack of resources and our great political difficulties in 1919, we succeeded in organizing the bulk of the industry
and in conducting the greatest strike in its history. We abolished the
twelve-hour day and seven-day week and we raised wages; but most
important, we showed that the steel industry could be organized in
spite of the ferocious steel trust opposition. And now comes the C.I.O.,
better equipped from every point of view, and completes brilliantly
the trade union organization work which we were not strong enough
to accomplish eighteen years ago.

In 1919 the reactionary leaders of the A.F. of L. sabotaged the steel

* We also started the great meat-packing organizing campaign of 1917 on a shoe
string. To begin this work, which resulted in organizing two hundred thousand workers,
the only resources we had was a promise of the Chicago Federation of Labor to pay the
expenses of our first mass meeting.

campaign and were basically responsible for its failure. In 1936-37 this same stripe of leaders again obstructed the organization of the steel workers; but this time the C.I.O. was strong enough to defeat them and to carry the movement on to victory in spite of them.

During the 1919 campaign I maintained that if the steel industry were organized it would result in the organization of further millions of workers in other industries. The C.I.O. campaign, with its big successes in auto, steel, electrical manufacturing, etc., which have resulted in some three million new trade unionists, proves that our 1919 analysis was correct.

The steel industry could have been organized twenty years ago, or at any time since, had the A.F. of L. leaders made an effort to accomplish it. But they were against it; they did not want the great masses of semi-skilled and unskilled in the unions. If the steel workers and the workers in various other mass production industries have remained unorganized and bitterly exploited for all these years, if the bosses have been able to whip many extra millions of profits out of their toil and suffering, the A.F. of L. reactionaries were alone to blame for it.

CHAPTER V . AGENTS OF THE ENEMY

In this chapter there are outlined a few characteristic experiences with labor spies, gunmen, scabs, vigilantes and police. As an active worker in industry and the labor movement, I have naturally come much into contact with such unofficial and official upholders of the capitalist system. The following incidents show how these elements operate against the working class.

JACK PETERS

In *The Labor Spy,* by Sidney Howard and Robert Dunn, the first stool pigeon cited—a sort of "Exhibit A"—is J. M. Peters of Wheeling, W.Va. Peters was a district secretary in the steel campaign and strike of 1919. Later identified as "R. O.," he was an undercover operative over twenty years for the Corporations' Auxiliary Company.

When we were about to begin organizing the Wheeling district, I requested the local trade union leaders to suggest a live man to take charge of the local campaign, and they nominated Peters. He was a member of both the Machinists' Union and the Amalgamated Association of Iron, Steel and Tin Workers, and was then working in a machine shop. About thirty-five years old, he was plain and unassuming and had an excellent record locally for honesty, trade union activity and long years of work in the steel industry. "Just the man we want," I decided.

Peters was always on the first line of the fight and an indefatigable worker. Nearly every night he was out to meetings till midnight, and six o'clock in the morning usually found him at some mill gate distributing leaflets. He actually worked so hard that his health was undermined, and this overwork contributed directly to hastening his death later on.

Under Peters' able and energetic leadership we soon had strong unions in all the plants in the Wheeling district, and eventually twenty-seven thousand workers struck, tying up every mill. All through the strike Peters was tireless. More than that, following carefully the line laid down by our national committee, he relentlessly fought the strike-breaking tactics of the reactionary leaders of the Iron, Steel and Tin Workers.

"A good job of organizing, a splendid organizer," we all agreed. Peters' prestige was very high among the whole steel campaign crew of organizers. I had complete confidence in him. Yet all the while this quiet, efficient, modest, capable organizer was a stool pigeon, busily selling out the workers to the steel bosses.

Peters was not exposed until after his death. At the time he was business agent of the Machinists' Union and president of the Wheeling Central Labor Council. He died from tuberculosis, which he had aggravated by overwork in the steel campaign. Widely mourned by the workers generally in the Wheeling district, he was given a big funeral. And then, the very next day, the bomb burst. Peters was shown to be a spy.

The exposure happened like this. In the two or three days between Peters' death and his funeral, a local girl, a friend of a Wheeling business agent, was called from an employment agency to work in the office of the Corporations' Auxiliary Company to substitute for a girl who was ill. She was put at copying undercover men's reports, and was amazed to find one from the just-buried Peters. She surreptitiously made a copy of it. Without delay, a trade union committee, with a plausible pretext, got access to Peters' room and there found many documents proving beyond doubt that Peters was a detective. The local trade union paper published a special edition on the astounding exposure. I, for one, could hardly believe it.

The steel campaign was infested with spies, and we looked sharply for signs of them. Peters knew this and carefully covered up his tracks. He worked diligently (as many spies do) to keep in a key position; he lived plainly, for he realized that by a show of prosperity he would arouse suspicion that he had questionable sources of income; he betrayed no curiosity in seeking information, and actually he often had to be pushed to attend our national committee meetings. A cunning, clever spy.

POLLARD

Jack Peters was an insidious stool pigeon; but a worthy mate for him was Pollard. I ran into Pollard, whose first name I never got to know, in Chicago during the big A.F. of L. campaign to organize the meat-packing industry in 1917-18, of which I was national secretary. Pollard was an impressive person. He was a cattle skinner, or floorsman, and reputed to be the most skillful worker in this most skilled craft in the packing industry. Pollard was intelligent and aggressive. About thirty years old, American born and fine looking, he dressed as flashily as a race track sport. An excellent speaker, a capable organizer and with a genial personality, he stood out like a lighthouse among the rough packinghouse butchers, most of whom were foreign-born. With his varied accomplishments he could have gone far as a workers' leader; but he had a rotten spot in him. He was one of those contemptible parasites upon the working class, a labor detective.

Pollard started out as a scab in Omaha during the national packinghouse strike of 1904. Clever and unscrupulous, he was picked up by the packers and made their star stool pigeon. For ten years he went from one packing center to another, breaking up attempts to build the Butcher Workmen's Union. Wherever the organization got a foothold, the boomer floorsman Pollard would drift in, and soon the fledgling union would go to smash, either by an ill-timed strike, wholesale discharges, internal quarrels or some other disaster skillfully engineered by Pollard.

By a peculiar chance Pollard was exposed. In New York City the union was beginning to establish itself in the local packinghouses. As usual, Pollard showed up, and another boomer worker who knew him remarked casually to the organizer: "Well, once that disrupter gets here, our union will soon be busted; he breaks it up everywhere." The organizer was struck by this statement, and a little investigation by him showed a trail of broken unions and discharged union workers wherever Pollard had worked for years past. A small union committee inveigled Pollard to a secluded spot and forced him to confess. He was then expelled from the union.

This happened about 1914. After his unmasking, Pollard disappeared. But he bobbed up again during our big stockyards organizational campaign, working in the large Chicago packing-plant of Wilson & Company. The workers in that plant, new to the Butcher Workmen's Union, did not know Pollard. And Jack Johnstone and myself, leaders of the Stockyards Labor Council, but coming from others of the federated craft unions in the packinghouse campaign, were also unacquainted with him. Only a few top officials of the Butcher Workmen's Union in Chicago knew him, but as they were not engaged in the field work they were unaware he had reappeared. So, Pollard joined the union in the confusion of organizing two hundred thousand workers nationally. He began energetically to build the union in the Wilson plant; the workers liked him, and almost overnight he became the outstanding leader in this big works.

So far, the Butcher Workmen officials who knew Pollard's record had not yet remarked his presence. Thus it went for some time, with Pollard's prestige rapidly rising, when suddenly he was discharged, allegedly for union activities. This at once produced a strike crisis in Wilson's. At the time we were preparing for a national struggle of the packinghouse workers, and the discharge of Pollard was doubtless an attempt by the packers to defeat our general strategy by forcing a premature local struggle. I became fully convinced of this when general secretary Lane of the Butcher Workmen informed me that the discharged Pollard was a notorious stool pigeon.

We got hold of Pollard at once. Imagine our surprise when the latter immediately gave us the same interpretation of his discharge that we held. The whole business was a provocation, he said, the object being to precipitate a hasty and disastrous plant strike. He announced himself completely opposed to such a strike as dangerous to the union, and proposed that his reinstatement case be handled in the routine way. Pollard then reviewed in detail for us his long and lurid record as a labor spy. He traced it all to the fact that as an ignorant young worker he started out as a scab. He professed great remorse and a determination to redeem himself. As proof of this, he pointed to his many weeks of good organizing work in Wilson's and his present refusal to lead the Wilson workers into the packers' trap. He backed up his proposals by going to the leading Wilson workers and explaining how the bosses were trying to rush them into an unprepared strike.

For us organizers the situation was a baffling one. We were sufficiently wise to the ways of trapped labor spies not to be taken in by Pollard's protestations of remorse and his good organizing work. But we were stumped by his refusal to go along with the packers' plan for a premature strike, as such a strike then in Wilson's big plant would have been disastrous. This actually seemed to be a friendly gesture towards the union, or a subtle strategy that went over our heads; because Pollard had so much influence among workers that he could have forced a strike even if we had denounced him as a spy, and he not only understood this quite well but told us so to our faces. Hence, although we could not trust a man with such a record, we were inclined to believe that for some reason or other he had actually come to cross purposes with the packers and was refusing to try to wreck the union.

This opinion was strengthened when we took up Pollard's case with Frazee, the superintendent of Wilson & Company, for reinstatement. Frazee violently denounced Pollard as a double-crossing rat and a spy. He would not let him work another day for Wilson & Company, he shouted. Dramatically, he took from his desk drawer a big sheaf of written workers' grievances not yet passed upon and declared that he would settle them all, at face demands, sight unseen, if we would withdraw the demand for Pollard's reinstatement. This we refused to do. As a parting shot, Frazee told us every packer in Packingtown was laughing at our defense of this spy. The more the packers attacked Pollard the more we were disposed to defend him. But we did not succeed in reinstating Pollard, the national arbitrator in the industry, supported solidly by the packers, ruling against us.

Pollard went on in the union and built up his influence to a dangerous point. We decided, therefore, that he had to be exposed. The job fell to Dennis Lane, national secretary of the Butcher Workmen's Union, for it was to his organization that Pollard belonged. Lane, himself an ultra-reactionary and highly unpopular with the men, feared the clever and popular Pollard as a possible rival. So he carried through the exposure of Pollard with especial gusto.

The actual exposure was highly dramatic. It took place at a full meeting of Local 87, key local of the fifty thousand organized Chicago packinghouse workers. Lane violently denounced Pollard. The workers, utterly astounded by the revelations, remained in dead silence. Pollard sat pale as a ghost under the withering attack. At its conclusion he arose, admitted Lane's charges, and brought forth as defense his remorse and his good union work. Then, fearing what was coming, he walked up the main aisle to the secretary's desk, turned in his union card, and stated he would serve the union loyally anyhow.

Pollard then started to walk towards the exit. But by this time the workers, recovering from their astonishment at seeing a trusted leader so unexpectedly revealed as a spy, began to shout out against him. Many arose in their seats. Pollard broke into a run for the door. For the last twenty feet he ran a gantlet of fists and feet of angry workers. But he managed to get out of the hall and he fled wildly down the street, pursued by several workers.

"Well," I thought, "that's the end of Pollard." But nothing of the kind. The slick and versatile Pollard was not to be so easily disposed of. He went to work in a small Chicago packing plant, and Lane, thinking him thoroughly killed off, made no opposition. There Pollard swiftly intrenched himself among the workers. This he could do, in conjunction with his own outstanding ability and persuasive tongue, by reason of a special situation.

During the years from 1904 to 1917, when the packing industry had been unorganized all over the country, the only plant in Chicago where the workers had succeeded in maintaining the union was the particular one in which Pollard had now gone to work. In the long non-union period this plant had become a sort of haven for blacklisted, militant union workers from the entire industry. The workers in this plant, in view of their record of struggle, had tremendous prestige among the masses of newly organized workers. Now it happened that during these open shop years this plant's workers had carried on a bitter guerilla warfare against the reactionary Lane. So, when Pollard came to work among them, he played upon their hatred and soon convinced them that he had been victimized by Lane. And, incredible though it may seem, he actually got the entire body of workers in the plant to sign a petition demanding his reinstatement into the union.

So great was the prestige of Pollard's militant worker friends in the old-time union plant that Lane could not withstand their demand. He had to make a maneuver. Thus he agreed to the reinstatement of Pollard as a member, but without voice or vote. Lane thought this would gag him and make him helpless. But the clever Pollard wrecked this scheme completely at the first union meeting. Arising, he politely asked the local president to please point out what clause in the union constitution provided for members without voice or vote. The president had to admit that there was no such clause; whereupon a friend of Pollard's made a motion that he be given full membership rights. This was carried overwhelmingly, to Lane's consternation.

Here was Pollard, whom we all thought done for, back in the union in good standing. The man who but a few weeks before had been driven forth from the union in the peril of his life, an admitted labor spy, was now returned as a hero. To anyone who understands the deep and unrelenting hatred workers have for labor detectives, this accomplishment by Pollard in getting himself reinstated must seem more than astounding.

And this was still not the end. The local elections came on in the strategic Local 87, and Pollard, with the backing of many of the old-time union members, became a candidate for local president. Large numbers of workers believed Pollard honest in his repentance. But we could not trust him and came out in open opposition against him. Only by the mobilization of all available forces did we defeat him by a handful of votes.

The incredible Pollard later dropped out of sight, nobody appearing to know just what became of him. And so I lost track of the cleverest labor detective I have ever encountered. Up to the last I was not sure whether Pollard was sincere in an effort to redeem himself, or whether he was making a super-maneuver to enable him to carry on his detective work more effectively than ever.

DONALD VOSS

When the McNamara boys, upon the bad advice of Clarence Darrow, Lincoln Steffens and others, pleaded guilty on April 11, 1911, to dynamiting the Los Angeles *Times* building, one of the stipulations with the District Attorney was that all existing indictments and proposed prosecutions of other labor men should be cancelled. But this agreement was violated flagrantly. Many others were indicted, and it was not long until W. J. Burns arrested Matt Schmidt and Dave Kaplan for complicity in the *Times* case.

The stool pigeon who turned them in to Burns was one Donald Voss. Voss was raised in Home Colony, near Tacoma, Washington. This colony had been founded by Anarchists, in the 'nineties, on a co-operative basis, but it had long since reverted to the principle of private ownership. I lived there a short time in 1912 and got to know Voss, who was then a gangling youth. He was to be singled out among the other boys of the village as a dull-wit, a sneak and as generally unreliable. One of his dubious accomplishments was clay-eating. Voss grew up in the midst of radical teachings but remained impervious to them.

Burns contacted Voss shortly after the *Times* explosion. He had brought several undercover men to Home Colony, Schmidt and Kaplan being known as Anarchists. He was also especially anxious to get something on Jay Fox, able editor of the local paper, *The Agitator,* and militant fighter since the days of the Chicago Haymarket. Burns' men posed as surveyors and hired lodgings at the Voss home. Thus Burns was easily able to draw into his service the weakling, Donald Voss.

Voss, because of his Anarchist mother, had an easy access to radical circles, and eventually was able to lead Burns to Schmidt and Kaplan. Kaplan was running a barbershop in a backwoods community not far from Tacoma, and Voss managed to ferret out this information. But Kaplan was not arrested immediately, as that would have alarmed Schmidt. The hunt was pressed for the latter, while Kaplan was kept under surveillance. Schmidt was hiding near New York City, but in contact with local Anarchists. Burns, through Voss, learned this; so one day, Voss showed up in New York and Emma Goldman stupidly allowed him to ascertain Schmidt's precise whereabouts. Then Burns picked up both Schmidt and Kaplan at the same time.

Although nothing was known definitely, it seemed pretty clear that the arrest of Schmidt and Kaplan had been caused by a stool pigeon. Some suspicion pointed to Voss, whose comings and goings of late had indicated possession of undue amounts of money. Finally he was exposed by accident. He had been stopping in San Francisco with Anarchist friends, and it so happened that when one of them left town he, by mistake, took Voss' suitcase instead of his own. I saw the grip when it was broken open. It contained many Pullman tickets, hotel bills, letters and other documents that showed beyond question the disreputable work of Voss. The latter took no chances in trying to explain away these things, but decamped as soon as he realized that his suitcase was gone.

Burns undoubtedly intended to use Voss further as an undercover man in the revolutionary movement but for his unexpected exposure. So Voss was put on the witness stand against Kaplan and Schmidt. Both were convicted. The rat Voss, his treachery completed, disappeared somewhere into the dregs of the underworld and was seen no more around his usual haunts.

TRAPPING A LABOR SPY

The 1919 steel campaign was saturated with steel company spies. We exposed many of them. One such case had to do with the systematic stealing of the minutes of the meetings of our National Committee for Organizing Iron and Steel Workers. A friendly contact in the employers' camp, whose name must still remain secret, tipped us off that the U. S. Steel Corporation was getting our National Committee minutes regularly, making photostatic copies of them and sending them out to its connections. This person showed us one of the photostatic copies and was in a position to get others whenever they were distributed. But he could not learn from what source the original minutes came.

Where was the leak? Who was the spy that had access to our documents? The minutes we were keeping close record of, only about forty-five copies being struck off, after which I personally destroyed the mimeograph stencils. Of the mimeographed copies, the bulk went to the heads of our affiliated unions and to National Committee members. The only others were two copies sent to the A.F. of L. and two that remained in my hands, and which I carefully hid away. On our National Committee there were three men whom I suspected of being spies (one of them, Robert Beatty of the Stationary Firemen, was eventually exposed as such), and I simply did not send copies to these suspected elements.

Notwithstanding my precautions, our minutes kept falling into the hands of the enemy. Therefore, I had to try to trap the spy, and I worked out a plan. This was to mark each copy of the minutes sent out, and then, when a photostatic copy of the stolen minutes was eventually turned in by our friend in the bosses' ranks, we could trace it to its source.

The job of marking the committee minutes was done like this. We used to include in our minutes the names of all those present at the meeting in question. So, to code the mimeographed copies of the minutes of our next meeting, I left out the name of E. N. Nockels, secretary of the Chicago Federation of Labor, and then had it typed in afterward so carefully that the difference between the typing and mimeographing could not be detected by the naked eye. The trap consisted of varying the spelling and Nockels' name (E., Ed., Edw., Edward, Nockles, Nockles, etc.) for each document and then keeping a record of the destination of each set of coded minutes.

We duly sent out the marked minutes. Then we waited impatiently during the week that must elapse before we could get hold of the photostatic print of the stolen copy. Who would turn out to be the stool pigeon? Our zest for the hunt was sharpened by the fact that our minutes went solely to high labor officials. Only three of us at the top of our National Committee knew of the trap.

Sure enough, our steel trust contact duly turned over to us the eagerly awaited photostatic copy. And there, big as life, was our code mark reproduced and evidently unnoted by eyes possibly searching for markings. Quickly we compared the photostatic copy with our record of the marked minutes, and this comparison showed unmistakably that the stolen document was one that had been sent to the national office of the International Brotherhood of Blacksmiths in Chicago. Investigation at this office found the copy of the minutes regularly in place in the files; but a little watching of the next set of minutes resulted in trapping a girl office worker, who was unceremoniously fired. Thus came to a successful conclusion our hunt for this particular steel trust spy.

A SCAB'S PAYOFF

For the same reason that employers glorify scabs the workers have for them a deep and blazing animosity. The workers hate scabs as cowards who are afraid to fight for their rights, as parasites who reap the advantages fought for by others, as traitors who desert in the battle. There is no term in the English language that expresses such concentrated contempt as the word "scab."

There are varying degrees of the workers' hatred for scabs. Bitter is their anger directed against actual workers who go back in a strike; but the most burning hatred of all is directed against scabs brought in from other industries and localities, especially professional strike-breakers. These are the real vultures, come to steal the bread from the strikers' children. It is about such a scab that this incident deals.

In strikes it is usually the strikers who suffer, but after the battle scabs are often paid off for their treachery. I knew of a very interesting case of this kind in a shingle sawmill in Ballard, near Seattle, where, years afterward, I was an organizer for the Timber Workers Union.

Shingle-makers, or "shingle-weavers," are highly skilled workers. Although relatively few in number in the great lumber industry of the Pacific Northwest, they were always very militant, and for many years had a strong union while the rest of the workers were unorganized. They work among whirling saws and, as they were then piece-workers and worked at great speed, their occupation was a dangerous one. Especially they used to saw off their fingers. At one convention of the old Shingle-Weavers Union a "show of hands" was had and it was found that a majority of the delegates had one or more fingers missing.

In Ballard the shingle-weavers had struck and fought resolutely, but the powerful lumber companies defeated them and destroyed their local union. The men, beaten and resentful, went back to work. The mills were loaded with scabs, many of them outsiders, and an extreme hostility existed between them and the returned union members. One leading scab, a professional strike-breaker who had decided to stick in the shingle mills for the high wages, was especially vicious in his attitude towards the defeated strikers. Protected by bosses and police, he felt quite safe in this persecution; but one day he came to grief in a way he little expected.

In order to understand what happened a few explanatory words are necessary. A shingle sawyer worked at two circular saws: one on his left and the other in front of him, and both spinning at great speed. With his left hand the sawyer cut the shingles off the block, and with his right hand he trimmed them up. Working between the two saws was very dangerous, especially as it was piece-work and done swiftly. Here many "weavers" lost their fingers.

Well, the star scab in question was working as a sawyer, or rather learning to become one. Beside him worked a union militant, one of the best sawyers in the industry. The two men hated each other and they quarreled as they worked. The scab sneered at the union, and the unionist returned the compliment in full. The unionist, sawing like clockwork and turning out three shingles to the scab's one, scoffed at the scab's clumsiness and estimated that after a few years' experience he might be able to earn a boy's wages.

This taunt enraged the scab. He was already deeply angered at the grace and ease with which the skilled union sawyer speeded ahead, while he himself blundered along vainly trying to keep pace. And this remark made him lose his head. Previously the scab had been more than cautious in keeping clear of the sinister saws, but now he grew reckless. Faster and faster he cut shingles with his clumsy hands when, bang, it happened. Awkwardly reaching for a shingle with his left hand, he grabbed the saw instead and in a jiffy three fingers were gone. That shingle mill henceforth had one strike-breaker less in its crew.

CHICAGO GUNMEN

Like other left-wingers, I have had many "run-ins" with gunmen in the gangster-controlled A.F. of L. unions. Once, in the packing-house campaign, I was on the list of a famous Chicago gangster to be "rubbed out," and was saved only by threats of my friends "to get" this gangster personally if anything happened to me. The following is a characteristic incident.

The time was 1916 and the organization the Barbers' Union. This local, like many other Chicago unions, was a prey of gunmen-grafters, who robbed and betrayed the workers by stealing dues and initiations, peddling jobs, selling out strikes, etc. The union, with several thousand members, was a rich prize, and a bitter fight for its control was raging between two gangster factions: one of them the beginnings of the eventual O'Donnell gang of bootleggers and hijackers, and the other a bunch of Sicilian black-hand gunmen who a few years later were to be part of the Al Capone outfit.

The union elections were at hand. Sluggings and gun-play were the order of the day. But suddenly both factions agreed upon a man for local president, the most contested job. The person so unexpectedly chosen was a newcomer named Buck, recently arrived from the state of Washington, where he had been vice-president of the State Federation of Labor. Buck delivered a rousing speech at a pre-election union meeting which made a big hit with the rank and file and he was nominated. The gangster factions, at a stalemate in their fight, made no opposition to Buck, both hoping to win him over later.

But Buck did not play the gangsters' game. He was for cleaning the union of corruption and terrorism. This antagonized both factions, and they began maneuvering to get rid of him. The Sicilian clique controlling the finance committee saw a chance to deal a solid blow at both their enemies, the O'Donnells and Buck, by adopting a proposal, in the name of economy, to fire several O'Donnellites who were on the union payroll. With real finesse, the finance committee gave Buck the job of doing the actual firing. They figured, and correctly enough, that the O'Donnell sluggers would violently resist losing their jobs and would direct their resentment against Buck.

At this point I blundered into the picture. One day I met Buck, who was a friend of mine, on State Street. Greeting me rather faintly, he asked me to go along to a little conference with the O'Donnell gangsters to tell them why their services were no longer required. He merely wanted me to help explain to these gunmen why they should give up their union meal tickets! After I caught my breath I agreed, and we proceeded to the office of the Motion Picture Operators' Union where the meeting was to take place.

The Motion Picture Operators' Union was then perhaps the toughest in all Chicago. Just the day before an auto load of its strong-arm men had an open gun battle on the streets with the Electrical Workers for control of the moving picture operators. Several were wounded on each side. It was only a little spat between two brother A.F. of L. unions. The union headquarters was like an arsenal. Armed guards stood at all the doors to repel an expected invasion by "Umbrella Mike" Boyle's gangster huskies from the electrical workers. Inside the office revolvers were scattered about the desks, and the two business agents, Armstrong and Malloy (the latter was shot to death a few years later), were in bandages from yesterday's fray. A fitting place indeed for our impending conference, with its unheard-of objective of firing the tough O'Donnell gangsters from well-paying union jobs.

We were duly ushered into the innermost room where we found the O'Donnell gunmen. They were ostentatiously armed, and also plenty mad. Immediately they saw us they blew up. Our "conference" was short and sweet. It consisted of violent threats against us, Buck in particular. The O'Donnellites wanted to settle matters then and there, but the Moving Picture Union officials said no. They had plenty of trouble on their hands already with the electrical workers. It might not be so bad to take care of Buck, a comparative stranger in town, but as for me I was business agent of the Chicago District Council of the Railway Carmen and working closely with the controlling Fitzpatrick group in the Chicago Federation of Labor. I had many strong friends in the labor movement, and an attack on me might have bad consequences. So we got out of the office with whole skins.

A couple of days later, however, Buck received a sinister visitor. The Barbers' Union occupied offices in the same building as the Chicago Federation of Labor on West Washington Street. The several rooms in its office suite were strung single-file-like along the corridor. On the day in question, as Buck was passing through one of the inner rooms, he was suddenly confronted by a gangster who stuck a gun into his ribs and told him he had twenty-four hours to leave town or he would "get his." Buck knew the gunman, a plug ugly at the time under sentence of twenty years for killing a man and out on bail upon appeal.

Buck courageously decided to ignore this ultimatum and the twenty-four hour deadline passed. That day I decided to drop into the Barbers' Union, a couple of floors below the Chicago Federation of Labor offices, to see how Buck was prospering. I found the situation plenty hot. Buck, with coat and hat on, was sitting at a desk in the employment office of the union, where about a dozen members were idling about, waiting for jobs. Buck's face was ashen gray. I sat down and inquired what was the matter. "Well, Bill," he said, "I guess they've got me. There are three gunmen in this room looking for an opportunity to plug me." And he indicated them to me. They had planted themselves at strategic points in the crowd. Glaring at us, their purpose was obvious. Buck had no gun, nor had I. We were at their mercy. I said to Buck, "What do you mean, they've got *you*? They've got *me,* too." I had walked right into the line of fire, so to speak. What was to be done? Evidently the gunmen were waiting until the workers left the room—then there would be no witnesses. It was already late in the afternoon and the workers began to drift out, one by one. Soon they would be all gone, and we would be left alone with the gunmen. So I said to Buck, "If we wait here the gangsters will shoot us as soon as the workers leave. There is nothing left to do but walk right out of the office now and take our chances. Let's pretend we're armed."

Buck agreed, and the two of us, holding our hands in our coat pockets as though we were clasping guns, walked out.

This action took the gunmen by surprise. They were afraid to begin shooting, because they thought we were armed, and also because the workers present might know them. Once outside, we started upstairs to the C.F. of L. headquarters with more speed than dignity. The gunmen by this time had come out of the union office. One drew a gun to shoot as we were piling up the stairs, but his companion grabbed his hand.

Buck hung on for a while as president of the union. His small group of progressives made a good fight, and we did all possible to help them from the outside. But the gunmen were too strong, the rank and file members too unorganized. Finally the gangsters ousted Buck both from office and from membership in the local union.

THE SHOOTING IN CARMEN'S HALL

Throughout the 1923-29 "prosperity" period the employers carried on an intense speed-up in industry. The A.F. of L. leaders fell right in line with the demands of the employers for faster and cheaper production. Strikes were declared obsolete. Labor now had a "higher strategy." More production would automatically bring high wages, short hours, steady employment, peace in industry and a contented working class. Marx was pronounced outmoded, the class struggle liquidated and the brotherhood of Capital and Labor established. Naturally in such a situation, wages and shop conditions degenerated, and the trade unions sank to the lowest point of morale they have ever known. For the first time in their history they lost members during a period of prosperity.

The Communist Party and the Trade Union Educational League opposed the prevalent illusions and sought to arouse the trade union masses against the fatal class-collaboration speed-up program of the bosses and the union bureaucrats. The union leaders replied by a policy of repression in the unions. The several years during which the no-strike policy prevailed were marked by the most intense inner-union struggle ever known in this country.

The opportunist Socialist union leaders joined hands with the reactionary A.F. of L. officials in putting through the "more production" movement. They greeted the rationalization of industry as a new and easy avenue to socialism and supported enthusiastically the speed-up, labor banking, employee stock-buying, etc., of the period. They were also the most militant in their attacks against the left-wing in the trade unions.

The Socialists were the first to use the weapon of expulsion against militant union elements. In August, 1923, in Chicago, the old guard Socialist leaders of the International Ladies Garment Workers Union expelled eleven Chicago Communist workers on the pretext that the T.U.E.L. was a dual union. Up till that time even the most reactionary A.F. of L. leaders had seldom or never expelled revolutionists from the unions. It was the old guard Socialists who taught them this splitting policy, then being used against Communists by the Amsterdam International in many countries.

The Chicago garment workers reacted angrily against the outrageous expulsion of the eleven militants and held a mass protest meeting on August 25th, in the Carmen's Auditorium. About three thousand were in attendance. Several I.L.G.W.U. officials came to the meeting. They violently interrupted the speakers, repeatedly throwing the crowd into commotion. With great difficulty the meeting proceeded and the workers, from the constant turmoil, were in a high state of tension.

Finally it came my turn to speak. I began to explain the meaning of the expulsions when, just as I mentioned the name of Sigman, president of the I.L.G.W.U., a man suddenly flung open a door on the extreme right front end of the hall and strode a couple of paces into the room. In his hand he held a glistening revolver and, before any one could stir, he raised it and fired three shots in my direction, the bullets lodging in the ceiling over my head.

Instantly the already much-agitated crowd was thrown into high excitement. Women began to shriek and men to shout. The crowd rose and many started for the exits. Fortunately, however, we on the platform, together with our ushers, were able to calm the excited mass and to avert the swiftly developing panic. Many might have been killed had the crowd stampeded down the several flights of zigzag stairways. Meanwhile, in the uproar, the gunman fled down the back stairs through which he had entered the hall.

Many present recognized the notorious gangster who did the shooting. We offered to present his name, together with those of the local union officials who were at the meeting, to a committee made up of representatives of the T.U.E.L., the national office of the I.L.G.W.U. and neutral elements; but the I.L.G.W.U. top-officials ignored this proposal. We sent a committee consisting of Alex Howatt, Otto Wangerin and myself, to Terre Haute to consult Debs on the matter. He promised to investigate, but nothing came of his efforts.

This Chicago affair was the beginning of a big expulsion campaign. The right wing declared open war against the left. It was not long before, throughout the needle trades nationally, large groups of revolutionary workers were being expelled. Other A.F. of L. unions generally followed the lead of the old guard Socialists in the campaign. Abolition of union democracy, expulsion, blacklisting and slugging of Communists and their supporters became the policy of A.F. of L. bureaucrats far and wide. The campaign reached its greatest heights in the needle trades, where it finally climaxed in the expulsion of thirty-five thousand New York cloakmakers and twelve thousand fur workers in 1925-26. The speedup and expulsion campaign—which lasted with varying intensity until the industrial crisis in 1929 shattered the Coolidge "prosperity illusions"—constituted one of the worst pages in the whole history of the American labor movement.

THE JOHNSTOWN KIDNAPING

During the 1919 steel campaign the struggle of the workers in Johnstown, Pa., was an heroic one. They faced every obstacle: slippery company unions, suppression of civil liberties, wholesale discharge for belonging to the unions, terrorism by vigilante gangs and all other union-smashing, strike-breaking tactics known to the Steel Trust. Despite everything, however, the fifteen thousand local steel workers, plus about three thousand steel-mill coal miners, organized themselves and struck on September 22, 1919. Their strike was so complete that for eight weeks the powerful Cambria Steel Company (now the Bethlehem) was unable, with all its resources, to put even a single department of its great mills into operation.

On November 7th, as secretary of our National Committee, I was billed to speak at a mass meeting in Johnstown. The mills were shut airtight, things had been quiet in town and we expected no trouble. But when I arrived at the railroad station two newspaper reporters met me and warned me not to go to the meeting hall. They said the Chamber of Commerce held a meeting the night before and decided to break the strike by violence. They had organized a vigilante mob, euphoniously called a citizens' committee, and were going to start work on me.

Pushing past these bearers of evil tidings, I went up to the Vendome Hotel, in the heart of Johnstown, where our chief local organizer, Martin Conboy, lived. I told him what the newspaper men had said, and he laughed at the whole business. It was just a trick, he declared, to trap me into leaving town, and it would have made a wonderful news story.

But I was unconvinced. I was sure something serious was about to happen. And even as Conboy and I sat eating lunch, the reporters came in and repeated their stories of projected violence by the employers. This time, more insistent than ever, they warned me that if, upon emerging from the hotel restaurant, we turned towards the meeting hall, I would be attacked. They urged me to leave town at once.

By now, Conboy began to take the situation seriously, as the reporters had previously been friendly. What should we do? We had no way of communicating with our people at the Labor Temple. Finally, we decided to go to the mayor and demand protection for our mass meeting. So we went out of the restaurant and turned towards the City Hall, in the same direction as our hall.

We had taken only a few steps when we were stopped by two city plainclothes men. These detectives told us about the imminent vigilante attack, said it would be at the risk of my life to go towards the union meeting place, and warned me to take the next train for Altoona. I refused and demanded protection for our meeting. They barred our way on the sidewalk. I then inquired if we were arrested, but they said we were not.

So, edging around the detectives, Conboy and I started for the union hall. But we had gone only a few feet when from various directions (out of the fire-house, restaurant, cigar store, etc., where they had been hiding) about forty men rushed us. Pushing Conboy off the sidewalk, they ganged up around me. The leader, sticking a gun in my ribs, told me to get going towards the railroad station, and I did. A dozen men marched closely about me, while a sort of advance-guard went on ahead and a rear-guard trailed behind. Evidently the whole business had been carefully planned. Conboy was left standing unmolested.

At the station, after buying me a ticket, and as the vigilantes were taking me through the underpass tunnel that led to the overhead tracks, the leader stopped, pulled from his pocket a "back-to-work" pledge card and said, "Let's make the son-of-a-bitch sign it." What a fine stunt if they could have accomplished that; what a big headline all over the country! The vigilantes crowded around me menacingly, but as I refused firmly, their leader soon abandoned the cowardly attempt to try to force me to put my name to the scab card.

On the overhead train platform the vigilantes placed me alone against a post, while several of the gang, all armed, stationed themselves nearby. Several others stood guard at the stairs leading up from the railroad station, and a score or so remained at the depot entrance to head off any possible rescue party.

We had about thirty minutes to wait for the eastbound train, and I was expecting momentarily to hear the workers coming to release me. It was a tense period. I figured that if they came, shooting would begin and I would be immediately plugged by the gunmen who had me. They could easily escape responsibility for it if there was a fight. But nothing happened. The workers did not come. The attack took them so by surprise that they were unable to organize in turn to try to free me.

About a dozen vigilantes boarded the train and rode as far as Conemaugh. They denounced trade unionism, marveled how a few "outside agitators" had so completely won the confidence of the workers they had controlled for years, lectured me on my unpatriotic activities and informed me that the steel company, the city officials and the business men of Johnstown were determined to break the strike at all costs. They declared they were returning to town to drive out the other organizers, which they did that same day. I continued on to Altoona, where I was billed to speak that night.

The deportation of the organizers seriously injured the strike. Due to the prevailing terrorism, it was several days before they could get back into Johnstown and resume their duties. In the meantime the company, with the help of vigilantes and police, succeeded in getting a number of strike-breakers into the mills. But the bulk of the workers fought bravely until the national steel strike was called off two months later.

My kidnaping created a sensation nationally in the newspapers. But nothing came of it. The Federal government did not interfere;

the governor of Pennsylvania, Sproul, was a Republican henchman of the Steel Trust, the mayor of Johnstown was of a similar stripe. And all the A.F. of L. did was to emit a feeble protest at the outrageous violation of civil liberty.

FREE ASSEMBLY

McKeesport was one of the many steel towns in Pennsylvania that suppressed the workers' right of assembly in the steel campaign of 1919. After a long and bitter struggle, in which we openly violated the restrictive city ordinances by speaking on the streets, the authorities of McKeesport were compelled by the great mass pressure to allow us to hire a hall.

But they hedged our hall meetings around with restrictions. The only hall they would let us hire was small and in a remote part of town; we were prohibited from having foreign language speakers and forbidden to hold our meetings under the auspices of the A.F. of L. The latter two provisions we violated openly, but a more serious problem was the bosses' system of picketing our meetings (as well as our union offices). Whenever we held a hall meeting the streets were thickly lined with company officials and gunmen, and every worker recognized by them lost his job next day. Once we considered supplying the workers with masks to shield them from this menace.

A meeting we held one night showed to what lengths the bosses went with their picketing. At this meeting, among other speakers were J. G. Brown (our general organizer) and myself. As we walked up to the hall the street in front was crowded. "Well," said Brown, "it looks like a fine meeting." We were surprised, in view of the campaign of terrorism then going on against the workers. We pushed our way through the dense crowd and entered the hall, which was jammed to the doors. Every seat was taken and the aisles were packed.

I felt there was something queer; the crowd seemed much better-dressed than usual, and more silent. But I thought that probably most of those present were skilled workers. Brown and I, with difficulty, got through the crowded aisle and took our places on the platform. We estimated there were about six hundred people in the hall and four hundred more outside who could not get in. Brown was chairman of the meeting. At eight-fifteen he rose to speak, in the midst of complete silence. Not one single person clapped. I sensed something unusual was about to happen.

"I call this meeting to order in the name of the American Federation of Labor," said Brown. But hardly had he spoken these words then, evidently by a pre-arranged plan, a well-dressed man in front jumped up and shouted, "Come on, let's go!" Whereupon practically the whole audience rose and stamped out of the hall, with threats, yells and cat-calls at us. Only four people remained, steel workers who had been discharged from the mills previously in the unionizing campaign.

We learned the same evening that the crowd, both inside and outside the hall, not less than one thousand all told, was made up of bosses, timekeepers, detectives, mill police, etc.—a general collection of company tools. They had been assembled by the superintendent of the National Tube Company, at McKeesport, and they hailed from U.S. Steel Company mills all over the Monongahela Valley, from Monesson to Homestead.

Under such circumstances as these, which prevailed nearly everywhere in Pennsylvania, open recruiting in mass meetings was largely impossible. Most of the work had to be done by small groups in workers' homes, in fraternal order halls and in saloons. The workers took to this method enthusiastically and signed up in flocks. Knowing they would be discharged if they came to our offices, they used to send us the initiation fees and lists of new members by their womenfolk, whom the timekeeper pickets could not identify. In McKeesport, as elsewhere, despite all such difficulties, tens of thousands of workers were organized, and they struck the big mills solidly on the day of the great national strike, September 22, 1919.

THE COLORADO RANGERS

My kidnaping by the Colorado Rangers (State Police), which caused a furor at the time, took place during the hard-fought national strike of four hundred thousand railroad shopmen in 1922. With its policy of stiffening the strikers' ranks and drawing the non-striking train and engine service workers into the struggle, the Trade Union Educational League had sent various speakers, including myself, into the field. On a national tour I spoke to scores of meetings of railroad workers. Coming from the West and billed to speak at the local Carpenters' hall, I arrived in Denver one hot August morning during the strike. I registered at the Oxford Hotel,* notified our people by phone that I had arrived and then, worn out by my strenuous trip, turned in to get a little rest before my meeting.

Things began to happen at once. Hardly had I got settled in the room when a knock came on my door. I opened it and three huskies in plain clothes, one with an automatic in his hand, stalked in. They ordered me to pack and come along. I demanded to know who they were. They said they were Colorado Rangers and brusquely refused to show a warrant. They laughed and said that the Ku Klux Klan had not got me—yet. I was by no means sure I was not being "taken for a ride" by the Union Pacific railroad guards; so, as we passed through the hotel lobby I made a bit of a commotion and my abductors had to identify themselves at the desk.

Then I was bundled into an automobile, driven off to Brighton, about twenty miles from Denver, and lodged in jail. I was not booked on a charge, and all my demands to communicate with my friends were refused. While I was in the front office the leader of the men who had arrested me called up Pat Hamrock, head of the State Rangers, and gleefully announced, "We've got him." This Hamrock was the thug in charge of the armed forces responsible for the killing of twenty-two

---

* Long afterward I learned that Bill Haywood had been slugged and arrested in the lobby of this same hotel many years before.

women and children in the Ludlow mine strike massacre ten years before.

Meanwhile things were popping in Denver. My friends were alarmed for my safety when I did not show up at the meeting. I had seemingly vanished. The evening papers announced my disappearance in blazing headlines. Hamrock disclaimed all knowledge of my whereabouts and denied that the Rangers had participated in my suspected kidnaping. The hotel people also professed ignorance. Rumor ran that I was in the hands of the Ku Klux Klan or railroad gunmen.

Next morning in Brighton I was loaded into a machine with four Rangers. We sped northward, with the high Rocky Mountain peaks far off to the west. At Greeley I was taken to the local county jail where, despite my protests, I was "mugged" and fingerprinted. Leaving Greeley, we again hurried to the north by automobile; but where we were bound for I had no idea.

As we were driving along an incident took place that showed the caliber of the Colorado State Police. We were knocking off about fifty miles an hour when another car roared past, making at least seventy. Shouts of greeting were exchanged and our car pulled up at the side of the road. The other car was going so fast that it could stop only about a hundred yards farther on. Four Rangers piled out of the first car and came back to ours. They asked who I was and then told my guard they were on their way to Canyon City penitentiary with two Mexicans sentenced to life imprisonment. "But," said one of the Rangers in our car, "how can you guys all go away and leave them alone in that auto a block away; ain't you afraid they'll try a getaway?" The others laughed: "That's just what we want the greaser sons-of-bitches to do; we'd pot them like jackrabbits."

After this gentle manifestation of capitalist law and order, our party resumed its journey northward. Shortly we came to the Wyoming state border, where we stopped. My guards looked about impatiently, and I soon gathered that it had been planned to turn me over to Wyoming police at this place. But the connections had failed. No Wyoming authorities were to be seen. So, with miscellaneous curses upon the stupidity of their Wyoming brethren, the Colorado Rangers drove right into Cheyenne, about thirty miles farther, and we halted at the County Building.

At this point I felt called upon to assert some of my alleged constitutional rights, though my experience along similar lines during the past twenty-four hours was not reassuring. I said, "Well, I suppose I get off here. You are officers of the state of Colorado and as we are in Wyoming you cannot hold me." The Rangers laughed at this, and one of them said, "Just try to go, you red bastard and you'll get what those Rangers were going to give those Mexicans." I did not press the matter further.

In the County Building the Colorado Rangers were told that the sheriff had gone to meet us at the border, but for some unknown reason had missed us. So, with more uncomplimentary remarks about the "hick" Wyoming police, the Rangers drove back to the state line. There, sure enough, sitting in a Ford car, was the sheriff of Cheyenne County, together with a deputy sheriff and a chauffeur. After a confab between the Colorado and Wyoming police, out of my earshot, I was transferred to the Ford car, and we started again on the road back to Cheyenne, the Rangers returning into Colorado.

By this time, it may be imagined, I was wondering what it was all about. I was particularly mystified when the Rangers turned me over to the Wyoming sheriff. Had I said or done something at my Wyoming meetings for which I was to be jailed? My wonderment grew when, as our automobile got back to Cheyenne from the state border, instead of turning leftward to the County Building, it veered off to the right and headed for the open country.

I wanted mightily to know where we were going, but I deemed it inadvisable to ask. All I could do was to check the speedometer so I could know how far we had come. This was possible, as I was in the front seat, while the two armed men sat in the rear. The Wyoming police said not a word about me or to me, and I could gather nothing from their small-time local talk as to where I was being taken or why. We drove for five or six hours through beautiful rolling hills, typical Wyoming cow country. It was sparsely settled, and I do not remember seeing as many as two houses together on the whole journey. The road was all new to me, but I felt that wherever we were going it was by a roundabout way.

Suddenly the sheriff told the chauffeur to halt and turn the car around. The speedometer showed that we had come one hundred and sixty miles from Cheyenne. The sheriff ordered me to get out. My two grips, about half the contents of which had disappeared in the Brighton jail, were thrown out after me. Then the sheriff, at last finding his tongue, said, "Now, you red I.W.W. son-of-a-bitch, beat it. The town is three miles down the road. If you ever come back again agitating along the Union Pacific you'll go home in a wooden box." He spoke as he actually was and felt himself to be, a company guard of the Union Pacific railroad.

So there I was, dumped out in the middle of nowhere, and more surprised than ever. So it was to accomplish this rather trivial end that I had been kidnaped and driven three hundred and fifty miles across Colorado and Wyoming, in flagrant disregard of all legal procedure.

I had not the slightest idea of where I was, not even what state I was in. I floundered along the road with my baggage. Soon an automobile drew up, driven by a traveling salesman. He was mystified to find me wandering about in this open cow country, but he offered me a ride. Making an evasive explanation for my curious predicament, I climbed into his car and we drove, not the sheriff's three miles to town, but ten. It was Torrington, Nebraska, and presumably the Wyoming police had unloaded me at the state border. I was just in time to catch a train to Omaha, where I duly arrived in a big blaze of newspaper publicity.

My kidnaping caused important repercussions in Colorado. The workers and liberal elements (but not the A.F. of L. leaders, of course) were indignant at the violation of my constitutional rights. The Democratic candidate for governor, Sweet, made my case a central issue in the developing state election campaign, stating that if elected he would abolish the State Rangers, who were responsible for the lawlessness. Sweet was elected and he abolished the Rangers by cutting off their financial appropriation. So Hamrock and his Ranger thugs lost their state jobs through kidnaping me. But no real damage came to them, because they were immediately hired as guards by the Union Pacific railroad, the Colorado Fuel & Iron Company and other big concerns. And the governor who eventually succeeded Sweet reinstated the State Rangers by reviving the appropriation for their maintenance.

During the hubbub of the political campaign the Civil Liberties Union organized a meeting for me in Denver. Hamrock announced in the press that if I re-entered Colorado I would be carried out feet first. I went, however, and the workers gave me a strong armed guard which, fittingly enough, took me off the train at Brighton where I had been jailed by the Rangers. A dozen State Rangers were at my meeting in Carpenters' Hall but, considering discretion the better part of valor in view of my strong defense guard and the aroused public sentiment, they made no attempt to interfere with my speaking.

A LOS ANGELES RECEPTION

This is the story of the greetings accorded the Presidential candidate of the Communist Party, a legal party, by the City of the Angels, in the election campaign of 1932.

Los Angeles had long been noted as one of the most reactionary cities in the United States. Dominated by great railroad, oil, motion picture and fruit-packing interests, it was also a haven for thousands of wealthy capitalists and big farmers from all over the country who came there for the mild climate. These rich elements, highly sensitive to their class interests, had been meeting with an iron fist all efforts of the workers to organize and to secure better conditions. In Los Angeles the path of the A.F. of L. was long a thorny one, and the Communist Party had always faced ruthless police brutality.

I was billed to speak at an election gathering in the Music-Art Hall on June 26th; but the Red Squad, headed by the notorious Hines, refused to permit the meeting. Hines' capitalist masters hoped our Party would be prevented thus from getting its election message to the receptive ears of the underpaid workers and starving unemployed of

Southern California. The mere detail of violation of the workers' constitutional rights of free speech and assembly did not in the least bother the Los Angeles authorities.

In line with the traditions of the revolutionary movement in such cases, our Party, unable to secure a hall, announced an open air meeting to take place in the Plaza, a small square in a working-class neighborhood, at noon on June 28th, and called upon the workers to demonstrate. At the time appointed, despite Hines' threats, three of us—a chauffeur, an alternate speaker and myself—went to the Plaza in an old Ford.

Our "meeting" was short indeed. The square was full of police; it looked as though half the Los Angeles force was on hand. The crowds of workers were kept moving along adjoining streets and not allowed to come into the Plaza. Into this mess of police we drove our Ford. But curiously enough, the police did not recognize us. So we were able to pull up to the point nearest the workers, and I arose to speak.

This touched things off. No sooner had I arisen then from all sides police came rushing. I said only a few words when I was yanked over the side of the car onto the street. Half a dozen police surrounded and held me. Hines punched me several times in the face while my arms were pinioned. Another policeman gave me a rap over the head with his club. They then shoved me into a police auto and whisked me away. I could not see what became of the other two of our group. The crowds of workers booed and jeered the police.

At the police station Hines told the desk sergeant, "Put this guy apart a bit; we want to work on him." And, sure enough, after being taken from my cell half a dozen times to be questioned by the police, interviewed by newspapermen and stared at by representatives of the American Legion and the Better America Federation, I was duly brought down to be "worked on." Three members of the Red Squad had the job in charge, their leader being known among the workers as the most fanatical red-hater on the Los Angeles police force. I never got to learn his name.

I was taken to the third degree chamber. The place was about eight feet by ten and was manifestly designed for the purpose of maltreating prisoners and extorting confessions from them. There was no window, and when the heavy door was shut the room was quite soundproof. One might then shout at the top of his lungs and not be heard even in the corridor outside. Here was where many Communist workers and other prisoners had been beaten up. Merely to go into this gruesome looking place was enough to give one the shivers.

For furniture the third degree room had only a small table and two chairs. The table was jammed tight in a corner and the chairs were placed against each of the two open sides of the table. This was a usual set up, the third degree method being ordinarily as follows: The police questioner sits upon the chair at the end of the table, while the prisoner is seated at the long side of the table. Two policemen then stand behind the prisoner and, when he does not give the desired answers, strike him from the rear. The fear of the blows coming unseen from behind is especially terrifying to prisoners.

The three Red Squad police proceeded somewhat differently with me than the usual routine. The leader seated himself and ordered me to sit down. The other two policemen stood behind me, but they did not strike me. The interrogator, who by this time had worked himself up to a maniacal fury, began to violently abuse me. He shouted, "Well, you god-damned bastard, so you came to Los Angeles to get a few police killed in a street riot, eh? We'll give you your belly full of that." And more of the same kind. I remained silent.

As this was going on, the leader of the three police inquisitors drew a pair of buckskin gloves from his pocket and put them on. I was much on the alert and at once noticed a peculiarity about these gloves—they had narrow strips of lead sewed lengthwise on the backs and halfway down the fingers. They also appeared well-worn from use.

Suddenly jumping up, the leader yelled at me, "You bastard, have you been searched? Have you got a gun? Hold your hands over your head so we can frisk you." I complied, and no sooner had I raised my arms than they were seized by the two police behind me, while the one wearing the leaded gloves began to punch me viciously in the stomach and groin. I could only squirm to protect myself.

After about a dozen blows the slugger stopped. His face was twitching and his eyes were blazing with hatred and excitement. Clearly he wanted to go on, but doubtless he had orders not to mark me up with the leaded gloves. After all, I was the Presidential candidate of a national legal party, with hundreds of thousands of worker supporters, and there might be an aftermath not so pleasant for Mr. Hines and his police thugs if I were badly beaten up. Covering me with abuse and denunciation, the Red Squad sluggers threatened me with a "real" workout later on and took me to my cell. Not long afterward a reporter of the Los Angeles *Times* called to interview me, and although I told him the whole story not a line of it appeared in his paper.

Meanwhile I was held on ten thousand dollars bail, although no charge whatever had been placed against me. The Communist Party, which was strong locally, began to prepare for mass protests, and nationally our Party also got into action. So Hines, or whoever gave him orders, decided I was not a profitable prisoner to hold. Therefore, the same night, at three A.M., I was suddenly released, this ungodly hour being chosen to forestall demonstrations by the angry workers.

JUSTICE A LA MODE

The I.W.W. fight in Spokane, in 1909, for the right to hold street meetings was, as I have indicated, an epic of police brutality and working class heroism. The workers were clubbed and jailed mercilessly. In the midst of this orgy of police thuggery and lawlessness there was one incident, minor in itself, which seemed to me to show up with special clearness the cynicism of capitalist class justice. It took place during the trial of Elizabeth Gurley Flynn and C. L. Filigno, I.W.W. members who were charged with conspiracy and confronted the possibility of six months' sentences.

"Gurley" Flynn, as she was always called, was in her early twenties and very attractive. She was a brilliant speaker and militant strike leader. At the trial she received much attention and the jury, all men, were visibly affected by her charms. Her co-defendant Filigno, on the other hand, was a plain immigrant Italian worker; a good fighter, but totally eclipsed by his captivating co-defendant.

The prosecution's case was so weak that the jury, although composed mainly of businessmen, found it difficult to convict the defendants. Half the jurors were for acquittal and half for conviction. Several ballots were taken, but there was no change in the lineup.

This was very inconvenient for the businessmen on the jury. For here it was late on Saturday and there was the dismal prospect of spending Sunday in the jury room. And for what? Merely a question of jailing a couple of "wobblies." Clearly a solution had to be found. Then a juryman got a bright idea. Why not compromise the whole business by letting Gurley Flynn go free and soaking Filigno? This happy scheme was greeted enthusiastically by all the jurors. No sooner said than done; the cases were separated and each voted on individually.

So Gurley Flynn was acquitted and Filigno convicted. Thus several birds were killed with one stone: the majesty of capitalist law was sustained by a conviction, the jurors saved their Sunday and they also were enable to express their "chivalry" toward a charming young woman and their hatred toward an immigrant workman.

THE WOMAN JUROR

The Communist Party, being illegal at the time, held its national convention of August, 1922, secretly at Bridgman, Michigan. Tipped off by undercover men, the Department of Justice agents and local police raided the convention, arresting thirty-two delegates, for violation of the state's criminal syndicalism law. Later forty more were indicted. I was among the number. The country was then being torn with the greatest series of strikes in its whole history, the war-time anti-red hysteria still lingered, and so the occasion was deemed opportune to railroad most of the top leadership of the Communist Party to the penitentiary for long terms.

The Communist Party, which had united front movements with the Farmer-Labor Party and many trade unions, launched a national mass defense movement, hired Frank P. Walsh as chief attorney, while the Department of Justice and the Michigan police gathered together a choice collection of frameup witnesses to convict us. The State, believing that I, because of my long activity in the trade union and revolutionary movements, would be the easiest to convict, chose me as the first to be tried. The charge was unlawful assembly and the penalty was five to ten years imprisonment in Jackson penitentiary. The trial took place in St. Joseph.

The Michigan authorities confronted us with a list of prospective jurors made up almost entirely of small businessmen, professionals and farmers. Consequently, we soon exhausted our peremptory challenges.

Then came a woman to be examined for the jury. Her name was Mrs. Minerva Olson and she was a militant leader in all the local patriotic work in St. Joseph. She had had two sons killed in France and was a member of the D.A.R. During her examination she defined a "red" as "an ignorant foreigner." She appeared very eager to get on the jury, manifestly to help carry out the prosecutor's aim of organizing the jury to convict me. To us she was so much poison, and Walsh exhausted all his skill to disqualify her. But in spite of our charges of bias, she was accepted as a juror. Our hopes sank, and the prosecution was obviously pleased.

The hard-fought trial lasted a week and attracted national attention. As it progressed, I naturally spent no little time studying the jurors, trying to figure out their reactions to the testimony. But there was small reassurance in this. The twelve faces in the jury box, especially Mrs. Olson's, looked cold and hostile. I could not perceive a friendly glance anywhere among them.

When the case duly went to the jury we expected a quick decision of guilty. But the hours dragged along, and no verdict came. What could be up? Our hopes rose with the passing hours. Who were our friends on the jury? We had not the slightest idea. Finally, at the end of thirty-six hours the jury reported; it was hopelessly split, six for conviction and six for acquittal. And so they were discharged as a hung jury.

Imagine my great surprise when I learned that it was Mrs. Olson who did the job! Wrecking the prosecutor's plans and upsetting all our calculations, she had from the outset carried on a strong fight for acquittal. She organized the six who voted for us. Her principal aide was a small farmer who, the whole week long, had stared malignantly at me. At one time Mrs. Olson had seven jurors lined up for acquittal, but as the jury walked out to lunch that day, a court official passed word to the seventh, an old and crippled railroad worker, that he would lose his job if he voted "not guilty." So we lost him. We were amazed, and so was the prosecution at the outcome of the trial.

Next day, my wife and I visited Mrs. Olson. She soon cleared up the mystery of her role in the hung jury. She was a firm believer in free speech and held that workers had the right to meet and discuss Communism if they so saw fit. She took seriously the idea that her two boys had died in France fighting for democracy. Besides, at the trial she had gained a new and more favorable conception of Communism.

Mrs. Olson's liberalism came as a great shock to the prosecution. They had not suspected the existence of such an element in the ultra-reactionary D.A.R. They never brought my case to trial again. Instead, they picked out C. E. Ruthenberg and convicted him by a more carefully sifted jury. He died as his appeal was going through the upper courts. The rest of the defendants never came to trial. But the state of Michigan kept us all under heavy bail, and it was not until 1933, after being eleven years in the courts, that our cases were finally dropped.

HOT SPOTS

Communists are particularly exposed to police frameups. Situations which mean nothing to other people may be full of danger for us. I have been in many tight corners, of which the following are a few I managed to squeeze out of.

Some years ago there was a big agricultural workers' strike in California, and the ranch owners had set up a real reign of terror. I was passing through San Francisco, and it was decided that I should confer with the strike leaders. There must be no press publicity, however, because if my presence in the strike area were known it would be a signal for fresh vigilante attacks.

In the strike center all went well until, by an ill chance, on the main street I ran smack into a reporter whom I had met in Frisco. It was impossible to avoid him, so instantly I decided to try to deny my identity.

"Hello, Foster," he sang out, "what're you doing here? I'm working on the local sheet; won't you give me a statement?"

As best I could, I put on a stony look of non-recognition and replied, "I'm afraid you've got the best of me; my name's not Foster and I don't know who you are."

He glanced at me incredulously. "What, don't you remember me?" he said. "I had a long interview with you the last time you spoke in San Francisco."

Then it struck me that to get angry was my best way out, so I growled, "What are you trying to do, kid me?"

At this, much bewildered, the reporter lamely apologized and made off down the street, occasionally glancing back and evidently undecided whether to believe his eyes or his ears.

The strike leaders were alarmed when I told them what had happened, as the reporter was unfriendly. So everything was arranged for me to leave town next morning. Early enough I got up and went out to buy the paper, expecting to see my name plastered on the front page. And in truth I saw even more than I counted on.

Big headlines shouted that the night before (while our committee was in session) some persons, allegedly two mysterious men seen lately in town, had set off dynamite under one of the ranchers' association warehouses. And then, right under this article, but with a separate headline, was the reporter's story of his peculiar meeting with me. It all looked very suspicious. What a lovely chance for the police to connect the two stories and to frame me for the dynamiting.

At first the committee thought I should call in the reporters and talk to them. But this looked to me like putting my head into the trap. True I had an alibi; but alibis count little for labor militants in such situations, and mine would have been destroyed by my damningly suspicious encounter with the reporter. I was in a tight corner, so I left town quietly. Strangely enough, nothing ever developed out of the whole matter. Thus, the small town police muffed a wide opportunity and I eluded a very serious frameup danger.

Another "hot spot," not without its humorous side, but which might have brought me a long prison term, was one that a friend and I blundered into some years ago in North Carolina. The locality was the scene of very bitter strikes, and when we arrived the whole town was in a state of internal excitement. A dozen or more Communist union leaders and workers had been arrested, and later several of them were sent to the penitentiary.

My trip had nothing to do with this local situation. I was on a national speaking tour and was merely driving by automobile through the town to make a train connection. When we reached the city the raids had already closed our headquarters and jailed our leaders and so, not knowing any private addresses, it would have been impossible for us even to contact the local people during our few hours' stay in town.

We took a room in a small hotel. The local situation was plenty exciting. Many workers and leaders were being arrested. If we were arrested also, this would only add fuel to the already blazing local persecution, not to mention the consequences to ourselves. And there was much danger of our being recognized, as my companion was well known locally and my picture had been running widely in the press.

To kill time before the train left, we went to a movie, after which we returned to the hotel. As we entered the small lobby, there, big as life, sat two State policemen. They gave us a sharp "once over" as we passed. "Well," said my companion when we reached our room, "that's that; they say the local hoosegow is not the worst, but we'll soon find out in person."

We gathered up our grips and went down to check out. Now only one cop was in the lobby. Where had the other one gone? Probably to telephone about us. We went over to the desk to pay our bills, furtively watching the State policeman the while. Suddenly he got up and strode right over to us. "This is it," whispered my partner, and while we waited for the "glom" we pretended a nonchalance we did not feel.

The policeman stopped right behind me. I did not look back, but I expected momentarily to feel him grip my shoulder. He seemed to hesitate a few seconds, while my friend and I literally held our breath. I saw the cop's hand reach in between us—he was about to seize us! But he only said to the clerk, "Buddy, give me the key, I want to go up to my room."

Talk about feeling as though you could be knocked down by a feather! As the policeman made his way to the elevator, my partner murmured, "For Christ sake, what do you think of that?"

Later, going towards the railroad station, we laughed over the whole thing. But we were mystified: never in our many years of traveling, during which we stopped at hundreds of hotels, had either of us ever before seen uniformed police as guests.

Still another "hot spot," this time abroad, was one I got into in Paris, in December, 1933. Sick as a dog from a heart attack of the year before, I was returning from the Soviet Union after several months hospitalization. In Vienna I had asked the Cook's Tours people to give me the address of a quiet, cheap hotel in Paris, being too sick to hunt one for myself. They had directed me to the Hotel d'Antin, in the Rue d'Antin, just off the Avenue de l'Opera.

I found the hotel satisfactory and prepared to stay for several days while waiting for a steamer. I could not travel alone, and as the friend who had accompanied me up to this point was to go no farther, I was scheduled to wait in Paris until I could contact another American who was about to leave Moscow for New York. So I wired this man in Moscow, giving him the name of my hotel, and we settled down to await his arrival.

All wheels turned smoothly until, a few days later, hearing a commotion outside my window, I looked out and found the narrow street full of people. Three automobiles had drawn up in front of the hotel, several cameramen were there and numerous police were holding back the big crowd. What could all this be? My partner and I guessed that probably a movie star or other celebrity was stopping at our hotel and this was some sort of a reception.

But we were soon undeceived. Going downstairs I found the small hotel lobby literally packed with police and newspaper reporters. A battery of a dozen cameras were trained upon the stairs and as I came down the stairway all eyes turned towards me. Edging my way through the crowd, I asked a reporter, in a French that was about as sick as myself, who was the celebrity they were waiting for.

"Why, don't you know?" he answered volubly. "In this hotel not long ago, the police arrested an American aviator, Switz, head of the biggest gang of international spies unearthed in France since the war, and now they have come to search his room and to take his wife for questioning."

That evening the papers were full of the case, with big front-page pictures of the hotel, etc.

This was a fine howdy-do for my partner and myself, especially me. Paris at the time was greatly excited over the Stavisky scandal, and this excitement culminated a few weeks later in fierce riots. The uncovering of the Switz spy ring added fuel to the excitement. Besides all this, the Communist Party was being sharply attacked by the government and the fascist organizations. And here was I, a member of the Central Committee of the American Communist Party, stopping at the notorious spy hotel. What a combination of circumstances for some officious French police inspector. Had my identity been known the least we could have expected was a considerable detention for investigation, a detention which, in my very bad state of health, would have been a severe hardship or even disaster for me.

The two of us discussed what was to be done. We relieved our feelings by cursing the bad luck that had led us to this miserable place, of all the hundreds of hotels in Paris. Then we decided we had better quietly move to some other lodgings. But we remembered with a shock the telegram I had sent to Moscow giving this hotel as my address. Telegrams to Moscow are always more or less suspect in France, and we wondered what police eyes might have scanned my Moscow wire, especially as the Hotel d'Antin was then so very prom-

inent in the daily press. Possibly we were already under police surveillance. In these circumstances we concluded it to be the better part
of wisdom to stand our ground, which we did. But our remaining
several days in the Hotel d'Antin were not restful ones. Nor did I
feel altogether at ease until, aboard ship, we finally saw the lights of
Havre fading into the distance.

A BRUSH WITH SCOTLAND YARD

My only tangle with Scotland Yard came when I was the delegate
of the Red International of Labor Unions, headquarters Moscow, to
the fourth annual conference of the National Minority Movement
(left-wing trade union), held in the Battersea Town Hall, London,
October 27-28, 1927. I knew beforehand that the Tory government
police would try to arrest and deport the R.I.L.U. delegate, so I had to
proceed cautiously.

After much quizzing and delay, the British consul in Brussels, not
knowing me, gave me a visa. Arrived safely in London, I made my
presence known to the N.M.M. leaders, who furnished me with regular delegates' credentials. When the conference opened, I took my place,
unnoticed, as a delegate in the body of the hall. It was a splendid gathering of several hundred militant trade unionists, although held in the
reactionary aftermath of the great general strike of 1926, which had
been betrayed by the opportunist Socialist leaders of the trade unions
and Labor Party.

N.M.M. leaders recognized several plainclothes Scotland Yard men
in the hall; they were sharply on the lookout for the R.I.L.U. delegate.
I kept myself lost among the large crowd of delegates and visitors.
Only Tom Mann, Harry Pollitt, George Hardy and a few others of
the top leaders knew me personally.

The first day of the conference passed without event so far as I was
concerned. I kept my anonymity, seated in the body of the hall, being
careful to speak to no delegates. To fool the Scotland Yard men seeking me, rumors were circulated in the conference that the R.I.L.U. man

would not arrive. And then, suddenly, late in the second day, I was sprung upon the conference.

It was done very neatly, the British workers having had considerable experience along such lines. At a given signal, all the doors of the hall were quickly closed and locked, and guards were placed at them to prevent anyone coming in or going out. Then, before the delegates realized what was taking place, a number of workers lined up in front of the speaker's stand and I, who had just a while before stepped behind the wings, emerged, took my place on the rostrum, was introduced and delivered my report.

The delegates applauded vigorously. The several known Scotland Yard men present sat quietly in their seats. Evidently, with the doors locked, a militant workers' guard in front of me, and with several hundred hostile delegates all around them, they did not deem it advisable to try to arrest me. They had to make the best of a bad situation. The crowd enjoyed their predicament hugely.

I spoke for about twenty minutes. After I concluded I was spirited out of the hall through a rear exit. Meanwhile, the doors remained locked and guarded. I made my way to the street with a delegate, who followed me for a few blocks to make sure I was not surreptitiously arrested. Soon I buried myself in the vast maze of London streets, and I saw no more of Scotland Yard.

That night I had the interesting experience of standing, unrecognized, in a street crowd on Mile End Road in the great East End of London, while a speaker of the unemployed movement reported on my afternoon's speech and related the whole incident of my appearance at the conference, to the vast amusement of the crowd.

FASCIST ROME

Twice I have visited Italy, and both times in bad circumstances. On the first occasion, late in 1921, things were in a wild ferment. The fascists, storming their way to power, were assassinating workers, burning labor temples, breaking up trade unions and creating a reign of terror generally throughout Italy. I was on my way back from Moscow to the United States, via Naples, from the first congress of the Red International of Labor Unions, but I passed unnoticed.

During my second visit to Italy, early in 1926, an incident occurred, however, which might have had serious consequences. There were four of us: my wife and myself and another comrade and his wife. Again we were returning from Moscow, and the most available steamer, to save a ten-day wait in Northern Europe, was one leaving Naples. So we decided to take it. At this time the fascists, having defeated the workers and peasants with bloody violence, were in full control of Italy. The Communist Party was outlawed and Communists were being subjected to brutal persecution.

Everything went well down through Milan, Turin and Venice, until we were approaching Rome early one fine morning. Our train was making its last stop at a station about an hour's run from the big city, and I stepped off and bought a morning paper. I know the Italian language a little, so I was able to make out from the great headlines and display news stories that Mussolini had been shot the previous day. I gathered that as he was attending a public function an English woman fired on him, wounding him gravely. The paper wildly shouted that it was a plot of the British government. It further reported that the nation was in high excitement, and the police were investigating all Englishmen in Italy and, for some reason not made clear, Americans also. All trains coming into Rome were being carefully watched. Several Englishmen and Americans had been roughly handled on the streets by hooligans. Rome was in a state of hysteria.

And here were we, four Communists fresh from Moscow, speeding straight to Rome and with less than an hour to go. What a fine chance for the fascists to link up the attack upon Mussolini with the Comintern or the Soviet Union. The situation was a critical one. Obviously we must somehow brazen the thing out. Before we reached Rome, we gave our baggage a swift going over, tearing up every scrap of printed or written material, however innocent in character, and throwing it through the window as we flew along. Then we sat down in considerable alarm to await our contact with the buzzsaw, the Blackshirts in Rome.

Our train duly arrived in the Eternal City and we piled out. Blackshirts were dotted along the platform, and at the exit we could see a reception committee waiting. Just outside the gate a detachment of about thirty Blackshirts were drawn up in a semi-circle. They stood four deep and were "staggered" so that the arriving passengers had to zig-zag to get through their ranks. They narrowly observed each person who passed them.

It came our turn to go out. Did the fascists know who we were?—that our party contained two members of the Central Committee of the American Communist Party returning from Moscow? Would they stop us? Loaded with baggage we started to run the Blackshirt gauntlet. And just nothing happened. Only the same sharp looks were given us that the other passengers received. Evidently we were unknown to the fascists, as we were not stopped or questioned. Getting through the cordon of Blackshirts without difficulty, we finally arrived at our hotel. What a relief!

When we were established in our lodgings, the first thing I did was to run downstairs and get another paper. This, a later edition, contained a sort of anti-climax. Doctors had pronounced the would-be assassin insane, and Mussolini, only slightly wounded in the nose, had stated that the matter was of no political significance. So the threatened wholesale arrest of English and Americans had been cancelled. All this explained why we were able to pass through the Blackshirt station guard so readily. Now we could breathe easier. But we did not feel quite certain about the whole matter until we were finally sailing out of beautiful Naples Bay, and Mount Vesuvius, with historic Pompeii at its foot, was sinking into the distance.

CHAPTER VI . . . . PRISON

This chapter deals with conditions, during 1930, in the New York County penitentiary, part of the huge prisons of Greater New York, which, including the city jails, reformatories and workhouses, contain a population of about seven thousand prisoners and are said to be the largest local prison system in the world. Here I speak principally of the sections of the penitentiary on Welfare Island, Riker's Island and Hart's Island. These island prisons are located along the East River, from middle Manhattan to the mouth of Long Island Sound. In this penitentiary Robert Minor, Israel Amter and I served six months, and Harry Raymond ten months, for participating in the great Union Square unemployment demonstration of March 6, 1930. Later on Mayor LaGuardia made somewhat of a cleanup on this prison situation.

CLASS LINES IN PRISON

American prisons are, of course, not built to hold rich malefactors but offenders from the oppressed classes. The capitalist system, based on the robbery of the workers and poor farmers, is the greatest stickup game in the world's history, and the capitalists who profit from it are the biggest criminals. But this mass robbery is justified by law, sanctified by religion and enforced by the state power. It is only those capitalists and mass scale crooks who go far beyond the rules of the capitalist robbery system—and then only when their crimes are especially stupid and flagrant—who are occasionally put into jail.

In accordance with the role of our prisons generally, the New York county penitentiary was populated almost entirely by workers, and declassed workers become slum proletarians. Ruthless capitalist exploitation and bad social conditions furnished a steady stream of workers, or the sons and daughters of workers, to fill this institution.

And the poorer and more downtrodden the strata of the population the greater their representation among the prisoners. The Negroes, oppressed of the oppressed, stood first in relative numbers, and after them came the poverty-stricken Latin-Americans.

Class lines were evidenced not only by the social makeup of the prisoners, but also by the whole process through which they got into jail. The poorer prisoners, arrested often simply on the basis of their "criminal records," had been kicked and beaten by the police in the station houses and railroaded for maximum sentences, usually without lawyers or jury trials. But the few racketeers and stray capitalist crooks there had been able to buy up crooked police, lawyers and judges. Those who could not purchase their freedom outright could at least get terms altogether inadequate to their crimes. And once in jail, they were able often to buy their way out. On Welfare Island and Hart's Island commutations of sentence were freely hawked about the prison yards on the basis of a hundred dollars for each month of sentence reduction, and it was a flourishing business.

For the workers and slum proletarians, a stay in New York's penitentiary was a real hardship—rotten food, brutal discipline, long sentences. But the handful of racketeers and "big shot" crooks, doing small "bits" to escape heavy "raps" in Sing Sing or Dannemora, "lived the life of Riley." On Welfare Island these well-to-do criminals had the best food that money could buy outside, they lived in the comfortable hospital, had their own servants, had special visitor privileges, and they ruled the crowd of prisoners through their organized gangs.

An outstanding example of class favoritism while we were at Hart's Island was the Tammany grafter, Maurice Connolly, former president of the Borough of Queens, in New York City. Connolly was convicted of participating in steals from the city's funds amounting to millions of dollars, and he committed his crimes so brazenly that all his pull could not save him from prison. He deserved a long term in Sing Sing, but served only ten months on Hart's Island.

While in jail Connolly lived at ease, catered to by the prison officials. He went as he pleased, quite free of the regular prison discipline. Any day he could be seen strolling about the island taking his exercise.

Upon his arrival at the prison he was personally escorted around by the top officials and shown the "sights." His home was in the hospital (where all the "big shots" were). There he had his own special diet and received visitors whenever he wished. It was said he often left the Island at night for trips home.

Connolly was kept separated from the rest of the prisoners. He joined in the pistol target practice of the guards on their special range and shared in various social activities of the prison officials. He treated the guards as though they were his servants, and they fitted into the role. The body of the prisoners cordially hated and despised this gilt-edged crook and favored grafter.

FOOD NOT FIT FOR HOGS

New York allowed the beggarly sum of but twenty-six cents per day to feed each prisoner. This was low enough in all conscience; but the garbage that actually reached us could not have cost more than half that, including all legitimate expenses of delivery and preparation. In jail with us were several food workers, arrested for union activities, and they declared that twelve cents a day would buy better food than what we received. The difference between this figure and the regular allowance found its way into the pockets of the Tammany grafters. Indeed, everything that went into the running of the penitentiary—clothing, bedding, building materials, medical supplies, payrolls, etc., as well as the food—was scientifically grafted upon. He would be naïve indeed who did not realize that the prison officials condoned and participated in this system of belly-robbing the prisoners.

The prison diet was made up mostly of meat, potatoes, beans, bread and rice, and it definitely lacked necessary vitamins and mineral salts. Only in summer did we get a few vegetables from the prison farm. Naturally, on such a diet the men's vitality and general health suffered. Especially constipation was widespread among the prisoners, many old-time prisoners being quite incapacitated from hemorrhoids. One, I remember, used to stop at his work, "push in" his protruding piles, and then go ahead again. No real farmer would feed his hogs such unhealthy food as New York City fed its prisoners. Cynically enough, the prison had a dietitian whose sole function, so far as I could see, was to draw his salary. The "big shot" gangsters and other fancy crooks in the jail who had money never ate the common jail food. They always had ample supplies of eggs, meat, canned goods, ice cream and whatever other foods they might want, stolen from the prison kitchen or surreptitiously brought from the outside. Some even maintained private ice-boxes to preserve their table delicacies. In the prison commissary, within narrow restrictions, fruit, cakes and tobacco could be bought by regular inmates, but few prisoners could afford these luxuries. Thus, in our dormitory on Hart's Island, out of seventy men only one-third were able to buy commissary tobacco and but one-tenth bought fruit.

Not only was the prison food grossly deficient in the variety necessary to health, but of an inferior quality as well. Often it was unfit for human consumption. Especially bad was the meat, which in summertime was usually putrid and fly-blown. On Hart's Island is located the Potter's Field of New York, and the great numbers of pauper dead are conveyed there three times a week, piled high on a steamer's deck and usually in an advanced stage of decomposition. On the off days when no "stiffs" were being transported, the prisoners' beef was carried by the steamer, exposed to the open air and flies, and stacked at the very same place which the day before had been occupied by ripe, dripping, pauper corpses.

Let the following incident show the condition in which the meat often reached the prisoners. One evening the Deputy Warden, who used to parade up and down the dining room ostentatiously, noticed that the men of one division sat at the table without eating their supper. He said nothing at the time, but later came into the division dormitory, lined up the men and asked what was the matter. At first no one answered, for even the mildest complaints brought a trip to the isolation cells. Finally, however, upon his urging, the men produced a matchbox full of maggots which they had gathered while at supper. The box had been quietly passed along from man to man at the tables, each contributing to it his share of maggots from the meat on his plate. Many men in the other divisions had eaten the filthy mess. The Deputy Warden, at sight of the crawling maggots in the matchbox, shrugged his shoulders and walked out.

To make matters still worse, the food was poorly prepared and filthily served. Everything was steam-cooked and about as appetizing as so much hay. The dishes were but half washed, with food from previous meals still clinging to them. This disgusting condition was made worse by the realization that also eating off the dishes were scores of men suffering from syphilis and other contagious diseases. As for myself, I avoided the rotten meat and wormy cereals by not eating them, but it was impossible to escape making use of the filthy dishes.

Among the prisoners the food question was always an urgent one. Next to the central fact of their deprivation of liberty it was their greatest hardship. In jail men can get accustomed to many hard conditions, but not to such swill as the New York penitentiary put upon the table. Even the oldest and most hard-boiled prisoners felt it acutely as a burning grievance, and more than once the tension among the men over it was so acute that a serious prison riot could have easily resulted.

UNSANITARY HOUSING

Formerly known as Blackwell's Island, Welfare Island gained such a terrible reputation from its horrible prison conditions that it was ironically renamed. Now this prison has been superseded by the newly-constructed one on Riker's Island.

On Welfare Island there were "accommodations" for thirteen hundred prisoners, but sixteen hundred were confined there. In the old cell block, built a century ago, the tiny cells measured only four feet wide by six and a half feet long. This gave barely room for a man to stand beside his cot. He could hardly walk a step. The cells were fronted by heavy banded steel doors that shut off at least three-fourths of the light and air. In summer they were stifling hot, and in winter cold and clammy. A prisoner, especially a newcomer, when confined in one of these cells, felt as though he were buried in a tomb. Altogether, they constituted a direct and swift road to tuberculosis and insanity.

There was no sanitary plumbing in the Welfare Island cells. The prisoners were compelled to use buckets, which were emptied only once a day. These horrible buckets were a crime against the health and comfort of the prisoners. In summer the stench was intolerable. Passing along a tier of cells, a person would be literally struck by a foul blast from each cell. The whole prison was constantly permeated with the horrible stink. This filthy and unhealthy condition had gone on for generations in rich New York City, in a land famous for its scientific plumbing. Many times, pestered by the abominable buckets, I wished the city fathers responsible for them could have been forced to spend a few summer months on Welfare Island.

On Riker's and Hart's Islands there was the dormitory system, with fifty to a hundred men in each dormitory. The overcrowding was general, the cots of the prisoners being only a few inches apart. So acutely did the men feel the crowding that often there were fist fights because one prisoner took even a single inch of floor space belonging to another. It was like trying to live in a bee hive. Such conditions, of course, increased prison vice. It was also very bad for the men's health. Often when one prisoner got a cold it soon spread to many more, and doubtless other more serious diseases were also passed from one to another because of the too-close contact. The lighting system was miserable, and we used to sleep under glaring red lights.

The bathing facilities were inadequate and the weekly process of bathing used to enrage and embitter the men. For some unknown reason we were allowed just five minutes from the time the first man entered the bathhouse until the last one left it. This meant a wild rush to undress, wet oneself under the shower, grab clean clothes (which usually did not fit) dress swiftly and then rush out. And pity the prisoner who could not hit the pace; he got a bawling-out, a violent shove or a kick in the behind.

The fire hazard was great in all parts of the penitentiary, especially on Welfare Island. Conditions existed similar to those in the Columbus, Ohio, penitentiary a number of years ago, when nearly four hundred prisoners were burned to death locked in their cells. In case of a serious fire at the Welfare Island penitentiary, the prisoners confined in the upper tiers of cells would have had virtually no chance for escape and the prisoners and everyone connected with the prison system knew this quite well.

Let me say a word here about the monstrous prison steamer, *Colonel Clayton,* which was used to transport prisoners up and down the East River between Welfare, Hart's and Riker's Islands. I do not know who Colonel Clayton was, but he certainly has a wonderful memorial in this notorious boat. To confine the prisoners, there was a bull-pen on the steamer not exceeding five feet by twelve in size, with steel walls. Into this small space were packed and locked as many as fifty men. We made the trip in summer and were jammed in so tight we could hardly move. The bull-pen adjoined the engine room and was terribly hot; it must have been a hundred and twenty degrees or more. Several of our group had to be taken out en route in a fainting condition and many more were just about knocked out on the three-hour trip up the East River. We were wishing that Mayor James Walker were with us.

The East River is the human refuse heap, the backyard of New York City. It is the home of the unfit, the defeated, the worn-out and the trapped of the huge metropolis. Its many islands are packed with institutions to hold the thousands of human cast-offs, broken and wrecked in this great whirlpool of capitalist society. Prisons, insane asylums, orphans' homes, places for the aged, poorhouses and hospitals for chronic and contagious disease, follow one after another along the river in melancholy sequence wherever they can find place among the many power houses and garbage dumps that line the river. A trip along the tragic East River is a depressing experience; it is a long panorama of human sickness, defeat, misery, hopelessness and death. And a fitting craft on this river of sorrows is the infamous prison ship, *Colonel Clayton.*

BRUTAL DISCIPLINE

The working theory of the New York Department of Correction was that to correct prisoners they had to be cowed at every turn and impressed by all possible means with a sense of utter worthlessness, inferiority and hopelessness. The men were not allowed the right to protest against even the most outrageous treatment. Discipline was established by the insult, the fist, the club and the isolation cell. The guards seemed to take a sadistic delight in abusing the prisoners. The prisoner who ventured to shield himself, if only by words, against the attack of a guard was kicked half to death by several guards and thrown into a punishment cell. Even if a prisoner merely protested to the Warden or the Department heads about any grievance, no matter how flagrant, he was fortunate not to be put in solitary for it. Consequent upon such conditions, the prisoners almost all believed that only by united action, by workshop strikes and prison riots, could they improve conditions, although they well knew the severe punishments that followed such movements.

On Welfare Island one of the methods of punishment for infractions of the prison rules was the "Number Two" cell. This medieval torture chamber was located in one of the main corridors where all the men could see it for the "good of their own souls." It was only eighteen inches wide and the same in depth. A man in it could neither sit up nor lie down. There he had to stand the whole twenty-four hours without food—a one day's sentence being the usual term. This was real torture. The presence of a man in "Number Two" always inflamed the body of prisoners, and his friends would take the greatest chances to bring him food.

For serious offenses there was the so-called "bing," or isolation cell. Such bings existed on Riker's and Hart's Islands, as well as on Welfare Island. Here men did as much as thirty days on bread and water, alternated every fifth day with one regular meal of the prison garbage. When a prisoner was thrown into the bing the officials thoughtfully removed his shoelaces so he could not hang himself in a fit of despondency.

Besides the brutality of the keepers, the prisoners were harassed by organized cliques of gangsters. These gangs carried on all kinds of grafting activities, with the connivance of prison officials. They sold narcotics and stolen prison food; they took a "cut" on the prison gambling; they peddled the better prison jobs and special prison visitor passes and they sold better cells and places in the hospital. Their leaders were also agents of the local officials in selling commutations of prison sentences. They ruled by sheer terrorism.

On Welfare Island there existed several well-organized gangs. Among these were the Irish-Jewish, the Italian, the Latin-American and the Negro. There was constant rivalry between these gangs and they often came into violent conflict over the extensive prison graft. Every once in a while some gangster would be swiftly surrounded in the prison yard or in a corridor and stabbed. One night, on Welfare Island, as we were eating supper, suddenly the dining hall doors were slammed shut and guards appeared with guns. We learned afterward that two outstanding gang leaders (who, of course, never ate in the dining room) had seized upon the occasion of the meal hour to knife another gang leader. The slashed man, almost dead, was carried to the hospital. As usual, no legal action was taken against the big shot gangsters. They were merely held in their cells a few days until the excitement among the men died down. The prison officials recognized and dealt with the prison gang leaders, first because they were a rich source of graft and secondly because they were definitely accepted as part of the prison control system.

The Negroes, of course, bore the brunt of the system of prison brutality. Their court trials were the most farcical; their sentences the most severe; they got the worst jobs in the prison; they were segregated in the sleeping, eating and working arrangements, and the guards made it a special point to abuse them. The prison segregation regime cultivated race prejudice by the whites and created a dangerous tension between the races. This resulted, during our term, in a serious race riot on Welfare Island. One day a large body of white prisoners, armed with knives and clubs and instigated by the big gangsters, suddenly attacked the Negroes. The latter, outnumbered and unarmed, were defeated, many of them being injured. The attack was well-prepared, and it is inconceivable that the prison officials did not know all about what was being planned. None of the white gang leaders were punished.

It seemed to me that the utter stupidity and brutality of the prison discipline was classically exampled by the following characteristic incident. One evening while we were at supper on Hart's Island, a Negro, a couple of tables away, raised his hand, indicating that he wished to go to the toilet. The regular routine in such emergency cases during meal times was for the guard to accompany the prisoner. But, in this instance the guard standing in the aisle six feet away ignored the signal. The Negro, in evident distress, motioned again. The guard threateningly waved to him to sit still. A moment or two later the Negro, manifestly unable to control himself, rose in his seat and once more signaled to the guard. Whereupon the latter came over and, cursing the prisoner loudly, menaced him with his club. The Negro sat down and signaled no more. A few minutes later we all filed out of the dining room. Then the same guard, noticing the place where the Negro had been seated, dragged him back, and with curses and blows made him clean it up. For his "violation" of the prison rules the Negro was given five days in the bing on bread and water. Such was the discipline in the prisons of the enlightened city of New York.

THE CARE OF THE SICK

In New York's prison system the guiding theory appeared to be that the prisoners were human riff-raff entitled to no serious medical care. Many were the stories afloat of men who had been allowed to die, practically unattended.

The hospital equipment was totally inadequate, and the prison doctors were, if possible, more brutal than the guards. The hospitals were used mostly as easy residences for big shot prisoners and were so occupied by these people and their friends that often sick cases could not secure admittance.

The medical examinations for new prisoners, lasting only a few seconds each, were a farce. No segregation was made of venereal diseases, nor was any treatment given except in acute cases. At Hart's Island there was a make-believe tuberculosis dormitory, with no medical attendance and with a diet totally unfit. It was indeed a hardy consumptive who could withstand the rigors of this "cure." Also, the drug addicts who, when "kicking the habit" were desperately sick, got no care whatever. Small wonder then that the prisoners deeply hated the prison hospitals and the doctors.

One night, at Welfare Island in a cell just below ours, a man fell sick with acute appendicitis. It was about eight o'clock and he groaned horribly throughout the entire night. No doctor or attendant came to him, and the guards paid no attention beyond yelling at him to "shut up." The other prisoners were in a great commotion and nobody could sleep. The sufferer was left thus for over twelve hours. Finally, at eight A.M., after an awful night, he was taken out. But, instead of carrying him upon a stretcher, they made him walk, actually bent double with pain and groaning feebly, about a hundred yards to the hospital. If he survived it was surely a miracle. If not, doubtless following the usual course, he was unceremoniously hurried to Potter's Field, with no questions asked.

Another day, at Riker's Island, a Negro youth, newly arrived and about to be put to work, told the doctor he had a very weak heart and could not do the heavy work allotted to him. The doctor, with typical brutality, inquired, "Do you eat well?" The lad answered affirmatively. "Then," said the doctor, "if you can eat you can work." The Negro was set to work on the dock, and that same morning he collapsed and died. The men called this murder. There was no investigation, of course.

Then there was the case of Bob Minor. He had been dangerously ill in jail from chronic appendicitis. Despite his protests, he was shifted from the Welfare Island hospital to Riker's Island, where there was no hospital. This was the worst of the three islands; on it was a mountainous garbage dump that stank up the high heavens for miles around; it was also overrun with hordes of huge rats. A fine place for a sick man. Bob was put at heavy laboring work. Result, an immediate and almost fatal crackup. His death was narrowly averted by an emergency operation.

The dental arrangements at Hart's Island were barbarous. The dentistry consisted only of extractions, except for those who could pay. A dentist used to visit the Island once a week. Hence, for the prisoners with bad teeth, there were many days of suffering between his visits. The official theory seemed to be that the men should time their tooth troubles to fit in with the visits of the dentist. Often I have seen men half crazy with toothache and absolutely no treatment to be had. During the summer the Hart's Island dentist took a month's vacation and there was no substitute to replace him. From my knowledge of this man I am sure his vacation enjoyment was quite undisturbed by the knowledge that nine hundred men were left on Hart's Island entirely without dental treatment.

WORK AND EDUCATION

To call New York's prison system the Department of Correction is a cynical joke. During our incarceration there was no attempt whatever to correct the prisoners, to give them even the most elementary education or to teach them useful industrial occupations. The boasts of the Department about its work of reclaiming prisoners were simple falsification. In reality the prisons were efficient schools for crime. If a first offender was green when he entered the New York penitentiary for a two or three year bit, he would be thoroughly posted on criminal methods and gang connections when he emerged.

On Welfare Island the majority of the prisoners did no work at all. They vegetated twenty-two hours a day in their cells—a demoralizing condition. Of the available jobs—in the dining room, hospital, clothes room and office—the best were controlled by the gangsters and their aids, who sold those that they or their clique did not want.

Most of the work was stupid and useless, of the "Stephen Girard" brand, such as moving things from one place to another and then back again. Thus Amter, Raymond and I, in the farm gang, spent many days weeding the potato and corn fields after the crops had been harvested. Often they had our gang hauling the farm wagons about by hand, while the horses grazed contentedly in nearby fields.

On Hart's Island there were a few so-called industries—shoe, bed, brush and clothes-making—but they were altogether farcical. The longer a man worked in them the more incapacitated he became for employment in real industry outside. No trades were taught the prisoners. Nor were the men paid a cent for their work. One of the worst mental tortures for a prisoner is to know that his family, with the breadwinner gone, is destitute and that he is totally unable to help, and the New York prisons intensified this gnawing worry.

Prison pastimes were few. On Welfare Island a daily hour for exercise and baseball, with motion pictures twice a week when baseball could not be played. On Hart's Island pretty much the same. On Sundays, church for the minority who were interested to attend. On Decoration Day and the Fourth of July, a band concert; on Christmas, a hall concert or show. A dull, deadly routine; in the overwhelming idle time nothing to do but play cards and reminisce over criminal exploits and plans.

The prison regime had a particularly disastrous effect upon the young prisoners. On Hart's Island there was a special dormitory as sleeping quarters for the boys, but they mixed with the older ones at all other times. The crops of boys grew into social weeds in the rank prison air. Coming mostly from the slums, the orphan homes and the State reformatories, these dark products of capitalism ripened into criminals. The boys were given absolutely no education or industrial training. They were treated as already developed outlaws for whom society had no place but the prison. The boys learned rapidly from the men all the methods, traditions and gang affiliations of the underworld. For the most part, they considered their lives definitely and inexorably shaped for criminal careers, and in the main they were not mistaken.

Typical of the many prison-made criminals was "Little Mac." I knew him and we often talked together. He was born in the slums of New Orleans, of an impoverished family of workers. Growing up with no schooling and in a poisonous environment, he was arrested in his early teens for a petty offense and sent to a reformatory. There he was thoroughly instructed in the ways of crime. From then on it was one prison sentence after the other for him. When I knew him he was finishing his twelfth term, or a total of twenty-five years, although he was only forty-six years old. He had been in eight penitentiaries during his long imprisonment and had not even learned to read or write; nor had he been taught any trade.

But "Little Mac's" criminal education was quite complete. He was an expert pickpocket and sneak thief. He was also a drug addict and an all around sex degenerate, accomplishments he had learned in prison. He was released while we were in jail, and during the last weeks of his term he counted the diminishing days as impatiently as any first termer. He declared he was through with prison life for good and all; he would go home to his old, heart-sick mother and find himself a job. But this was only his routine; the reality was that he was hopelessly caught in the net of a criminal's life and could not escape. He was free only two hours, or just long enough to peddle his prison suit on the Bowery for a dollar and a half (as released prisoners are given only twenty-five cents) and then to hasten to "Sixty-two" Street to buy a deck of heroin. There he was arrested by a detective who, knowing his weakness, had followed him. "Little Mac's" thirteenth term was for two years, and he set out to "do" it, kidding himself the while that when he finally got out he would go home to New Orleans, get a job, set up a home and all the rest of it.

DRUG ADDICTS

Drug addicts are sick people who require curative care, but New York treats them as criminals. Its theory, which coincides with that of the Federal government, is that not only the sale but also the use of narcotic drugs is a crime. Arrested drug users are ordinarily given sentences up to two years. An addict does not have to be caught actually taking the drug or having it in his possession; it is enough that he be found carrying a common eye-dropper or a teaspoon, things used in the practice of his habit. Some have even been convicted on blood tests.

The New York penitentiary was crowded with drug addicts, or "junkies" or "cokies," as they are called. Fully half the prisoners were victims of the habit, and in our dormitory at Hart's Island they ran to eighty per cent. The place might well be called a prison for addicts. Practically all these unfortunates were workers or the poorer strata of criminals, the large numbers of addicts among the wealthy being left unmolested by the police.

The junkies use every known narcotic drug—opium, cocaine, morphine, marihuana and many others. But the master drug of all is heroin. Almost unanimously the junkies sang the praises of its magic lure. They declared it was the only real habit-forming drug, the enslaving powers of opium and other narcotics being mild in comparison. Addicts often sat with me for hours and related the beauties of their drug-god, heroin, much as a love-sick man separated from his woman might talk of her.

Every junkie that I knew declared that heroin produces no alluring dreams like opium, or wild fantasies like cocaine. They pictured its effect as one of indescribable well-being. Inoculated with the drug, they were completely at peace with themselves and the world. They called it "God's medicine that cures all diseases and all worries." Such were the sensations, however, only in the early stages of the habit; later on, they said they had to have the drug merely to keep "normal."

The prison treatment for the drug habit was a compulsory tapering-off process, in which the addicts received diminished quantities of heroin each day for a week. But this was almost as bad as the "cold turkey" method in which the drug was shut off suddenly and completely. In either case the addicts remained desperately sick for many weeks. Sometimes they became despondent and committed suicide.

The only way the drug habit can be cured, if at all, is by voluntary action of the addict, by a great effort of his will. Imprisonment, no matter how long and severe, is quite useless to cure the confirmed heroin taker. It tortures him, but it does not break his habit. After several months' imprisonment without drugs and after unspeakable suffering, a heroin addict apparently loses the physical craving for his beloved drug, but the mental longing persists for years undiminished.

Addicts have told me they would never abandon heroin, regardless of the consequences. They counted as quite negligible imprisonment, poverty, physical breakdown, social ostracism and early death. The New York penitentiary held hundreds of heroin addicts who had done from two to a dozen long terms in jail, but they had not the slightest intention of giving up the drug. Heroin was the goal of all their ambitions, the center of their entire cosmos, their only reason for living.

There was a young, fine-built Finn. He had been taking the drug only a few months when he was arrested and given the usual two years. He and I talked much about his habit. I warned him of the many drug wrecks all around, and their miserable life, mostly spent in jail. But all my talk was utterly useless. When he spoke of heroin his eyes glittered. He said he would get it at all costs when he got out. The world was well lost if only he had heroin.

Women, food, drink, theater, travel, the usual joys of life mean very little to the heroin user. One day, on Hart's Island, this was graphically illustrated. Nearby lies City Island, where were anchored many palatial yachts, including Morgan's and Astor's. On this day a big steamer yacht, after loading aboard a gay party, headed away towards the sea. A prisoner, eying it enviously, said, "Jesus, I'd like to be on that one. I'll bet there'll be plenty of wine, women and song." Whereupon a junkie in our farm gang looked at him scornfully and remarked, "Listen, do you know what I'd like? If we were all on that yacht together you guys could enjoy yourselves in the swell cabins with the fine dames and booze and grub; but give me plenty of heroin and you could put me down in the hold alone, in the filthy bilge or anywhere, and I'd have a much better time than you." Every junkie would agree with that sentiment.

With such a craving, the addict moves heaven and earth to get his supply of heroin. He will commit crime, if necessary. And unless he is an extraordinary individual he is a helpless victim in the hands of the police, who only have to withhold his supply of drugs to make him tell all he knows. This is why cleverer criminals beware of drug addicts in their organizations.

In prison, if the addict had the price he found narcotic bootleggers on hand to serve him. They kept the New York prisons well supplied. They got the stuff in by a variety of means—by throwing it off the Queensboro Bridge or from motor boats, by sending it in with articles received through visitors, by saturating letters with it, etc. But the main quantities were carried in directly by prison guards who worked with the prison narcotics rings. This was one of the prison officials' richest sources of graft, and everybody knew about it.

On Welfare Island one could see, any day during the exercise periods, addicts freely buying the dope and injecting it into their arms. There was no secrecy whatever about the matter. One of the terrible features of such indiscriminate use of narcotics was that the men passed the blood-covered safety-pin, which served for a hypodermic needle, from one to another without any sort of sterilization. Thus, as there were many syphilitics among them, they must have freely infected each other. Many times I saw addicts with great ulcers on their arms where they had injected heroin into themselves by this most unsanitary and dangerous method. In our dormitory there were several known syphilitics, and they all freely used the safety-pin with other addicts.

When released, the poorer addict finds himself in a difficult position. Broke and incapacitated for work through drug-using and jail terms, he often is driven immediately into crime to get money for his supply of heroin. And the drug habit is an expensive one, costing a minimum of three to five dollars a day. The usual thing for an addict upon his release from a "bit" in the New York "pen" was to hasten down from the parole office to the Bowery, trade in his prison suit for a dollar or so "to boot," and then streak it up to New York's bootleg retail narcotic market on "Sixty-two" Street, as they call it, west of Amsterdam Avenue, and buy himself a "deck of junk." The police were well aware of all this and often followed the addicts directly from the parole office and arrested them immediately after they bought their "junk." Cases were common of addicts being seized within a few hours after finishing a two years' sentence and then being sentenced to two more. Often also addicts were framed up and jailed by members of the Federal and City Narcotic squads to whom they refused to pay graft. An addict's word in court was worth precisely nothing against that of a policeman.

To make headway against the terrible drug-taking evil, the basic thing to do is to treat the addicts upon the basis of hospitalization, rather than of imprisonment. In my opinion addicts should be enabled to buy their minimum supply of drugs from city clinics, and the bootleg narcotic traffic should be ruthlessly exterminated. But more than this is necessary. The heroin addicts, as part of their cure, must be accorded an opportunity to work and live free of grafting police and drug peddlers. As things stand, the situation becomes constantly worse. The number of addicts grows steadily, and the maze of exploiting drug peddlers parasitically sucking the life out of these unfortunates expands accordingly. It is just one more of the insoluble problems of a decadent capitalist system.

PRISON VICE

Sex abnormalities were widespread in the New York penitentiary, as in other American prisons. Every known substitute for normal sex relations was practiced by the sex-starved prisoners. The youthful prisoners on Welfare Island were especially endangered, for to a sex hungry prison "wolf" a young lad has very much of the allure of a girl.

On Welfare Island in 1930 there were over one hundred known homosexuals, who made up a special prisoners' division. Like the drug addicts, they were barbarously treated as criminals. These unfortunate creatures, with the bodies of men and a monstrous caricature of women's instincts, called themselves by the names of actresses, queens and other famous women, and bought whatever women's articles were available in the prison commissary. Whenever they could, they let their hair grow long and they powdered and painted. The other prisoners called them "girls" or "fags," and always referred to them in the feminine gender.

The fags worked in the laundry, and lived apart in the prison. But they managed to carry on violent flirtations with the other prisoners. From the laundry windows, or as they went to and fro between their work place and their quarters, they would make love signals to the objects of their strange affections. Many fags took a delight in knitting socks and sewing clothes for their men sweethearts.

Despite the official segregation, there was much direct contact between the fags and other prisoners. The rendezvous was in the hospital, and the big shot gangsters were usually the other parties to the "love-making." They would select one of the more comely of the "girls," and through a keeper she would be instructed to report sick and be sent to the hospital, where the big shot prisoners lived. I stayed one night in the Welfare Island hospital and there were half a dozen prisoners being entertained by a smirking fag. Next day, "cured," she was returned to her own quarters. Of course, the guards knew all about such affairs. The fags were paid in cigarettes.

Only those fags were segregated into the special gang of perverts who had been arrested outside for their special offense, or who were actually caught at it in prison. But there were many more of them, arrested for other offenses, among the body of prisoners. These were not segregated, however, because as the prison tradition had it, in the past a prisoner, unjustly segregated as a fag, had won a heavy damage suit against the city. The unsegregated fags were prolific sources of vice, and also of fights between rivals for their affections.

On Hart's Island there was an unsegregated fag in our dormitory, a young Puerto Rican. "She" had all the usual characteristics. "She" looked like a girl, affected feminine ways and was never done singing in her high falsetto voice. I used to marvel at her gaiety, for measured by any normal standard she had enough difficulties to take the song off anyone's lips. Besides being a sex pervert, she was doing a two years' sentence, she was a drug addict and, as if all this were not enough, she was also being eaten up by a malignant case of syphilis. Yet she laughed and seemed carefree. I concluded that in addition to her other troubles she must also be insane. This fag carried on a love affair with a syphilitic drug addict in our dormitory, the two being inseparable companions. In the farm gang, where we worked, they were to be seen sitting hand in hand under the trees, a true prison love idyll. Her lover guarded her jealously from the attention of other prisoners, and he had need to.

THE PRISON GUARD

The occupation of guard in a prison usually brings out all that is mean and brutal in a man. With practically helpless human beings under their domination, few are the prison guards or "screws" who do not become intolerable tyrants. In the New York penitentiary the guards, for the most part, rode roughshod over the prisoners, freely venting their spleen upon them and making them the victims of their miserable will-to-power.

Guards lorded it over their helpless prisoner charges, and dared to bully men whom they would quail before in ordinary life. To the guards a prisoner had no rights that they were bound to respect. Some of them sold dope to the prisoners, others grafted upon them in various ways and some even played up to the prisoners' womenfolk who came to visit them. They were callous to the mental and physical suffering of the prisoners; and the insult, the blow and the isolation cells were their answers to those prisoners who crossed their imperious wills. Of course, some guards retained their balance and treated the prisoners with consideration; but these were decidedly not the predominant type.

The degeneration of the guards into petty tyrants **was** facilitated by the universal rule of the prison officials that the guard was always right when his word was pitted against that of a prisoner. This vicious system put a premium upon arbitrary action by the guards. Incidents that were actually trivial in character became transformed into serious breaches of discipline when related by the guards to the Warden. The latter always accepted these cock-and-bull stories for truth as a matter of course. The prisoner, accused by a guard, might as well keep his mouth shut. Only in the most obvious and scandalous cases of brutality would the prison officials accept the word of a prisoner.

Just a little incident to illustrate the arbitrariness of the guards: One day we were at the bath-house, engaged in the usual weekly scramble to get a bath in the allotted five minutes. Rushing along with the rest, trying to beat the deadline time, I got into the clean overalls given me, only to find that they hardly reached below my knees. Politely, I requested a pair that would fit me. The guard's answer was, "You son of a bitch you'll wear the ones you've got, and if you say another word I'll bust you in the nose." So that was that. I had to wear the knee-high overalls, at least until I reached our dormitory, where I dug up a better pair from a friendly prisoner.

Naturally, the prisoners hated the guards deeply, save, of course, the humane ones. There was one guard who especially aroused my animosity. Towards the prisoners he bore himself with an offensive air of cynical aloofness and disdain, seeming to consider them as inferior beings unworthy of his serious attention. He would look right through a prisoner without giving a sign that he even saw him. His reputation was that of a strict disciplinarian over his work gang. Altogether I sized him up as just the kind of man who would make a real strike-breaker or company gunman.

This guard was not attached to our division, and I was thankful for that. In the months that Amter, Raymond and I spent on Hart's Island we were, in view of our very spectacular arrest and conviction, objects of considerable interest, both to guards and prisoners. But this cold fish never spoke a word to us; nor did he even so much as glance at us so far as I could notice—and I used to study him.

Then came the last day Amter and I spent on Hart's Island. We had packed up our few things and were on our way to report at the mustering-out point. As we were walking through the long prison dormitory corridor, whom should we meet strolling towards us but this guard. He was evidently waiting for us, and I wondered what he had on his mind. But my imagination could not picture what actually took place.

As the guard advanced towards us I could see that his customary supercilious stare had given place to a friendly, human look. With a conciliatory gesture, he halted us and said, in substance: "Before you boys leave I just wanted to tell you that I know all about your fight for the unemployed and I am in full sympathy with it. We guards have had our wages cut too, and we're plenty sore about it. Many others feel as I do. Keep up the good work." Then, with a glance over his shoulder to make sure he had not been observed, he passed on.

I was so amazed I could say nothing to him except a few formal words. And Amter and I, as we joined the motley group of prisoners being freed that day, speculated about the strange and devious ways and places in which the mounting discontent of the masses expresses itself.

POTTER'S FIELD

Instead of disposing of its dead by a sanitary cremation system, New York still clings to its filthy, disease-breeding Potter's Field on Hart's Island. Used for about seventy years, this island is said to contain more dead than anywhere else in the world in an equal space. The bodies are buried en masse in bare pine boxes, a hundred and fifty to each trench. In summer, the "stiffs," without ice, arrived by steamer in a high state of decomposition. During the depth of the industrial crisis the number of dead paupers greatly increased.

About half of Hart's Island was devoted to the Potter's Field. One horrible section was the "baby-trench." This was a great grave containing hundreds of babies whose mothers were unable to pay for burial elsewhere. To save the small job of reopening the grave each day, one end of it was always kept uncovered. The polluted air all around would "knock you down." Great rats fed upon the exposed baby bodies, and when surprised these monsters often scurried away dragging all or part of a dead baby body with them.

Although the prison officials made a great show of religion, they wasted no ceremony or niceties upon the pauper bodies. They just piled them in the huge graves in tiers of several each and let it go at that. Protestants were supposed to be buried in one set of trenches and Catholics in another, the latter in "consecrated ground." But this distinction furnished one of the standing jokes of Hart's Island. Thus, if a shipment of bodies contained only a few Protestants among many others, the guards, rather than go to the slight trouble of opening up the Protestant trench, would crack their regular joke, "Let's make them Catholics," and then bury them all in the consecrated ground. Or Catholics might be similarly turned into Protestants.

While we were at Hart's Island, the endless stream of pauper dead finally filled the many acres of available space. But not in the least troubled by sentiment, the authorities began the burying process all over again. Starting at the graves filled up about seventy years ago, they began to re-fill them with a new set of bodies. This involved the filthy and dangerous task of digging down through several feet of coffins, human debris and mud. I wondered if any of the small-pox, syphilis, cholera, yellow-fever and the other contagious disease germs that killed many of these men were still malignant. The remnants of the old coffins and clothes were gathered up and burned in bonfires on the spot, and what was left of dozens of skeletons was thrown pell mell into pine coffins and reburied. Clearly, the vast armies of men buried on Hart's Island will have quite a job untangling themselves when Gabriel blows his horn.

The men who did this disgusting work in Potter's Field were the "cemetery gang." This was a disciplinary gang, prisoners being sentenced to work in it indefinitely for various real or imagined infractions of the prison rules. It contained about forty men. The prison paid them nothing, not even a weekly sack of tobacco for their filthy and grewsome labor. It was autumn when they were re-digging the old graves, which contained several inches of water and muck, and the men had neither rubber boots nor gloves. Nor did they have a change of clothes, and they could bathe only once a week. Nobody wanted to sit near them in the dining hall.

All the work of the cemetery gang was bad enough, but the most noisome jobs fell to the lot of four men known as the "buriers." It was the task of these men to exhume bodies claimed by friends for burial elsewhere, the rude pine coffins being supposedly registered in their specific places in the mass graves for possible later identification.

Words cannot describe the disgusting scene when the buriers were digging up a corpse buried for several months in the midst of a mass grave of a hundred and fifty decaying bodies. For a hundred yards around the stench would turn a skunk's stomach. Perhaps the buriers unearthed the right body, and perhaps not. But any port in a storm, for as the grim joke had it the customer would never know the difference anyhow. For such disinterments the private undertakers received a hundred dollars or more and, in the fullness of their hearts, they would give a dollar, or maybe two, as a tip to be split among the four buriers. No better indication of the poverty of the average prisoner at Hart's Island is needed than the fact that, because of these occasional tips, the horrible job of burier was a preferred one in the cemetery gang.

THE PAROLE SYSTEM

The parole system in force in the New York Department of Corrections was as vile as the rest of the institution. As I have already remarked, sentences in the penitentiary did not extend beyond three years, long termers going to Sing Sing, Auburn, Dannemora and other state prisons. A prisoner, on being sent to the New York penitentiary, usually received the so-called "penitentiary indefinite" term, or "pen indef" as the men called it. The "pen indef" was a sentence of three years, part or all of which had to be served in prison and the balance, if any, on parole. The "pen indef" was the sentence received by Amter, Minor, Raymond and myself.

The length of time a prisoner had to serve of his sentence in jail, and how much on parole, was determined by the parole commission, a body of Tammany Hall politicians who sat behind closed doors. This situation presented a rich opportunity for favoritism and graft of every kind, and it was not neglected. The parole commission operated entirely in secret so far as the prisoner was concerned. The latter never knew when his case was coming up, and neither he nor his attorney could be present. It was a star chamber trial. Meanwhile the prisoner remained in suspense in prison for months on end, waiting to learn what his actual prison sentence was to be. This waiting was nerve-racking and demoralizing, and it lasted until the leisurely parole commission saw fit to act. Often a man served out the whole three-year term without ever being informed as to what his jail sentence was.

All "pen indef" prisoners, when freed, even those who did only the briefest jail terms, were required to serve the balance of their three years on parole. For a released prisoner, freedom on parole was a kind of "out of the frying pan into the fire." He found it very difficult to hold a job because the parole officers, as a routine, notified his employer that he was an ex-convict, and they were forever snooping around to see if he was on the job. Consequently, he frequently got fired and was very often forced back into crime in order to live. One of the greatest hardships of the paroled prisoner was that he might be re-arrested at any moment for a real or alleged violation of his parole and railroaded back to the penitentiary to serve out the balance of his three-year term. In such an event he had no trial, no bail privileges and no attorney, but was just rushed offhand back to prison on the parole officer's complaint. He might not know of what parole violation he was accused.

This vicious parole system rendered the average paroled prisoner absolutely helpless in the hands of his parole officer. If the latter were a grafter he could milk his victim freely. A prisoner who had money could buy immunity, arranging it so he did not have to report in person to the parole officers. But if he did not "come through" the parole officer could, without difficulty, have him fired from his job, or returned to the penitentiary as a parole violator.

Innumerable prisoners were victimized in this way, and the men told many stories of grafting parole officers. It is small wonder therefore, that when upon their release on parole the great city of New York gave them the munificent sum of twenty-five cents and a cheap prison suit with which to start life afresh, many prisoners tore up their yellow parole cards, fled to parts unknown and became fugitives from justice. The parole system was just one more of the many ways by which New York manufactured habitual criminals.

CHAPTER VII . . . . . . PARTY LIFE

During nearly forty years I have been a member of a number of political parties, among them the Socialist Party, the Wage Workers Party, the Labor Party of the United States, the National Farmer-Labor Party, the Federated Farmer-Labor Party, the Workers Party and the Communist Party. I have also been affiliated to several anti-political organizations, including the Industrial Workers of the World, the Syndicalist League of North America, the International Trade Union Educational League and (in its early syndicalist days) the Trade Union Educational League. The following incidents are a few typical experiences, some humorous, some serious, taken from this long and varied participation in workers' political organizations.

SOAP-BOXERS

In pre-war days, from about 1900 on, soap-boxing reached a high stage of development in the Socialist Party. Very effective educational work was thus done, but many humorous incidents occurred. There was the case, for example, of Callaham, a printer in Seattle, in 1906, who deeply cherished the usual ambition to become a soap-boxer. Finally, those of us in charge of this work locally agreed to give him a chance. He would begin in the usual manner by opening one of our Sunday evening meetings and introducing the principal speaker.

Callaham was intelligent and well-posted but badly afflicted with stage fright, and as his first trial at facing a street crowd approached his heart sank. But he carefully memorized his five minute speech. When the long-feared time came Callaham, with many quakings, mounted the platform.

"Fellow workers," he began, "tonight in the two hundred churches of Seattle two hundred preachers are at this moment entering their pulpits to preach. And what have they to say to the people? Nothing, just nothing!"

As Callaham went on his stage fright visibly increased, and when he reached the point, "Nothing, just nothing," it quite overcame him. He became speechless; not another word could he utter, and he slid down from the box unable even to introduce the next speaker. He, too, it appeared, like his preachers, had "just nothing" to say. The crowd, catching the point, laughed good-naturedly and Callaham retired in confusion.

Then there was Floyd Hyde, a well-known S.P. street speaker in Seattle during this period. Floyd was a Southern mountaineer, and he had an inveterate habit of "drawing the long bow," which often led him into fantastic exaggeration.

Typical was his description of a rich New York woman and her sick poodle dog. The original story, as it appeared in the daily newspapers, was to the effect that the dog of a society leader fell sick, and she took him to Florida for his health.

Now Floyd waxed plenty wrath over this outrageous solici- tude for a dog while thousands of babies were dying in New York tenements for want of milk and other necessities. He told the story night after night, and under the combined effects of his just indigna- tion and fertile imagination it grew in the repeated telling until it became almost unrecognizable.

Monday night Floyd told the story substantially as it appeared in the morning papers. Tuesday night, however, it began to develop: the woman, according to Floyd, had taken with her to Florida also a trained nurse to care for the indisposed poodle. Wednesday night Floyd indignantly had not only the owner and a nurse, but a doctor as well, accompanying the sick dog to balmy Florida, all in special Pullman compartments. Thursday night Floyd introduced some addi- tional medical members into the dog's entourage and had the whole outfit traveling in the aristocratic lady's private railroad car.

By Saturday night Floyd had so developed his dog story that the canine invalid had for its voyage South a special train with several doctors and a battery of nurses and maids. Each time he told the elastic story with added trimmings, the outraged Hyde seemed, if anything, to believe it the more implicitly. Nor did our amused protests that perhaps his nightly street corner crowds might remember his previous, more modest, versions have any effect in checking the growth of this fabulous tale. I often wondered what it would have eventually grown into had not its evolution been stopped abruptly on Saturday night by some big strike developments which distracted Floyd's attention from the adventures of the sick society dog.

Ed Lewis was another whose street meetings were colorful and humorous. He was the star street speaker of the Socialist Party on the Pacific coast at the time. His knowledge of the labor movement was broad, his philosophy was homely and his delivery flowing and brilliant. He was a real mass orator, and his brother Tom was a speaker of hardly less ability.

Ed was famous not only for his great power as a speaker but also for his occasional "bulls." He had a positive genius for using wrong words of similar sounds, often with amusing effect. Startling was his reference, at a Frisco street meeting one night in 1907, to the dire fate which, he said, threatened the leaders of the American revolution of 1776.

In line with the prevalent Socialist Party contempt for American revolutionary traditions, Ed charged that many of the fathers of the revolution were mere land stealers and smugglers. He denounced them as criminals and, with one of his grand flourishes, shouted, "They were outlaws and thieves, and, had the revolution not succeeded, a dozen or so of the biggest of them would have been hanged on an English *giblet*." And the crowd never blinked at this strange fate that had menaced the revolutionary patriots.

About 1910, the so-called "Irish Federation" of the Socialist Party consisted of old Tom Flynn, father of Elizabeth Gurley Flynn, and a few other Irishmen. Their soap-boxers could be found almost any fine night along Broadway, near Times Square, holding forth to the unresponsive pleasure-hunting crowd thronging the Great White Way. Their "soap-box" was an elaborate affair, with a high back to it, surmounted by three flags—the Irish on one side, the American on the other and the red flag in the center.

One of their speakers was an old-timer who knew little of socialism but who was possessed of a ready wit. There were a few of us local I.W.W.'s who, having no love for the S.P. generally, decided that it would be helpful to heckle and kid this tough old Irish speaker a bit. So we worked out a question to ask him, blithely ignoring history, military technique, etc., in its formulation.

That night at the Irish Federation street meeting the old Irishman was on the box, and when it came to the question period one of us posed the following fantastic query:

"Mr. Speaker, in your judgment did the facts that in the first Peloponnesian war the Athenians used the short sword and phalanx formation, while their enemies, the Spartans, used the long javelin and the column formation, tend to either hasten or retard the development of the Protestant Reformation in Germany?"

As our man unfolded his pseudo-learned question, a look of surprise came over the old Irishman's face. He, like most of the crowd, had probably never even heard of the Peloponnesian war, much less its alleged connection with the Protestant Reformation; but this did not trouble him for a second. With a wave of one hand he declared: "My answer to you, sir, is both yes and no. Next question please." The crowd haw-hawed and our man giggled weakly. It was an embarrassing question, but not for this nimble-witted speaker of the Irish Federation.

ANTI-POLITICS

The hatred of the old-time Western "wobblies" for political action was wide, deep and all-embracing. This was one of the basic reasons for the decline of the I.W.W. The special object for their scorn was the Socialist Party. Sometimes this assumed comical forms.

Thus, one day, in Spokane, Wash., in 1909, a dozen or so typical floating workers were idling about the local I.W.W. headquarters when a rather pretty girl came in to talk to the secretary. The workers, most of them, as usual, homeless and familyless and thoroughly sex-starved, eyed her trim figure hungrily as she walked the length of the hall. Finally, one standing not far from me, remarked, "Jesus, I'd like to have that girl."

There seemed to be general agreement with this sentiment until "Brawley Blackie," a real Western hard-boiled direct actionist, spoke up. With a pitying look at the one who had expressed the amatory wish, he sneered, "Oh, hell, she'd be no good, she's just a Socialist Partyite." And having delivered this crushing rejoinder, he stalked off in disgust.

Or take another instance of I.W.W. hatred of politicians and all their works. When the I.W.W. was formed in 1905, much of the initial funds to start it, amounting to several thousand dollars, came as loans from wealthy Socialists, as the Socialist Party at that time backed the organization. The I.W.W. was not able to repay these loans in its early years, and when it later fell into the hands of the anarcho-syndicalists, ardent haters of the S.P., it neither could nor wanted to pay them. Each year at the I.W.W. conventions these old loans were read to the delegates. Here is how the matter was handled at the 1912 convention.

Vincent St. John, general secretary, known as "The Saint," was in the chair. As a routine matter he droned off the amounts owed to the hated Socialist politicians. When he had finished, a typical "direct actionist" from the West took the floor. "Fellow-worker Chairman," he shouted, "I make a motion that we don't pay those bills." A burst of applause greeted this proposal.

"The Saint" demurred, however. He, too, thoroughly despised the Socialists. "But," he said, "we borrowed the money and are obligated to pay it back." This line of argument created some confusion in the convention and no one knew now just what to do with the troublesome debts.

Finally, another Western anti-political delegate got a bright idea. "Fellow-worker Chairman," said he, "I make an amendment that we just let the debts run on." This happy suggestion was hailed with a roar of approval. It solved both phases of the problem: the despised

Socialists were not paid and the financial honor of the I.W.W. was saved. The amendment was adopted unanimously.

A TAMMANY ELECTION

It is an old story that Tammany Hall in New York City, similarly to corrupt political machines in scores of other American cities and states, has falsified innumerable elections by wholesale buying of votes, stuffing of ballot boxes, failing to tally opposition ballots and by various other crooked devices. The following episode points its own moral.

A Socialist speaker, a prominent figure locally in the New York S.P., was delivering a speech at a street corner on the lower East Side, during the 1912 elections. At that time most of the garment workers still lived in this congested slum area, and the Socialist Party had a strong following among them. There was a large crowd, and the speaker made an effective speech. On the edge of the gathering stood the Tammany Hall precinct leader, much interested.

When the speaker had concluded and climbed down from his portable platform, the Tammany heeler sidled over to him and said:

"That was a fine speech you made, me boy. I think you'll poll sixteen votes for it on election day."

This made the Socialist a bit wroth and he replied:

"What do you mean, sixteen votes? This precinct is one of our Party's strongholds. We'll get many times that; we'll carry the precinct."

By now the Tammany man was also hot under the collar and he shouted:

"I told you sixteen votes, didn't I? Well, that settles it. Not a single one more will you get!"

Now, indeed, the Socialist speaker was angry. He reported the matter to the city committee and it was decided to make an extra effort to carry this particular precinct. Accordingly, additional speakers were sent in, many meetings were held and special house-to-house work was done. The workers responded well and as the election took place the Party local leaders were positive they had won the precinct.

But when the detailed election returns were made public, there, sure enough, the Party in the precinct was credited with the famous sixteen votes. And so the thing stood. Nor could all the Party's protests and demands for a recount change matters.

A PERPETUAL VACATION

One of many manifestations of the conservative A.F. of L. bureaucracy is the so-called chair-warmer type of organizer. Such organizers draw big wages and do nothing constructive. About the only time they can be galvanized into action is when it is a case of fighting back some progressive movement struggling to improve the unions, on which occasions they display an amazing vigor and activity.

Chair-warmer organizers have long been targets of attack by progressives and revolutionaries in the labor movement. But I never knew a criticism more effective than one made off-hand by Samuel Gompers, himself the king of labor chair-warmers, to a typical A.F. of L. conservative, do-nothing organizer in Pittsburgh.

Gompers happened to be in Pittsburgh, and in the course of his conferences, the organizer, an old veteran, requested that he be granted a month's vacation. Gompers, with a drink or two under his belt, listened to his request and then inquired:

"Now, let's see, Tom, how long have you been on our payroll?"

"It'll be twenty-five years next November," replied the organizer.

"Well," said Gompers with a sly grin, "don't you think that's vacation enough?"

AMALGAMATION FROM THE BOTTOM

During the World War and for some years afterward, under pressure of the high cost of living and profiteering by the trusts, the masses displayed much independent activity on the political field. There was a strong growth of labor parties in Illinois, New York and various other states. Farmer parties also sprang up in the Middle West and Northwest—in Minnesota, the Dakotas, Iowa, Washington. Likewise, the city petty bourgeoisie developed considerable organization, which finally crystallized nationally as the "Committee of Forty-Eight," headed by J. A. H. Hopkins.

When the 1920 elections drew near, these groupings of workers, farmers and middle class tended to unite, and in consequence they assembled in two separate conventions in Chicago, in July of that year, to work out some kind of a joint program. The Labor Party forces had no great difficulty in coming to an agreement with the relatively small delegations of farmers. But when it came to uniting with the middle class elements of the Committee of Forty-Eight many obstacles developed. The rank and file of both groups clamored for amalgamation of the two conventions, but the leaders could not agree over knotty questions of program, organization and candidates.

The situation was this: the labor and farmer convention was meeting in Carmen's Auditorium, while that of the Committee of Forty-Eight met in the Morrison Hotel, about two miles away. The delegations of both conventions waited impatiently, while their leaders ran back and forth fruitlessly negotiating. Finally, after reports were made to the delegates that a couple of days' attempts to arrive at an agreement had failed, a few of us Labor Party delegates got into touch with some live wire delegates in the Committee of Forty-Eight and urged that their whole delegation march over to Carmen's Auditorium, take seats in our convention, and by this action bring about amalgamation in fact.

This idea ran like a prairie fire among both delegations and, without a by-your-leave to Hopkins, the several hundred members of the Committee of Forty-Eight convention suddenly pulled up stakes and paraded in a body over to Carmen's Auditorium. As they came streaming into the hall the assembled worker and farmer delegates gave them a roaring welcome.

The Forty-Eighters simply took seats in the hall, thus organiza-

tionally fusing with the convention already in session. This unprece-
dented action instantly threw a whole maze of problems into the laps
of the leaders. But after many creakings between the organized and
disciplined trade union workers and the unorganized and confused
middle class, a working arrangement was finally effected and the
convention got down to work. The workers were outnumbered by the
Committee of Forty-Eight delegates, but by force of their better discipline, leadership and program they, properly enough, were the
decisive force in the amalgamated convention. A program was worked
out, candidates, P. P. Christensen and Max Hayes, chosen, and a
national party, the Farmer-Labor Party, formed. Thus, in this unprec-
edented convention was given a practical demonstration of the common interests and practical organized unity of workers, farmers and
middle class which today, under new conditions and with the ideo-
logical leadership of the Communist Party, manifests itself as the
Democratic Front.

A BABY ON OUR DOORSTEP

The Farmer-Labor Party, formed at the 1920 Chicago convention,
did not do well in the ensuing elections, its Presidential candidate,
Christensen, polling only a quarter of a million votes. This gave the
new party a serious setback, and its difficulties were intensified by the
John Fitzpatrick leadership's political ineptitude and organizational
sluggishness. Then there began to develop the Conference for Progressive Political Action. The C.P.P.A., led by the railroad unions and
including many other labor unions, farmers' organizations and middle
class groupings, totaled over three million, and climaxed in the
La Follette Presidential campaign of 1924. This great movement immediately took the political lead out of the feeble hands of the Fitzpatrick Farmer-Labor Party.

For a time it looked as though the C.P.P.A. would launch a farmer-
labor party, but in December, 1922, it rejected this perspective and gave
endorsement to the general A.F. of L. non-partisan policy. It also

refused to seat the delegates of the Workers Party (the Communist Party). For these actions Fitzpatrick violently condemned the C.P.P.A. as "scabs," and he reaffirmed the necessity for building a farmer-labor party.

Upon the proposal of the Workers Party, many of whose Chicago leaders, including Jack Johnstone and myself, had worked closely with Fitzpatrick for several years, the Fitzpatrick group agreed to call a general national convention of all farmer-labor forces, in Chicago on July 3, 1923, to form a new, federated party. The Workers Party, invited to attend, became very active, together with the T.U.E.L., in building up the convention.

In the meantime, however, important developments were taking place that were causing Fitzpatrick to lose his taste for the convention. For one thing, there was a new conservative current running in the trade unions as the Coolidge "good times" began, and he was feeling it very much; the Gompers machine was cracking down on him, cutting off his subsidy and demanding that he abandon the whole convention and his alliance with us; and besides, the main stream of the workers' political movement was moving towards the C.P.P.A. As the July 3rd convention approached Fitzpatrick, therefore, began to shy away from us, and he put forth the argument that he had led the labor party movement long enough; now let Minnesota or someone else assume the responsibility.

We should have been warned by all this that Fitzpatrick was ready for a split, but we were not sufficiently alert. The convention was a fairly good one, some six hundred thousand organized workers being represented. Fitzpatrick seemed in a trance, but when we pushed on with the agreed-upon plan to build a federated party, he finally came in with proposals to expel the Workers Party from the convention and to reject the formation of a new party. Almost the whole convention delegation voted against this splitting proposition and decided to form the Federated Farmer-Labor Party; whereupon Fitzpatrick and a few followers walked out of the convention. The new-born political baby was in the lap of the Communists.

Fitzpatrick, as he had been threatening to do, quit the labor party movement cold, and has never since given it an ounce of support. His loud charges that we were responsible for the split were only so many rationalizations to cover up his retreat into the camp of Gompers, where he has remained ever since.

For a time it looked as though the new F.F.L.P., with Joseph Manley as general secretary, was going to be a success. But before long the true trend of things became evident: the F.F.L.P. was soon reduced pretty much to the Workers (Communist) Party and its immediate supporters. We put all available men and money into the F.F.L.P., but to no avail; the new party was still-born.

Then evil effects from it all began to show themselves for the Workers Party. First, through the Chicago split it had lost many valuable contacts with progressive elements in the labor movement and was increasingly threatened with isolation from the masses. Secondly, the drain by the F.F.L.P. upon the resources of the Workers Party and the former's tendency to be merely another Communist Party under a different name menaced the latter with actual liquidation. And worst of all, the whole situation revolving around the F.F.L.P. provoked an intense factional fight in the Workers Party that almost tore it to pieces. The launching of the F.F.L.P. had turned out to be a very serious mistake.

Obviously it was necessary to merge the F.F.L.P. into the main political currents of the masses. So, with what progressive contacts it still had left, the Workers Party caused another farmer-labor convention to be held in St. Paul on June 17, 1924. This also was a good convention, and out of it came a new National Farmer-Labor Party. Into this the ill-fated F.F.L.P. was merged. The new party put up as its Presidential candidates, Duncan McDonald, formerly head of the Illinois district of the Miners Union, and William Bouck, President of the Western Progressive Farmers.

But the new party could no more find a place for itself than could the old F.F.L.P. La Follette was maneuvering at the time to take the field, and the masses were looking towards him as their leader. Shortly afterward, in Cleveland, the combined forces of the A.F. of L., C.P.P.A., and farmers' organizations nominated him for President. We refused

to support La Follette, chiefly because he would not break completely
with the Republican Party. These developments left our new Farmer-
Labor Party high and dry, quite detached from the masses. Clearly it
could perform no useful function in the elections. So we did the necessary thing: we induced McDonald and Bouck to withdraw their can-
didacies and then allowed the National Farmer-Labor Party to expire.
The Workers Party put up its own Communist candidates in the
1924 elections, the first in our Party's history.

JIMMIE HIGGINS

In his book, *Jimmie Higgins,* Upton Sinclair immortalized a basic
and vital type that every participant in the trade union and revolutionary movement knows well. Jimmie Higgins is that active rank
and file element which the French call the *militant.* He is the type of
tireless, devoted, disciplined, self-sacrificing and brave worker—the very
salt of the working class. Wherever there is hard, slogging work to
be done, Jimmie Higgins is on hand. When the going gets tough and
dangerous, he is always in the front line inspiring the masses to
struggle. He is the rank and file builder of every union, party and
other working-class body. And his reward is simply the feeling of his
proletarian duty well done. Usually he is quite unknown to fame or
glory, except in the esteem of his circle of contacts, who admire and
love him.

The Jimmie Higgins' are the natural heads of the toilers. All dynamic
working-class leaders have been of this category. It is especially among
them that the Communist Party recruits its members. In making a
Communist of Jimmie Higgins, the Party enormously increases his
efficiency by teaching him the true meaning of Labor's struggle, by
infusing him with class consciousness, by transforming his primitive
proletarian militancy into burning revolutionary zeal.

I have always been inspired by the Jimmie Higgins' militants. Their
modesty, sincerity, selflessness, courage and invincibility are the qual-
ities of the great heart of the proletariat itself. My experience in the

trade union and revolutionary movement has been lighted up by innumerable devoted actions of these unknown but heroic working class fighters. Let one simple incident reveal Jimmie Higgins at his post in the class struggle.

It took place in the concluding phases of the bitterly-fought 1929 textile strike at Gastonia, N.C., led by the National Textile Workers Union of the T.U.U.L. The strike was in a bad way, the union being pretty badly smashed, and the mills were operating. The leadership was in jail on the charge of killing Police Chief Aderholt in his raid upon the relief headquarters; a reign of terror prevailed in the surrounding country; the gifted strike-leader and labor song-writer, Ella May Wiggin, had been murdered by company gunmen on the public highway; several organizers had been brutally flogged and a vigilante gang had just raided the union headquarters and half-wrecked it. Altogether it was a situation of fierce class struggle.

On the day in question a few of us had been to visit the newly-made grave of Comrade Wiggin, a few miles outside of Gastonia; and by the time we got back to the local union center it was already quite dark. The vigilantes, a real K.K.K. outfit, had threatened to return that night to finish wrecking the headquarters, and we had resolved to take measures of defense.

As our Ford drew up to the union building, we were loudly hailed by a union picket. He was armed, but quite alone and evidently entirely unafraid. I asked him if he did not know of the imminent K.K.K. raid and he replied that he did and was prepared for it. He did not seem to think it any way strange that he, one man, had been given the dangerous task of guarding the hall. In the previous raid the K.K.K. had torn down the big union sign on the building front, but the workers had replaced it, and the picket seemed particularly resolved to protect it. In his Southern drawl he quietly told us that the man who should climb up to take down that sign would surely die, no matter what happened to himself. And I had not the slightest doubt that he would have been as good as his word had the occasion developed.

We scurried about and dug up a dozen other union members as guards, and for that night at least, the headquarters was safe. In the years that have passed, the figure of that lone union picket has stood out clear and bright to me as Jimmie Higgins at his best. It was such valiant proletarian fighters who carried through the Russian Revolution, who are holding back the fascist legions in Spain and China and who will finally, by their unconquerable spirit, put an end to capitalism everywhere.

A SMASHUP

It was my privilege to be the Communist candidate for President in the campaigns of 1924, 1928 and 1932. In these Presidential campaigns I spoke to approximately five hundred thousand people in three hundred meetings, not to mention uncounted numbers that I addressed in radio speeches, newspaper stories, station demonstrations, parades, etc. All told, I traveled some sixty thousand miles by train, auto, bus, airplane, steamboat, wagon and afoot, that is, by practically every mode of travel except the bicycle; and I repeatedly covered every state and important city in the Union.

In the 1924 national campaign our Party was officially credited with thirty-six thousand votes; by 1928 its vote had mounted to fifty thousand; and in 1932 to one hundred thousand. These figures did not, however, represent our true voting strength, because we were not on the ballot in many states, and also many of our votes were not counted by the usually very hostile election officials. Moreover, tens of thousands of our supporters were disfranchised by being foreign-born or unemployed; while thousands of others did not want to "throw away" their votes by voting for such a small party. Perhaps our true vote in each election would have run to at least three times what we were credited with officially.

Far more than the campaigns of the major political parties, those of the Communist Party were enormously overloaded with work for the candidates. They were real labor and no mistake, what with incessant traveling, perpetual speech-making, bad food, miserable hotels, boresome newspaper interviews, being talked half to death or kept from badly needed sleep by comrades who felt it to be the function of a Presidential candidate to adjust every local grievance, by after-meeting home-gatherings, "banquets" and untimely talk-fests. Usually, trying to make the much-too-heavy schedule of meetings, I found myself, despite a strong constitution, in a chronic state of exhaustion. In my time I have made eleven lengthy national speaking tours, several of them beating my way as a hobo, but the three Presidential campaigns were in a class by themselves when it came to hard work.

The 1924 and 1928 campaigns were severe enough, but the 1932 campaign almost killed me. I had been chronically overworking myself for many years in strikes and agitational work, and at the beginning of the campaign I was already in a run-down condition. I had just come from conducting a five months' coal mine strike and had written a book, *Towards Soviet America,* on the side. I should have taken off at least a month to rest up in preparation for the five months' grind ahead (our campaign began early in June). But, believing my strength inexhaustible, I did not do so.

I was greatly alarmed when, on the very day that I began my speaking tour of thirty thousand miles—with one hundred and five major speeches and innumerable radio talks, local conferences, station demonstrations and "banquets" ahead of me—I developed alarming heart symptoms. Previously I had hardly ever known I had a heart. I urgently needed rest, but how could I get it? I was the Communist standard bearer; the campaign was just beginning; I had to carry on somehow. Therefore, I hung on, traveling and making big meetings, when I should have been in a hospital. Many times I spoke when I had to hold myself erect by clinging to the speakers' stand, and often I drank glass after glass of water to keep from fainting.

I thought that my naturally rugged health would pull me through the campaign somehow, and eagerly I checked off each meeting as I completed it. But I simply could not last it out. After three months' campaigning, traveling twenty thousand miles and addressing two hundred thousand people in seventy-seven major speeches (not to count innumerable short speeches), I collapsed at Moline, Illinois, on September 8th. Even then, I thought a short rest would set me on my feet again. But "the pitcher had gone once too often to the well."

It was a heart attack—angina pectoris, the doctors called it—and for the next several weeks I was knocking sharply on death's door. I spent five long months in bed, suffering indescribable torture. When I finally got on my feet again there came many months of barely crawling about, sick to the core and such a nervous wreck that I was almost as helpless as a child. It was nineteen months after my crash before I could even put foot in my office, and three years before I could make even a ten minute public speech.

I have never ceased to wonder how the human body could possibly heal itself again after being so badly wrecked. Nor could I ever have pulled out of the terrible crisis I was in had it not been for the intelligent, tireless and loving care of my devoted wife, the loyal assistance given me by the Party, and my own determination not to die or to become a hopeless wreck but to live on and fight in the workers' struggle for emancipation.

ELECTION CAMPAIGNING

My three Presidential campaigns were not all hard work, however. They were also literally packed with human interest. Especially the tragic days of 1932. All over the country the terrible industrial crisis was rampant. On all sides factories and mills were closed; great breadlines of unemployed wound their way to their goal of miserable handouts; filthy flophouses were overflowing with the homeless, freezing unemployed; along the railroads myriads of hobo workers traveled and camped; in every city there were the monstrous "Hoovervilles" of tin can shacks on the city dumps or along the railroad tracks, filled with utterly destitute workers; in many Western towns there were tent colonies of dispossessed farmers. And the brutal Hoover government was doing nothing to relieve this mass misery caused by the breakdown of the obsolete capitalist system.

One night I was riding a South Side elevated train in Chicago when a Negro youth just in front of me collapsed. Starvation. Next day a small note in the paper stated that he had died. In Philadelphia an elderly immigrant couple told me that just a week previously they had lost their home by foreclosure; their whole life's savings were gone at one blow, and the old husband was sick and unemployed. In Pittsburg, Kansas, a miner insisted that I stay at his home while I was in town. But in my room I picked up a book to read and found in it, as a marker, an unpaid grocery bill for ninety-six dollars. I learned later he had not done a day's work for two years. And so on, I met with endless manifestations of the terrible mass destitution of 1932.

But my campaigns also produced many humorous incidents, and I could appreciate them as a relief from the hard work and mass pauperization. In the 1924 campaign there was, for example, the case of Poniatowsky's baby. Stanislaus Poniatowsky was a miner in the anthracite district of eastern Pennsylvania. He had a big family and, being a confirmed rebel, concluded it was very fitting to call his children after outstanding revolutionaries. In this sense, he distributed upon his first three offspring the names of the great international leaders, Marx, Engels and Lenin. Then he began to use names of American militants, including Debs and Ruthenberg, upon other newly-arrived children.

Eventually, Stanislaus' wife presented him with still another baby, a bouncing boy. What should this one be called? The miner was sorely troubled. He had two names urgently in mind; but he was afraid to use either, as he had reason to believe this would be his last child, and then he could not use the other name. It was indeed a difficult situation. But Stanislaus boldly cut the Gordian knot with one sweeping stroke. He decided to give both names to the youngster. So, a week before I saw the kid in 1924, he called him William Z. Foster Alexander Howatt Poniatowsky, and let the matter go at that.

During the 1928 election campaign I made a speaking trip through the South. I had just concluded a meeting the night before in Atlanta, Ga., and was on my way to make another in Richmond, Va. As the train pulled into Raleigh, N.C., the station was full of a noisy throng.

A band played, flags waved, the crowd yelled and a committee of a dozen "distinguished citizens" stood in front and looked important. Then a general invasion of our train took place. The committee, plus a score or so more, filled the car I was in, while the band and the *hoi polloi* jammed into the other coaches. I was not long in learning that it was a campaign reception committee going up the road an hour or two's ride to meet the train bearing the Democratic Presidential candidate, Al Smith, who was speaking that night in Raleigh. The delegation was headed by the pompous Josephus Daniels, Secretary of the Navy under Wilson. Nobody recognized me, but Daniels, politician-like, bade me a formal "How-do-you-do?" I wondered what he would have thought had he known I was the candidate of the hated "Commune-ist" Party.

The committee was in a hilarious mood, and evidently the moonshine "cohn likkah" that passed freely from hand to hand had a key part in livening things up. The delegates laughed and sang and joked. They outdid each other in making wisecracks at the expense of Calvin Coolidge, who was Al Smith's opponent and, incidentally, mine also. The best of these cracks was made by a preacher in the group, who, quite jolly and not a bit shocked at the open violation of his revered Prohibition amendment, delivered himself of the following.

"Do you know," said he, "Coolidge is such a musty conservative that every time he opens his mouth a moth flies out?"

The crowd laughed uproariously, and I, too. It was doubly funny to me, because of its coming from such Bourbons, tools of the cotton mill child labor exploiters, Jim Crowers of Negroes, hypocritical bible-pounders and Prohibitionists—even then on their way to welcome Al Smith, as reactionary a man as Coolidge ever dared to be. It was the pot calling the kettle black.

PAUL SINGER'S FUNERAL

During 1910-11, I spent a year in France and Germany studying the labor movement. When I pulled into Berlin from Paris in the dead of winter, 1911, I did not know a single word of German. I had secured a pretty good grasp of French in my previous six months in France, but German was all "Greek" to me. Therefore, I had the devil's own time on that first Saturday, my arrival day, in getting located in a cheap lodging house; for I had only twenty dollars in my pocket and could not afford to go to the high-priced places where they spoke English.

The morning of my second day in Berlin, Sunday, was bright and clear, but what the French picturesquely call *froid de loup* (wolf-cold). I decided I would take a walk about the city. I had not gone far when I noticed many little groups of men, most of them with high hats, all hurrying along in one general direction. I could not make out what was up, and of course I was unable to ask anyone. At first I thought all these people were going to church, but I soon saw this was not the case.

Moved by curiosity, I decided to follow a group and learn what was afoot. So I "tailed" one and it led me towards the center of the city. The farther we went the larger the number of high-hatted groups and the bigger the crowds. Finally we came to where a great demonstration was taking shape. The streets were jammed in all directions.

From the banners I made out that it was a Socialist turnout, but I did not know what it was all about. Soon, however, I saw a newsboy selling copies of *Vorwarts,* the Socialist daily paper, which had a full front page picture of Paul Singer, noted Social Democratic leader, surrounded by a heavy black border. So that was it: Paul Singer was dead and the Socialist Party was burying him. And what a mighty demonstration—the claim was made that a million people took part and that it was the biggest funeral in the history of Germany.

At the time I was a syndicalist, and as such had no confidence whatever in the revolutionary pretensions of the German Social Democracy. And this first view of the organization itself in action only intensified my unfavorable opinion. For one thing, coming from six months' contact with the militantly revolutionary French trade unions, I was struck by the absence of red flags in the demonstration. There were hundreds of the national colors, but so little red that I was at first barely able to recognize it as a Socialist demonstration.

Besides this, I saw hardly a single policeman in all the gigantic throngs. The Socialists had set up an elaborate policing system of their own and taken over the job of maintaining order along the line of march. The regular cops had a day off, it seemed. This gave me all the more of a shock as in France the class struggle was acute and the workers so militant that even the smallest working-class demonstrations were heavily guarded by police and often led to violent clashes. Such a great demonstration as this in France, if permitted at all, would have been menaced by thousands of police and troops.

But what impressed me most unfavorably about the demonstration were the many high hats worn—I counted sections where they averaged as much as ninety-six per cent of the total. It was then, and maybe still is, the custom of the German big and little bourgeoisie to wear "stovepipe" hats at funerals; but I was astonished to see a workers' organization aping this master class custom.

In general, I got such a bad impression of the demonstration that I wrote a personal letter to the editor of *La Vie Ouvriere* in Paris, then the left-wing organ of the General Confederation of Labor, detailing my reactions. I had no idea my letter would be published; but the editor, without consulting me and without even correcting my very faulty French, printed it. This evoked a heated protest from the General Committee of the German Social Democratic Party. They denounced this nobody from America who had the effrontery to assert that their Social Democracy was saturated with German nationalism and petty bourgeois legalism.

For six months I remained in Germany and I came to know the Social Democracy intimately—its Party, unions and co-operatives; its leaders and its literature—and my original bad opinion of it was fortified. I became more convinced than ever that the whole movement was dominated by a reformist bureaucracy alien to socialism, and who were tailing after the capitalist class. And ensuing events justified my unfavorable judgment to the full. It was only three years later that the Social Democratic Party supported the war. Then, after the war, its leaders co-operated with the reaction in shooting down the German Bolshevik revolution, thereby saving European capitalism. And for years afterward they worked in every possible way with the exploiters to breathe the breath of life again into the tottering capitalist system. By their slander of Soviet Russia and their support of Bruening and Hindenburg, by their refusal to develop a united front anti-fascist struggle with the Communist Party, they cleared the way for Hitler, and when he came to power they surrendered to him without even a semblance of struggle. Indeed, the Social Democracy fully lived up to the bourgeois ideology that could even be seen sticking out all over it in Paul Singer's funeral.

KAUTSKY

For some years after the turn of the century Karl Kautsky was the outstanding Marxist theoretician in the German Social Democratic Party. He led the fight against the opportunist tendency, the principal champions of which were Eduard Bernstein the revisionist theoretician, and Karl Legien the reformist trade union leader. Kautsky, in those years, won much praise from Lenin.

But gradually Kautsky's revolutionary line weakened. Little by little, he surrendered to the growing opportunism in the Party. So that, when the World War came, repudiating his international principles, Kautsky supported the war, together with the reformist Socialist Party and union leadership. In the post-war revolutionary struggles Kautsky, still further degenerated politically, joined with the Noskes, Scheidemanns, Eberts and other traitors in suppressing the German revolution and re-establishing capitalist control. Kautsky has also always bitterly denounced the Soviet Union in filthy, lying terms that Hearst has never exceeded. Finally having discarded his Marxism and become the leader of the reformist tendency in the German Social Democracy, Kautsky theorized the political retreat of that movement which culminated in its surrender to Hitler without even striking a blow.

Kautsky, who recently died, was a fit pal for his present-day counterpart, Leon Trotsky.

I once had an instructive talk with Kautsky, in 1911, in Germany. I had read all Kautsky's books and principal pamphlets and, being a syndicalist, I differed sharply with his point of view. I decided to interview him, which I did at his home at Friedenau in the outskirts of Berlin. Kautsky, then a man in early middle life and still at the height of his reputation as a revolutionary Marxist, received me cordially. We talked in German, as his English was even more fragmentary than my German, and he quizzed me at length about the American trade union and revolutionary movements.

Then I got down to my point. I told Kautsky I had read his major works, but that I could not find the revolution in them. I remarked that although he constantly referred to the great power of the German Social Democracy, I was unable to discover precisely how this power was going to be exerted to bring about the overthrow of capitalism. I queried him as to how he thought the revolution would be accomplished, inasmuch as he then was avowedly not an advocate of the gradual-buying-out of capitalism (the reformist line), nor of the revolutionary general strike (the syndicalist conception), nor did he definitely advocate revolutionary insurrection.

In reply Kautsky entered into an extended discussion of what he meant by the power of the Social Democracy. This consisted mainly of a recitation in detail of the rapid expansion of the three main sections of the movement, the Party, the trade unions and the co-operatives, and the great increase in their mass influence. All this made an imposing presentation statistically, but I did not think it answered my question. To me it appeared very much akin to the usual reformist Socialist conception of the workers taking over capitalist industry and the state bit by bit. And I stated so frankly.

My remarks made Kautsky angry. Turning on me sharply, he said (in substance): "If you are proposing that the Social Democracy lead the workers before the guns of the German army, let me tell you it will never happen. That's precisely what the Kaiser wants, and we don't propose to walk into his trap."

In the years that followed I often thought of this statement of Kautsky's. It forecast his later political renegacy and the tragic surrender policy of the Social Democracy. Indeed, as Kautsky said, the Social Democracy (unlike the Russian Bolsheviks, who overthrew capitalism in armed struggle) never "led the workers before the guns" of the capitalists, and the world has seen the fatal result of their failure to do so. They refused to go through with the revolution at the close of the war and they rejected the Communist proposals to fight Hitler. And precisely because the German Social Democracy failed to fight the capitalists in these critical moments is why German capitalism was able to maintain itself after the war, and why fascism now confronts the world with this frightful prospect of a new world war. And all along this reformist path of working class betrayal and defeat the erstwhile revolutionary Marxist, Karl Kautsky, led the shameful way.

KARL LEGIEN

At the Budapest conference of the International Trade Union Secretariat in August, 1911, as delegate of the I.W.W., I challenged the credentials of James Duncan, vice-president of the A.F. of L. and demanded a seat for the I.W.W. This brought me into a head-on collision with Karl Legien, chief of the German Federation of Trade Unions.

Legien was chairman of the Budapest conference, and he undertook to steam-roller me, a system he had highly developed in the autocratically ruled German Socialist unions. My challenge against Duncan was on the grounds that as a member of the National Civic Federation he was unfit to represent American labor, and my protest should have been acted upon before the conference took up its regular order of business. But the arch-bureaucrat Legien started off the conference as though I and my protest had no existence.

A "wobbly" from the West and not so easily squelched, I took the floor and caused such a hubbub that the conference debated the issue for the rest of the day. There were but two delegates (the highest union officials) from each country, and the only ones who supported me were the French syndicalists, Jouhaux and Yvetot. That night, penniless, I was arrested for sleeping in a moving van on the outskirts of town, and I narrowly escaped six months in jail.

Legien, with whom I had this brush at Budapest, was more responsible perhaps than any other Socialist leader for the opportunism that finally led the German Social Democracy to its abject surrender to Hitler. This fatal reformist policy was based on the anti-Marxist theory of the gradual growth of capitalism into socialism. Its practical expression was the collaboration of the working class with (or more properly, its subordination to) the capitalist class. Bernstein was the theoretical leader of this revisionist tendency, but Legien and his fellow-bureaucrats gave it flesh and blood by building the trade union movement upon its treacherous principles.

The class-collaboration policy was many years in growing. In the early days of German capitalism Bismarck had tried to suppress the Social Democracy by passing the so-called Anti-Socialist laws. But the Party and the unions grew in spite of this persecution, and they maintained a sharply revolutionary outlook. So the shrewd Bismarck, backed by the employers and big landlords whom he represented, resolved to tame the Social Democracy through a policy of making small concessions, economic and political. Consequently, in the early 'nineties the anti-Socialist laws were repealed and the Social Democratic Party and its unions were "recognized." Then followed forty years of class collaboration, which took all the socialism out of the Party and union leadership.

The trade union leaders, with Legien at their head, took to German imperialism and class collaboration like ducks to water. The Party itself succumbed more slowly. Bernstein and other intellectual revisionists played a big role, but the story of the Party's political degeneration was largely the record of the rise in influence in its councils of the grossly reformist trade union leaders, especially Karl Legien.

The definite victory of the trade union revisionists in the Party came in 1907. It happened in this way. The central problem that confronted the Party in those years was to change the restricted suffrage laws. On the face of the prevailing undemocratic provisions it was impossible for the workers and their sympathizers to get a majority in the Reichstag; hence the main political demand of the Party was for equal, secret, free and universal suffrage. But how was this demand to be achieved, as the legally packed Reichstag would not concede equal suffrage and the workers had no parliamentary means to secure a majority to change the law?

After long years of agitation of this knotty problem, the German Social Democratic Party, largely led by the still-revolutionary Kautsky, decided in its congress, under the influence of the gigantic strikes of the 1905 Russian revolution, to win democratic suffrage for the workers by a general strike. This decision by the Party at once provoked a revolt of the trade union leaders, who saw all their beloved class collaboration structure threatened. Headed by Legien they, in their trade union congress, by an overwhelming majority condemned with sneers and sarcasm the Party's plan for a general strike and forbade even its discussion in the trade unions.

The issue of policy and leadership was thus drawn sharply between the Party and the trade unions; the former having declared for the general strike and the latter against it. A conference was called between the executives of the two organizations, and as a result the Party leaders surrendered outright, abandoning their general strike plan completely. The victory of Bernstein-Legien class collaborationism was decisive. Kautsky soon gave up his struggle against it and became its greatest champion, leaving only Karl Liebknecht and a few other militants to fight for a policy of class struggle. The way was thus opened wide for the betrayal of internationalism a few years later in the World War, for the shooting down of the German revolution, and for the eventual surrender to Hitler. Legien, a true lackey of capitalism, had led the German Social Democracy to political suicide and the working class to a disastrous debacle.

COMINTERN CONGRESSES

When Lenin led in forming the Communist International in 1919 he called it "the general staff of the world revolution." In the break-up of world capitalism that is now taking place, the C.I. has faced a maze of intricate problems in developing the revolutionary strategy of the international working class, with the great complex of industrial crises, strike waves, colonial upheavals, fascist movements, undeclared wars, etc. While the Second International has floundered about, shattered by these kaleidoscopic events, the Comintern has gone ahead making a penetrating Marxian analysis of decaying capitalism and building up the policy that is more and more becoming the program of the world's exploited myriads.

It has been my good fortune to be present at several World Congresses and enlarged executive meetings of the Comintern, as well as at a number of similar gatherings of the Red International of Labor Unions, during which important advances were made in developing this epochal world analysis and policy-making. These Congresses and Plenums were made up of the best Marxians in the world, militant revolutionary fighters who, for the past generation, have been in the heart of every great strike movement and revolutionary struggle from London to Shanghai and from Toronto to Buenos Aires. These international meetings constituted the most interesting and instructive experiences of my political life.

The first time I saw Lenin was at the Third World Congress of the Communist International, in Moscow, during 1921. As I caught sight of him, he was standing modestly near an entrance to the speakers' platform in the erstwhile tsars' palace, listening closely to a delegate's speech. It was one of the most inspiring moments of my life. There, indeed, was the great leader of the world's oppressed millions, the man who was a veritable nightmare to exploiters in every corner of the earth. I regarded him so intently as he went about in the Congress that his whole personal makeup and characteristics literally burned themselves into my memory.

My interest in Lenin was all the more acute because at that time he was exercising a most profound effect upon my ideology and my life's work. Attracted at first to the Communist Party by Lenin's stand on the trade union question, I was, during the period of the Third Congress, engaged in reading deeply of his writings. Over many years, I had read far and wide among socialist, anarchist and syndicalist writers, and had also much practical experience in their respective mass movements, but Lenin's masterly theoretical presentation was startlingly new and overwhelmingly convincing. It was easy for me to agree with his brilliant analysis of imperialist capitalism, his devastating criticisms of revisionist socialism, syndicalism and anarchism, his conception of the dictatorship of the proletariat, and to accept the general program of Communism—backed up as they were by the living reality of the Russian Revolution and world conditions generally. After more than twenty years of intellectual groping about, I was at last, thanks to Lenin, getting my feet on firm revolutionary ground.

Lenin spoke at the Congress, for he was at that time still in possession of fair health and very active in the struggle. I did not consider him an orator in the usual sense. Nevertheless he held the Congress in breathless interest for the whole period of his speech. He was such a deep thinker and plain speaker that every time he wrote or spoke he bared the very heart of the question in hand.

One of the many great political steps taken by the Communist International, which I witnessed at first hand, was the putting forth of its famous analysis in 1925 to the effect that post-war capitalism had succeeded in checking the revolutionary wave that followed the war and had achieved economically and politically a "partial, relative and temporary stabilization." This courageous and correct conclusion, for which Stalin was chiefly responsible, was based on the reality that although the revolution was victorious in Russia, it had been temporarily defeated, through betrayal by the reformist Socialist leaders, in Germany, Italy, Hungary, etc. The crest of the revolutionary wave had passed, and stricken European capitalism, largely with the help of American loans and the co-operation of opportunist Socialists, was lamely struggling to its feet again. The Comintern leaders, being realists and not wishful thinkers, recognized this unpalatable situation and analyzed it boldly and plainly. The analysis meant that, for the time being, no broad revolutionary movement in Europe would be looked for.

With glee the capitalist press of the world greeted this declaration as proof that the whole policy of socialist revolution was wrong, and they eagerly awaited and prepared for a new period of capitalist development. The capitalists' enthusiasm was outdone by that of the reformist Socialists, who looked upon the Comintern statement as a confession of defeat for its basic political line and a justification of their own. They, too, foresaw a long era of peaceful capitalist upswing.

But the Comintern pointed out that the stabilization was shaky and could not last, and that capitalism would soon plunge into still deeper crisis. The present world situation, with its profound industrial crises, fascism and wars is a striking demonstration of the correctness of this C.I. forecast. The whole "partial, relative temporary stabilization" incident was a brilliant example of clear-seeing, bold and realistic Communist thinking and leadership.

Another outstanding phase of the evergrowing Communist world analysis that I saw take shape was the Comintern's signalization of the world war danger at its Sixth Congress in the summer of 1928. At that time world capitalism was drunk with prosperity illusions, especially in the United States, then in the midst of its great Coolidge boom. Thoughts of crisis and breakdown were far from the minds of capitalist economists and reformist Socialists. The latter especially were spinning theories of super-imperialism, of an organized capitalism that would know no more wars, industrial crises, poverty and class struggle.

But the Sixth C.I. Congress rudely put its boot through the dreaming of this fool's paradise. With relentless Marxian-Leninist analysis it showed that the "partial, relative and temporary" stabilization achieved by world capitalism in the past few years was being rapidly broken down and that capitalism was heading into a fresh round of wars and revolutions. The Congress strongly stressed the danger of a new world war. This thesis was primarily the work of Stalin, who at the same time correctly forecast the early coming of an industrial crisis in the United States.

This analysis of world affairs evoked a chorus of raucous laughter from capitalist and reformist Socialist leaders alike, who were trustfully looking forward to a world-wide expansion of industrial activity. Especially they ridiculed the Sixth Congress' warning against a new world war. This, they said, was pure fantasy, a sign that the Cominterm was bankrupt, a desperate effort on its part to manufacture an issue upon which to live. "Did not everybody realize," they declared, "that mankind would never again repeat the monstrous folly of 1914-18?"

The sequel has conclusively shown that the analysis of the Sixth Congress was wholly correct. The shaky capitalist stabilization exploded a year later in the greatest industrial crisis capitalism has ever known, and year by year the war danger has grown until now the whole world stands aghast before its menace. The entire development is a complete justification of the Comintern political line and a repudiation of the reformist line of the Second International.

Still another great advance in Communist world analysis and policy that I saw in the making occurred at the Seventh Congress of the Comintern in the summer of 1935. The German proletariat had recently suffered its great reverse by the rise to power of Hitler, a defeat caused by the anti-united-front, reformist policy of the German Social-Democratic Party. The Second International, its policy obviously bankrupted by the breakdown of capitalist post-war partial stabilization and the intense sharpening of the class struggle, knew only one course—to retreat, helpless in the face of the ruthless march of fascism. It could not lead the masses, who wanted to fight.

But the Seventh World Congress gave effective leadership to these masses, by its development of the policy of the People's Front, the theoretical work chiefly of Stalin and Dimitroff. The People's Front is a broad alliance of the anti-fascist, democratic, peace-loving elements— the workers, farmers and lower middle class—against fascist big capital. There are two general phases to this great policy, both linked inseparably together. The first is a defense of democracy against fascism in the respective countries by the broad People's Front; the second is an international bloc of the democratic nations to curb the fascist war aggressors through a policy of collective security.

The People's Front is the effective answer to fascist terrorism and aggression. Its eventual victory over fascism, both on national and international scope, will, while preserving and developing the democratic liberties and living standards of the masses, also definitely facilitate these masses' advance to socialism, the only fundamental cure for the world's economic and political ills. By this great policy, which is rapidly becoming the accepted strategy of the masses in every country, the Comintern has placed itself at the head of the world's oppressed millions. The Seventh Congress of the Comintern which elaborated the People's Front policy will take its place in history as one of the most important gatherings ever held in the whole course of the international revolutionary movement.

RUSSIAN PARTY CONTROVERSIES

I was fortunate enough to be able to attend various Congresses and Central Committee meetings of the Communist Party of the Soviet Union and thus to get a first-hand acquaintance with almost all the outstanding Russian leaders, and also to watch the great drama of the Revolution as it unfolded itself in the big Party discussions and controversies.

From 1924 to 1926 I attended several such meetings when Trotsky was making his bid for Party leadership. This exciting struggle shook the whole country. The burden of Trotsky's platform was that the Party had gone to the right, that the Soviet Union was sinking into capitalism and that a more "left" policy was necessary at home and abroad. The several years' long debate wound up with Trotsky being defeated by many overwhelming votes in the Party Congresses and in the Party units. Trotsky refused to abide by these democratic decisions and revolted against the Party. For this he was gradually removed from his official posts, later expelled from the Party, then isolated, and at last exiled from the U.S.S.R. His eventual degeneration into a counter-revolutionary wrecker and fascist agent is well known.

Another important struggle that I saw was the defeat of Zinoviev in the convention of the Russian Party in the winter of 1925-26. Zinoviev was at the time head of the Comintern and also of the Leningrad Soviet, and he was ambitious to become the leader of the Party as a whole. Zinoviev had opposed Lenin and Stalin in organizing the seizure of power in 1917, but had lately supported them in fighting Trotsky. But when he made his big try for the Party leadership his platform bore the same earmarks of pseudo-left demagogy that Trotsky's did.

At the 1926 Party convention Zinoviev met his Waterloo. His ultra-left platform was overwhelmingly rejected, and Stalin's position received a heavy endorsement. Even while the convention was in session the Party units in Leningrad were withdrawing Zinoviev delegates and replacing them with others favorable to the line of the Central Committee. Kirov was leading the fight against Zinoviev in Leningrad, and it was because of this activity that several years later he was assassinated by Zinovievites who had turned counter-revolutionary.

During this great convention battle I spent much time observing Trotsky who, despite his long and persistent opposition, was still allowed to remain a member of the Political Buro (top committee) of the Party. He sat on the raised platform, saying nothing, but with a cynical smile on his face as he watched Zinoviev going down to defeat. I have often wondered since whether Trotsky was not already planning the later-to-be oppositional bloc with Zinoviev that was to eventually lead Zinoviev to the firing squad and Trotsky himself to exile and eternal obloquy as a traitor.

Still another great internal struggle in the Russian Party that I saw come to a climax was the fight of Bukharin, Rykov and Tomsky in 1929, against the Party majority led by Stalin. This was the right-wing opposition, and the decisive clash took place at a joint meeting of the Central Committee and Central Control Commission. I attended the week-long sessions and had a word-by-word translation of the whole historical debate.

The immediate fight turned around the question of the Five-Year Plan. The general leftist position of the Trotsky and Zinoviev groups had been that Stalin was going too slow; that the Party was not industrializing the country fast enough, that it was making too many concessions to the peasantry, that it was not cultivating the international revolutionary movement. But Bukharin and his right-wing affiliates took the other horn of the dilemma. They asserted that the Party was industrializing the country too fast and that it was cracking under the terrific strain; they were opposed to Stalin's struggle against the kulaks and they were also for less militancy on the international field. The essence of both the Trotsky-Zinoviev and Bukharin positions was that socialism could not be built in the U.S.S.R. alone, although these groups arrived at this same counter-revolutionary conclusion with dissimilar arguments.

The great debate was a splendid illustration of the democracy within the Russian Communist Party. Prior to the joint session of the C.C. and C.C.C., the whole controversy had been aired in every unit of the Party, and also far and wide in the Soviets, trade unions, co-operatives, etc. At the joint session, virtually unlimited time was granted the oppositionists. Although only a handful, their speeches made up fully half of the week's discussion, Bukharin, Tomsky and Rykov speaking from two to four hours each.

Stalin spoke last. He was preceded by a brilliant array of Party majority speakers, who literally tore the opposition's arguments to shreds, and I wondered what could possibly be left for him to say. But he made a masterful presentation. With remorseless dialectic he demonstrated the correctness of the Party policy—its tempo of industrialization, its attitude towards the peasantry, its international policy, its internal regime. It was one of the greatest speeches of his career. Bukharin's thesis was utterly wrecked. In the vote not a dozen out of the several hundred delegates present supported it.

This controversy was a key point in the life of the Russian Revolution. Like the Trotsky and Zinoviev controversies, the fight against Bukharin greatly clarified the Party ideologically and solidified it organizationally. It also enormously enhanced Stalin's already high prestige. In these great struggles the Party definitely broke both the right and "left" alien influences in its ranks. It was thus enabled to surge forward victoriously with its great Five-Year Plans, while the corrupt and discredited Trotsky-Zinoviev-Bukharin groups, affiliated together on a common counter-revolutionary program, took the downward path that led them into eventual campaigns of assassination, wrecking of industries and spying for fascist Germany and Japan.

SABOTAGE

The dispossessed capitalists and landlords of old Russia have used every weapon of violence to recover their rulership, and one of their most destructive means has been the sabotage of industry. On the eve of the Revolution in 1917 they were already making widespread use of it by shutting down their factories, reducing production, etc., to defeat the advancing revolution. And ever since then their agents have lost no opportunity to disorganize industry and agriculture in the hope of weakening and eventually breaking down the Soviet government. The recent trials of the Trotsky-Zinoviev-Bukharin traitors and wreckers illustrated dramatically afresh the way every counter-revolutionary seizes upon the weapon of sabotage to fight against socialism.

This sabotage, especially when applied by enemies in key positions, assumes many destructive types—waste of huge sums of money in construction, production of bad goods, introduction of inferior machinery, shipping of wrong or insufficient materials, actual destruction of plants and machinery, and a thousand and one other forms. All industries (and also agriculture) have been subjected to severe sabotage, especially the railroads, which play such a vital role in the economic life and military defense of the U.S.S.R.

A dozen years ago a friend of mine gave me a running account of how sabotagers were crippling the railroads. He was an expert bridge engineer, with long experience on several large American railroads. He went to Soviet Russia to give the new socialist society the benefit of his ultra-modern technique. He got a job in the railroad bridge building department, but immediately found himself up against a dead wall so far as doing any constructive work was concerned. The department was entirely in the hands of a group of old-time engineers, reactionaries who, because of the shortage of reliable technical experts, had managed to hang on to their strategic positions under a thin veneer of loyalty to the Soviet government. These engineers not only turned flint faces against my friend's efforts at introducing modern American methods of railroad bridge building but, even measured by their own antiquated Russian system, they were flagrantly committing sabotage.

Their sabotage took many forms. They ordered serviceable bridges reconstructed; they built bridges manifestly too light to carry the heavier traffic that was planned for the next few years, with the result that the bridges would soon have to be rebuilt; they used twice as much steel in bridges as was necessary; they needlessly tied up long stretches of railway line by their construction jobs; they wasted many millions of rubles etc. All this sabotage they justified on the basis of their obsolete, pre-war bridge-building technique.

My friend was pretty frantic at all this. Week after week, indignantly he used to recite to us incidents of the manner in which the reactionary engineers were sabotaging the railroad system. And he seemed powerless to do anything about it. Several times he wrote to the Commissar of Railways, Rudzutak, and got no satisfaction. More or less in desperation, he decided to apply himself to educating the classes of young bridge engineers. But here, too, he found the sabotagers in control and busily impregnating the budding engineers with their antiquated technique and poisonous social views. To fill his cup of misery to overflowing, the old engineers, who resented his "interference," busily plotted his removal.

Some years later I again met this engineer. This time he was quite happy. Somehow or other the old gang of sabotagers had been cleaned out and at last he was able to do constructive work. He had been promoted to a higher post and was making progress at introducing modern bridge building technique on the Soviet railroads.

An interesting aftermath to this incident is the fact that Rudzutak, Commissar of Railways at the time and the man to whom my engineer friend protested in vain, was exposed later as a spy. Long before the Revolution he had been a tsarist undercover agent in the Party, and when the Germans captured Riga in 1918 they found his name in the police files. Since then the Germans had used him as their agent. The Soviet government managed to dig up this information, and Rudzutak admitted his guilt. It was such sabotage as this of the bridge engineers, protected by secret wrecker enemies in high places, that was largely responsible for the many years' relative lagging of the strategic Russian railway system and that also accounted for needless economic difficulties on many fronts.

CONQUEST OF THE ARCTIC

One of the most striking achievements of the Soviet government is its development of the huge Arctic regions within its borders. Hitherto the Arctic zone has been considered in many countries as almost completely a desert of ice and rock, a place for polar bears and a few wandering Esquimaux. But the Russians, by great effort and real pioneering, are opening up the Arctic to civilization and showing that this long inhospitable area is full of riches and possibilities for settlement.

The Russian conquest of the Arctic was especially dramatized a couple of years ago by the establishment of the Soviet polar station and the world's record transpolar flights from Moscow to California. Behind these spectacular features lay a vast network of Russian Arctic enterprises. In years to come the Soviet's winning of the Arctic will probably be considered the most important economic development of this period. It is the completion of man's conquest of the globe.

In the summer of 1935, I saw some of this vast Arctic development, on a trip from Moscow to Murmansk, via the new Stalin Baltic-White Sea Canal. This great ship route, one of the largest artificial waterways in the world, was opened on August 2, 1933. It is two hundred and twenty-seven kilometers long and establishes a direct passage from the Baltic to the White Sea. Formerly ships bound from Leningrad to Archangel had to sail all the way around Norway, Sweden and Finland; the new canal cuts the distance to one-fourth, besides keeping the route entirely within Soviet waters.

The Stalin Canal provides transportation for the wealth of lumber, apatite ore, building stone, iron, coal, wood pulp, fish, furs, etc., now being produced in the great Arctic regions to the north of Leningrad. By connecting with the Neva and the Volga Rivers, the Stalin Canal also provides a direct waterway from the Arctic to the Caspian Sea. The canal, a part of the First Five-Year Plan, contains nineteen locks and many dams, floodgates, dykes and inner canals. The whole job was finished in the unbelievable time of two years, although the work had to be done under severe Arctic weather conditions. The Panama Canal took eleven years to complete. Once, bound from New York to Honolulu, I passed through the Panama Canal, and to me the Stalin Canal appeared the bigger job.

The canal was built by prison labor under the direction of the O.G.P.U. The intelligent way in which the prisoners were handled, and the splendid regenerative effects upon them, constitutes one of the proudest social achievements of the Soviet government. For good work done many of the prisoners were decorated with the Order of Lenin and large numbers were freed with other honors.

The Stalin Canal was enormously interesting, and so was Murmansk at the northern end of the route. This city is two hundred and fifty miles north of the Arctic Circle. In winter it is completely dark for a couple of months, and in the summer nights while we were there it was like broad daylight, except for an hour or so of dusk. Only a few years ago, Murmansk was an obscure small town, but it is now a bustling metropolis of over one hundred thousand people, and growing like a bay tree. It is a new socialist city, with a host of new Soviet cultural institutions. There are no churches. Many industries are springing up in the city and surrounding territory. One of the most interesting sights we saw was the raising of fruits and vegetables in tropical luxuriance under glass. The workers, with great pride, showed us what they claimed was the first watermelon ever grown north of the Arctic Circle.

Many construction projects were being completed with incredible speed, as the canal itself had been. We visited a big hydroelectric plant a few miles out of Murmansk, on the raging Tula River. Three years had been allowed for the job, but it was being completed in two. A year before, on the powerhouse building site, there had been nothing but a bear's den and a few fishermen's huts. The workers told us they chased the bears away and gave the fishermen jobs as builders.

Murmansk itself was simply one great building job, and the authorities were trying to hire ten thousand more workers. The head of the local Soviet told us that the city plan the year before, among many other jobs, called for building six big schools. He could not see how, with all their other tasks, these schools could also be built, and he had so expressed himself at a Soviet meeting. Whereupon the leader of the building workers proposed that the number of schools be increased to seven. And, sure enough, they were all completed on time. The plan for the following year also provided for seven more schools. The Soviet official said he believed it impossible to build them but he was sure, nevertheless, that they would be finished.

Such was Murmansk and such the tempo of industrial and social development in the Soviet Arctic. And the district we visited was only one small corner of the several thousand miles of Russian Arctic front, from the Finnish border to far-off Vladivostok.

HEROISM AND HUNGER

When in November, 1917, the Bolsheviki overthrew the Kerensky capitalist government and set out to transform Russia into a socialist country, capitalist economists all over the world ridiculed the whole proposition. And especially sarcastic were the reformist Socialist leaders, who with pseudo-Marxian language declared it entirely out of the question to reconstruct backward Russia into a socialist economy without its first passing through a long period of industrialization under capitalism.

The task has turned out to be the greatest ever undertaken by mankind in all its history, but in the main, it has been accomplished. Under the leadership of the great Communist Party, first headed by Lenin and now by Stalin, the workers and peasants have laid the structure of socialism in the Soviet Union. They have made of their country the forerunner of the new world order that is emerging from the worn-out and collapsing capitalist system. But this has been done only by dint of the gravest struggles, hardships and sufferings. The story of the revolution is one long heroic battle against war-devastation, foreign and domestic enemies, famine, pestilence, sabotage, assassination and economic backwardness.

On my first visit to Soviet Russia, in 1921, I went via London, Libau, Riga and Reval to Leningrad. All through Lithuania, Esthonia and Latvia, which were parts of old Russia, the ravages of the World War and the civil war were in evidence; the countryside was devastated, many bridges were lying in the rivers, the people were poverty-stricken, trenches and barbed wire were still there.

Leningrad was in terrible shape. Half the population had fled into the countryside to escape starvation. The streets were almost empty of people, and the stores along the famous Nevsky Prospect were nailed shut, their boarded windows plastered with revolutionary posters, many dating back to the workers' seizure of power in 1917.

As our train, consisting of a few coaches and a long string of box cars, drew up in the Leningrad station, a great mass of ragged humanity unloaded from it. Men, women and children, it looked as though there were several thousands, and they had been riding wherever a human being could hang on. Each carried a sack full of food stuffs, gathered somehow in the country. These unkempt travelers were the famous "bagmen," and this was their way of fighting starvation. Maxim Litvinov was on our car, and as we stood watching the throng of bagmen surge past he told me what a terrible problem it was to provision the cities.

Soon I had a taste of Leningrad hunger conditions. Several of us foreigners were whisked off from the train in a rickety automobile to the International Hotel for breakfast. The waiter brought us each a cup of "tea" and two small slices of black bread, amounting to about three ounces. I disposed of mine in a few bites, but our guide munched his slowly. After some twenty minutes of sitting there, with the waiters paying no further attention to us and I hungry as a wolf, I finally asked the guide when they were going to serve us breakfast. "Breakfast," said he, "why, you've had your breakfast. Your next meal will be in six hours."

Moscow, like other Russian cities, was in a terrifying condition. The whole population, except the children, were living on the edge of starvation. Everybody looked thin and wasted. I never saw one fat person during my several months' stay. Indeed, to be stout was to be suspected of food hoarding. As men and women walked along the streets, their slow pace betrayed their semi-starvation. Most people also had not had any new clothes for several years, and many were virtually in rags. I visited factories and schools where the workers and students had their shoes tied up with strings wound round the soles.

The fuel shortage was an acute agony during the hard winter of 1920-21, with the temperature ranging, for weeks together, as low as thirty degrees below zero. Moscow's coal supply was cut off, the mines being ruined by the civil war and the railroads unable to transport what little coal there was being mined. The supply of wood was also entirely inadequate. To make matters worse, from years-long lack of repairs the roofs of thousands of houses leaked and the upper floors became uninhabitable. In desperation, the freezing people began to tear out the flooring, rafters, doors and other woodwork of these abandoned upper stories to shield themselves from the arctic cold.

Disease ravaged the city. During this terrible period the American Communist, Jack Reed, perished of typhus. I visited several Moscow hospitals and saw hundreds of cholera and typhus sufferers; there was a great shortage of medicines and other hospital supplies, because the tight international economic blockade prevented their importation. People requiring major operations simply died, as there were no anesthetics to be had.

The city's transportation system was at an almost complete standstill. Once in half an hour maybe, a forlorn, unpainted, half-wrecked street car, packed with humanity fore and aft, inside and outside, would go creaking its way through town. There were few wagons to be seen, except occasional bread trucks, hauled by half-starved horses and accompanied by soldier guards. Once in a while also a lone, dilapidated automobile would limp along the streets, which were full of great holes from years of disrepair.

The lighting system was almost entirely out of commission. Only the most important government buildings had electric lights. There were no street lights, and the people at home had to use candles or whatever else they could contrive. The drinking water system was crippled, and the telephone service was in a state of collapse.

Everywhere the city presented a lugubrious and deathlike appearance. Half-empty streets; listless-going people; unfinished buildings standing as they were when the World War began seven years before; stove-pipes sticking out of apartment house windows, the steam-heating plants having long ago expired; broken window panes plastered over with paper, as glass was unprocurable. It was a depressing picture of ruin and decay. Yet through it all the theaters, only half-lit, freezing cold and packed with semi-starved people, kept going at full blast with performances which for artistic perfection could not be equaled in any other city in the world.

Hunger was acute all over the country, and cholera and typhus raged everywhere. Just emerging from seven years of imperialist and civil war, Russian industry and agriculture were almost completely prostrate. With the factories at a standstill, and with a severe international economic boycott existing against Soviet Russia, the workers could not furnish the farmers the necessary tools, fertilizers, farm machinery and other supplies. Farming thus became almost impossible and, to make matters worse, the richer farmers carried on a wide campaign to restrict production to the minimum possible, hoping thereby to force the Soviet government into collapse. The workers in the cities were starving and the peasants also faced famine conditions. This hunger situation, developing since the middle of the World War, became especially desperate in 1920.

War Communism prevailed, and everybody in the cities was living on rations, the famous "*pyok.*" In Moscow the workers got about half a pound of black bread per day, or even less, with a small supply of cabbage and, once in a while, a little meat or fish. We foreigners got the so-called "diplomatic ration." This, not quite so terrible, was based on one pound of bread per day, with sometimes a small bit of meat. Once I lived several days on apple parings and black bread. Of butter and milk we got none for many weeks on end; nor was there any fresh fruit, such delicacies being reserved for children. Our "coffee" and "tea" were bizarre concoctions of unknown origin. Sugar was not to be had, and the "tobacco" was not tobacco at all.

Worst of all was the bad quality of the food. The bread had a heavy admixture of clay and was full of small sticks and pebbles. As the always inadequate refrigeration system had now vanished completely, often the meat was putrid. The rank odor of the cooking soup seeping through the house used to gag me. I simply could not eat it, although I was chronically hungry.

After three and a half months of the "diplomatic ration" I had lost twenty-five pounds, and I was anything but fat to begin with. Food conditions were far worse among the Russians than with us foreigners, except in the case of the children, who were well taken care of even during the several hunger years. Just how bad the situation was I saw graphically illustrated one day in Moscow. Somehow the river had been contaminated, and thousands of small fish were floating downstream, belly up, dead or dying from the fatal water. To my horror, hundreds of people lined the river banks and were wading into the polluted stream and seizing the poisoned fish for food.

Real starvation stalked through every Russian city, but most terrible of all were conditions along the Volga where, because a severe drought added to the general war collapse, crops had completely failed. The frightful famine of late 1921, which cost hundreds of thousands of lives, was just getting under way. It was an appalling situation, and it was at this time that Herbert Hoover, arch-hater of the Soviet government, came in with the American Relief Administration and tried vainly to undermine the Soviets by controlling the distribution of the food generously provided by the American people to relieve the famine.

A couple of years later, making a trip through the Volga former famine districts, I heard the most harrowing stories of hunger and death, how whole villages had been wiped out by starvation and pestilence, how hundreds of workers had actually died of hunger in the shops heroically trying to set the wheels of industry going. No people in modern times has faced such a desperate situation as the Russians did in this period.

SOCIALISM VICTORIOUS

What a tremendous advance the situation in the Soviet Union of 1939 is over that of 1921! Socialism is victorious on every front, despite the bitter resistance of its enemies at home and abroad. The entire country, in all branches of constructive life, has literally leaped forward, in a way quite without parallel in history. Under the leadership of the great Communist Party the workers and peasants have accomplished a thousand "impossibilities." And it has been my profound privilege to see at first-hand this vast revolution developing.

During the World War and civil war, Russian industry, weak and feeble, and made up mostly of German, Belgian, French, English and American-owned plants, was almost completely wrecked. Hostile armies systematically flooded mines, dumped locomotives into rivers, burned factories, removed key parts of machinery, dynamited railroad bridges, etc., over nearly the entire country. The operating engineers either fled abroad during the Revolution or remained at home to sabotage. The half-starved workers, totally inexperienced in managing industry, were left with an utterly primitive and ruined industrial system. It was altogether an "impossible" situation.

Just how impotent Russian industry was in 1921 I saw vividly illustrated in Moscow. It was a garment shop, and the place was crowded with women workers, sewing by hand—while on one side were stocked up many sewing machines (one of which could do the work of a score of hand workers) all out of commission because small parts were worn out and could not be replaced by the prostrate metal industry; nor could they (because of the capitalist economic blockade) be imported from abroad. It was such conditions that reduced Russian industry in 1921 to only one-fifth of pre-war production.

But all this is now only tradition. The workers have established a free labor discipline, stabilized the ruble and balanced the government budget, cleared out the sabotagers and trained vast armies of skilled workers and engineers, broken the international blockade, mastered and improved modern industrial technique, set up unique Socialist forms of industrial organization, amassed great quantities of capital. All these problems were held by capitalist economists (and their reformist Socialist yes-men) to be utterly insoluble. But they have been solved, and the Soviet Union has surged forward into an era of the swiftest and most far-reaching industrial development in the history of the world.

During this stupendous advance the Soviet Union has been transformed from a backward agricultural economy into a modern industrial nation. It is the first industrial country in Europe, having outstripped Germany and England, and it is now rushing on with giant strides to overtake the world industrial leader, the United States. At present the industrial output of the Soviet Union is seven times that of pre-war Russia, and since 1913 the percentage growth of Russian industry has been twenty times as fast as that generally of the capitalist world. The new great power dams of Dnieprogres, the huge steel mills of Magnitogorsk, the great White Sea and Volga canals and the thousands of other monster industrial enterprises of today are indeed a far cry from that garment shop of 1921 with its unfixable sewing machines. During my many visits to the U.S.S.R. and my trips about the country I have watched, year after year, this stormy advance of Soviet industry.

Socialism has been no less brilliantly victorious in agriculture. Just a short while ago Russian farming was incredibly primitive, almost what it was a thousand years before. As late as 1929 wooden plows outnumbered iron ones by two to one. But now what a profound transformation! The world has never before seen the like. Soviet agriculture in the past few years has literally catapulted forward. The former twenty-five million primitive individual farms (with ninety-nine per cent of the total sown area) have been organized into a quarter million socialist collectivized farms. These farms have been equipped with the most modern machinery (four hundred thousand tractors, over one hundred thousand combined harvesters, etc.), are being cultivated according to the newest farming techniques, furnished vast supplies of manufactured fertilizers, etc. Soviet agriculture is also developing many new cultures—tea, rubber, citrous fruits and various industrial crops. The pre-war production of grain has been far outstripped. In short, Soviet agriculture has leaped from the position of the most backward in Europe to that of world leader.

This revolution in Soviet agriculture bears the profound political significance that the huge masses of peasantry, abandoning individual production for collective effort, are marching shoulder to shoulder with the industrial workers in building socialism. All the capitalist world said that the Russian peasants would never become socialists, but this "miracle," like so many others, has been accomplished. The collectivization of the Russian peasants is one of the most important events in modern history.

Whenever one travels now in the Soviet Union there confronts the eye a vast panorama of building and growth. On every side there are being constructed giant factories, docks, canals, apartments, public buildings, hospitals, sanatoria, workers' clubs, libraries, theaters. The older cities are being rebuilt from top to bottom, and scores of new socialist towns, all teeming with the new life, have sprung up almost overnight. The whole country throbs with a vitality such as no capitalist country has ever known. What a deep contrast to the terrible days of 1921, to the dark time of tsarism.

In this tremendous advance of socialism in the Soviet Union, the living standards of the masses have kept pace. From 1924 to 1936 the national income leaped from twenty to eighty billion rubles. The real wages of the workers have doubled since 1932 and quadrupled since 1927. The improvement in the conditions of the farmers is also altogether without parallel in any other country. While mass living standards fall in all capitalist lands, the Russian workers and farmers have finally overcome the old-time terrors of hunger and famine and are swiftly marching into a new and flourishing prosperity.

As part of all these socialist strides upward in industry, agriculture and living standards there also develops a great cultural revolution. Mass education of the workers and farmers is proceeding at a swift pace and on an entirely new basis. There is also a socialist renaissance in science, art, literature, the theater, the cinema. And, while popular liberties are being strangled by fascism in many countries, democracy is growing and expanding in the Soviet Union. The new Stalin Constitution is by far the most democratic in the world, guaranteeing the people political freedom, religious liberty, the right to work, the right of the worker to his product and the farmer to the land, the right to organize, the right to education, the right to full medical care, the right to rest and recreation, and the most complete system of social security to be found anywhere. Old Russia, the home of hunger, misery, ignorance and oppression, has now become a land of song, laughter, culture, hope and happiness.

Enemies of the Soviet Union, from the fascist Hearst to the pseudo-left Norman Thomas, try to belie and obscure these Socialist victories in the Soviet Union. They pass over the great achievements of the U.S.S.R. (the progress of industry and agriculture, the rise in mass cultural and living standards, the abolition of illiteracy, unemployment and industrial crises, the liquidation of anti-Semitism, etc.) simply as though they did not exist. Then they concentrate upon all the failings and weaknesses (and these are necessarily many) that they can find, or conjure up and never cease harping upon them.

The building of socialism presents innumerable new problems, and the steps taken by the Soviet government to meet them are novel and not easily understood in capitalist countries. Necessarily there has always been a serious lag internationally in realizing the true meaning of Soviet internal and external policies, even among the political friends of the U.S.S.R. Hence, it has been easy, for a time at least, for enemies of the Soviet to misrepresent its policies, and this has been done systematically with every important one of them, including the seizure of power in 1917, the Brest-Litovsk treaty, the New Economic

Policy, the launching of the Five-Year Plans, the campaign for collectivization of the farms, the development of Stakhanovism, the affiliation of the Soviet Union to the League of Nations, the Soviet peace policy, the defensive alliance between the U.S.S.R. and France, the cleaning out of the Trotskyist-Bukharinist-Zinovievite wreckers, etc.

But the Revolution eventually catches up with and destroys the slanders of its enemies. The accomplishments of the Soviet government are so huge and unmistakable that all the world is being compelled to recognize that. the new socialist system is a success. The socialist sun is in the ascendant, and more and more the Soviet Union is becoming the beacon light of hope to the oppressed toilers of the earth.

Postscript

Since the foregoing was written, showing the tremendous socialist growth in the U.S.S.R., that country has indeed been sorely tried in the fire of war. Its people and institutions have had to withstand the greatest military assault in all human history and they are meeting the test in a manner that continues to amaze the world. In the crucible of war, socialism in the U.S.S.R. has proved itself to be possessed of a strength that the capitalist economic, political, and military experts did not dream it had. And it is indeed fortunate for humanity that the first Socialist Republic displayed such vast strength else the fascist hordes by this time would have overrun and subjugated the world.

When on June 22, 1941, the Hitler armies treacherously invaded the U.S.S.R. they, with their allies, outnumbered the Red Army by three to two, and, with the vast industries of all Europe behind them, they had a production advantage of about two to one. These terrible odds, together with many years of underestimation of the strength of socialism, convinced the experts, both in the capitalist democracies and in the fascist countries, that Hitler would smash the Red Army in a few weeks, capture Moscow, and drive the U.S.S.R. out of the war. And for a time, indeed, the situation of the Soviet Union was almost desperate. With

SOCIALISM VICTORIOUS 315

terrific offensives, the Hitler armies overran Soviet territory containing 77,000,000 people, or almost 40 per cent of the total population of the U.S.S.R. Together with these great losses, the Soviet Union also lost about 40 per cent of her cultivated land, 54 per cent of her coal production, and at least 50 per cent of her steel output. Besides all this, not less than 10,000,000 Soviet civilians have been butchered by the Nazis and from two to three million Red Army men killed in battle.

Despite these terrific losses, enough to have defeated any capitalist country, the Soviet Union, making the greatest military effort ever made by any nation, is now driving the Nazi invaders from its borders. The defense of Leningrad, Moscow, and Stalingrad, the two great winter offensives, and the summer-winter offensive of 1943 are military achievements, without parallel. They are a few more "impossibilities" in the long line of "impossibilities" accomplished by the Soviet Union since its birth. And they have been made realities through the unequalled national unity, economic centralization, and fighting spirit of the gallant Soviet people and their socialist regime. Hitler signed his own death warrant when he sent his "invincible" troops marching across the Soviet border.

In his speech on November 7, 1943, the twenty-sixth anniversary of the establishment of the Soviet Union, Stalin explained that the Soviet system proved to be the source of strength during the present war. He spoke as follows:

"The Soviet state was never so stable and solid as now in the third year of the patriotic war. The lessons of the war show that the Soviet system has proved not only the best form of organizing the economic and cultural development of the country in the years of peaceful construction, but also the best form of mobilizing all the forces of the people for resistance to the enemy in time of war. The Soviet Power set up twenty-six years ago has transformed our country within a short historical period into an impregnable fortress. The Red Army has the most stable and reliable rear of all the armies in the world.

"This is the source of the strength of the Soviet Union."

At Moscow, Foreign Ministers Eden, Molotov and Hull have implemented the Atlantic Charter by co-ordinating the military strategy of the three great powers and by providing for post-war collaboration of all peace-loving nations. This agreement dealt a shattering blow not only to Hitler, but also to the professional Soviet baiters in the United States. In the big movement for allied solidarity, upon which the peace and future prosperity of the world depend, the strong, young, democratic, socialist U.S.S.R. may be depended upon to do its full, loyal and progressive share.

November, 1943.

Books and Pamphlets by William Z. Foster

BOOKS

PAMPHLETS